# RHETORICAL EDUCATION IN AMERICA

# Rhetorical Education in America

CHERYL GLENN
MARGARET M. LYDAY
WENDY B. SHARER

The University of Alabama Press
*Tuscaloosa*

Typeface: New Baskerville

∞

The paper on which this book is printed meets the minimum requirements of
American National Standard for Information Science–Permanence of Paper for
Printed Library Materials, ANSI Z39.48–1984.

Library of Congress Cataloging-in-Publication Data

Glenn, Cheryl.
Rhetorical education in America / Cheryl Glenn, Margaret Lyday, Wendy Sharer.
p.   cm.
Includes bibliographical references and index.
ISBN 0-8173-1424-5 (cloth : alk. paper)
1. English language—Rhetoric—Study and teaching—United States. 2. Rhetoric—
Study and teaching—United States. 3. Rhetoric—Political aspects—United States.
4. English language—United States—Rhetoric. 5. Rhetoric—Social aspects—
United States. I. Lyday, Margaret, 1946- II. Sharer, Wendy B. III. Title.
PE1405.U6G58 2004
808′.0071′173—dc22

2004005274

An earlier version of chapter 7 appeared in *Gender and Rhetorical Space in American
Life, 1866–1910,* Carbondale: Southern Illinois University Press, 2002. Reprinted
with the permission of Southern Illinois University Press and the board of
Trustees, Southern Illinois University.

Materials quoted in chapter 8 are used with the permission of The United States
Department of the Interior, National Park Service.

Materials quoted in chapter 11 appeared in *Cyberliteracy: Navigating the Internet with
Awareness,* New Haven: Yale University Press, 2001. Used with permission.

# Contents

# Rhetorical Education in America (A Broad Stroke Introduction)

*Cheryl Glenn*

By the time Harvard launched its first-year writing program in the mid-1800s, teachers and scholars of rhetoric and writing were already discussing the methods and models of rhetorical education in America.[1] If a college education were to prepare its all-male students for active participation within a citizenry, for leadership positions in the church, state, and trades, what specific skills and knowledge would equip them?

Ever since Isocrates (c. 370 BCE) argued against the Sophists, teachers have tried to define precepts of a rhetorical education that would enable students to govern knowledgeably and virtuously both their own households and the commonwealth. Centuries later, the Romans called for education that trained students for *vita activa,* the active life in the polis. Although Cicero felt that aristocrats held a rhetorical advantage, he devised a system of rhetorical education that could compensate for nonaristocratic birth and develop successful rhetors for the public sphere. Two millennia later, Walter H. Beale writes that the purpose of a rhetorical education is twofold: to cultivate both the character of the individual and the success of a culture (626). Bruce Herzberg tells us that rhetorical education is the linchpin of a participatory democracy, centering as it does at the nexus of civic virtue and public as well as academic discourse (396). Thomas P. Miller and Melody Bowdon argue that rhetorical education goes beyond the teaching of composition to inhabit civic action, whether that civic action takes the form of political debates, community literacy programs, or service learning (591). And writing about the public deliberation on war against Iraq, Chidsey Dickson describes his own rhetorical interventions as "symbolic action in the civic sphere." However broadly it might be defined, however and wherever it manifests itself, rhetorical education perpetuates the principles of participation appropriate to a specific cultural moment.

Ideally, rhetorical education shapes all citizens for public participation, "with political deliberations, judicial negotiations of conflicts, and celebrations of public values" (Miller and Bowdon 593–94). Practically, rhetorical education has traditionally shaped only men of the upper class for leadership positions in the public sphere, for *vita activa,* usually for the advantage of those same aristocratic men even when such an advantage is at the expense of Others. In fact, the concerns of Others were not an issue until these Others made their way into the academy. The entrance of white women of every class, bourgeois and working-class men, African-American and Native American men and women, and immigrants—and their concomitant expectations of rhetorical education—threatened the status quo. Their cultural traditions, language practices, and reading and writing skills did not correspond with those endorsed by the universities, yet university curricula could not change as quickly as the student demographics. If these Others also expected to be educated for participation in the public sphere, then who would lead? Who would follow? Rhetorical education is inherently slippery—as a concept, theory, practice, or application. And questions of who should receive rhetorical education, in what form, and for what purpose, continue to vex it.

As the essays in this collection demonstrate, rhetorical education enables people to engage in and change American society—but not always. Well-born males continue to receive the very best rhetorical educations, the best preparation for participating in the public sphere (an assessment of any judicial or legislative branch of government or of the Fortune 500 business leaders will attest to that statement). If this were not the case, then female students at the Seven Sisters colleges, male and female students at historically Black and Native American colleges and universities, students at land-grant universities, deaf and hard-of-hearing students at Gallaudet University, and students educated in clubs, organizations, and cyberspace would receive the same measure of rhetorical education as those white male students at Ivy League schools. Male, female, rich, poor—students of every age, color, and physical ability—would reap the benefits of rhetorical education in this democracy we refer to as America.

But the problem of equality in rhetorical education is not in its quality so much as in its distribution, and then not so much in its distribution as in its reception. Indeed, many of those denied formal rhetorical instruction successfully learned by other means (church, family, library, politics) to be eloquent public speakers and writers. But American society at large has not always welcomed the rhetorical productions of Others (the oratorical displays of Native Americans were systematically mistranslated, romanticized, or ignored[2]). When, despite great odds, members of traditionally marginalized groups received a measure of rhetorical education, they were often prevented from displaying their education and expertise (women, for instance, were not permitted to deliver their compositions and were discouraged from speaking publicly). When they did exhibit their rhetorical expertise, that expertise was received with suspicion. Nontraditional rhetors were sometimes ridiculed if not threatened by those who feared the potential of their suasory abilities, particularly when it disrupted traditional notions of who could behave as a citizen (many women, Blacks, and Native Americans attended college before they were granted U.S. citizenship). And when they used their rhetorical educations to assert their "inherent right and ability [ . . . ] to determine their own communicative needs and desires," what Scott Richard Lyons calls "rhetorical sovereignty," they were often challenged (449). In fact, when Others took the pen, stage, or pulpit, they were expected to do so as "Americans" representing the dominant culture. They were expected to have erased, as best they could, the traces of color, accent, and gender from their self-presentation. (Consider Richard Pratt's motto for the Carlisle Indian School: "Kill the Indian, Save the Man.") In other words, even though rhetorical education "attempts to shape a certain kind of character capable of using language effectively to carry on the practical and moral business of a polity," its goals circle right back to the preservation of dominant culture (Beale 626).

In *Distinction: A Social Critique of the Judgment of Taste,* French sociologist Pierre Bourdieu perceptively explains the tautology, for every educational program fulfills a specific function: to legitimate social inequalities that exist before, after, inside, and outside its educational operations. The cultural tastes of dominant classes are given institutional form and then, with deft ideological sleight of hand, their taste for this institutionalized culture (i.e., their own) is held up as evidence of their cultural, and ultimately social, superiority. Bourdieu's concept of cultural capital (of who assumes, claims, or is awarded the right to rule, lead, speak publicly) plays out in rhetorical education, particularly in America, where different groups of students at different locations are educated differently, prepared to take—or to not take—a range of rhetorical roles in the public sphere. Bourdieu enables us to understand that, by definition, rhetorical education promotes a culture and, in doing so, works to erase those cultures, languages, and traditions that are not those of the dominant class.

The problems of inequity inherent in rhetorical education are very much with us today. Yet despite those problems, millions of students, half of whom speak a language other than English in their homes, and thousands of teachers embark every year on a course of rhetorical education. These courses reside in such diverse and overlapping settings as in first-year writing and public speaking courses, undergraduate writing programs, English as a second language programs, graduate programs housed in English or Speech Communication departments, university writing centers and writing-across-the-curriculum programs, textbooks or seminal texts (such as Caleb Bingham's 1803 *Columbian Orator*), women's clubs, parlor performances, literacy programs and movements, churches, and political programs and movements. Teachers and students in these traditional and alternative settings continue to search for ways around the obstacles and toward the opportunities rhetorical education presents.

The relationship of rhetoric to education and the ways that rhetorical awareness is developed in educational institutions still remains to be clearly and fully articulated. After all, rhetoric always inscribes the relation of language and power at a particular moment, even as it concerns itself with the audience for and purpose of literate acts, with the actual effects of discourse, and with real possibilities rather than ideal certainties. Therefore, the contributors to *Rhetorical Education in America* have converged to explore the purposes, problems, and possibilities of rhetorical education in America on both the undergraduate and graduate levels, and both inside and outside the academy.

In doing so, the contributors join with scholars who have appraised, furthered, and changed the face of rhetorical education in America.[3] Beginning with Adams Sherman Hill's late-nineteenth-century publications on the subject, the critiques of rhetorical education in America picked up momentum in the last half of the previous century, bringing to bear studies varying broadly—from Brenda Jo Brueggemann's *Lend Me Your Ear: Rhetorical Constructions of Deafness* and David Wallace Adams's *Education for Extinction: American Indians and the Boarding School Experience* to Anne Ruggles Gere's *Intimate Practices* and Jacqueline Jones

Royster's *Traces of a Stream*.[4] Thus, the contributors continue the general vein of previous scholarly work, interrogating the contested phrase itself, its equally contested applications, its history, and its accumulative accompanying critiques. Their individual essays are responses to these questions: What students have been prepared for what action? How exactly have they been trained to behave, interact, and insert themselves into the economic, academic, and social politics of America? How have they accumulated and circulated their measure of cultural capital? Collectively, then, the essays that constitute *Rhetorical Education in America* explore and interrogate the practices and functions of rhetorical education in light of the links Bourdieu and others have made between institutional policies and the maintenance of the status quo. At the same time, we intend these essays to suggest that rhetorical education, through practices such as those described by Shirley Wilson Logan and Susan Kates, can be a means of empowerment for marginalized groups that wish to disrupt the status quo.

An edited collection can contain but a slice of scholarship on a particular topic. As we worked to establish a manageable scope and suitable arrangement for this collection, we focused on the readers who, we believe, are most likely to engage it. We suspect that our primary audience will include many newcomers to the field of rhetoric and composition; thus, we have selected materials that address some of the most important questions newcomers to the field might have. Many of these questions, we discovered, are also actively discussed among seasoned scholars of rhetoric and composition, and we hope these scholars will find the collection useful as they continue to search for answers.

Two of the most obvious questions one confronts when teaching rhetoric are "Why does rhetorical education matter?" and "What can rhetorical education do?" As Shirley Wilson Logan suggests, when teachers of rhetoric introduce their students to the means of persuasion, the texts of significant rhetors, and the various communities of discourse in the academy, the professions, and the public, those teachers must also engage in "discussions of the question, 'Rhetorical education for what?'" (36). Part 1, "The Implications of Rhetorical Education," provides a historical overview of rhetorical education in America while it also asks readers to consider the effects of that education. What should rhetorical education enable? To what ends should we pursue this amorphous project called rhetorical education?

In the first essay in part 1, William Denman proposes that the proper end for rhetorical education is the development of the citizen-orator. The ancient model of the citizen-orator, Denman explains, purposefully links rhetoric, civic life, and democracy. This model, however, declined in the face of nineteenth-century individualism, economic competition, and professionalization. The ideal of the citizen-orator, Denman contends, ought to be restored to the rhetorical curriculum today so that once again students will learn to communicate effectively in democratic life. "The ancient links between rhetoric and the development and maintenance of democracy," Denman concludes, "are too important for us to continue to ignore in our basic courses" (16). Denman's essay is suggestive of what rhetorical education might mean, and it provides a useful overview of scholarship on rhetorical education from the field of communications. We hope that this overview will encourage readers to pursue such scholarship further.

Thomas Miller also argues for a pedagogically and publicly reinvigorated model of rhetorical education within rhetoric and composition in his essay, "Lest We Go the Way of Classics: Toward a Rhetorical Future for English Departments." Miller suggests that English departments have embraced a "literary-research paradigm" that devalues the teaching of rhetorical skills for public participation. English departments, Miller continues, need to recast their purposes, to move away from literary research and instead prioritize a curriculum of "courses that combine historical analysis, institutional critique, and service learning to teach the literacies of citizenship" and assist in the development of articulate, activist citizens (34).

In the final essay of the first part, " 'To Get an Education and Teach My People': Rhetoric for Social Change," Shirley Wilson Logan discusses the contexts in which nineteenth-century African Americans studied rhetoric as a means to social change. Logan suggests that, unlike those nineteenth-century students, current students do not learn to see rhetoric as a powerful force in efforts to shape human interaction and political circumstances. "I am proposing" Logan writes, "that more attention be paid in composition classrooms—and in all classrooms—to the ways in which rhetorical competence influences and enables meaning and enhances the ability to manage human affairs" (38). The traditions of rhetorical education Logan traces among nineteenth-century African Americans provide powerful examples of how enabling rhetorical competence can be.

In addition to wondering about the implications of rhetorical education, newcomers to the field of rhetoric and composition will certainly wish to know some of the different forms that rhetorical education in America has taken throughout its rather lengthy history. Because many of our readers will encounter this collection in an academic context, part 2 explores "Rhetorical Education in Diverse Classrooms." Contributors to this section raise questions about how rhetorical education has been configured within university classrooms.

Jill Swiencicki considers rhetorical handbooks as sites where scholars, teachers, and students negotiate conflicting discourses of identity. Through a detailed study of *The Columbian Orator* in both its 1803 and 1998 editions, Swiencicki demonstrates that "artifacts such as rhetoric handbooks are places where our desires for coherent national, cultural, and political identities contend with the very differences that threaten to unravel seams of difference that are carefully stitched together" (58). Rather than simply presenting our students with contemporary textbooks, Swiencicki urges teachers of rhetorical education to use handbooks from the archives of rhetorical education. These historical texts—with the guidance of a skilled teacher—can engage students in a "critical dialogue about rhetoric, subject formation, and knowledge production—a dialogue that sees writing as action" (73).

In "Politics, Identity, and the Language of Appalachia: James Watt Raine on 'Mountain Speech and Song,'" Susan Kates invites readers to consider rhetorical education at nontraditional institutions such as Berea College, a four-year school in the Appalachian region of Kentucky. Kates explores how James Watt Raine, a professor of rhetoric at Berea in the early twentieth century, espoused the value of the Appalachian dialect in his publications and pedagogy. Raine's text, *The Land of the Saddle-bags: A Study of the Mountain People of Appalachia,* "mounts an articulate defense of the culture and, more specifically, the language of the people of the mountain region of Kentucky" (75). This defense of the Appalachian dialect, Kates suggests, is relevant to contemporary debates about the relationship between language and identity. In order to respond effectively to language-in-education controversies, such as the Ebonics debate and the English Only movement, scholars and teachers of rhetoric, Kates argues, would benefit from a "more complete portrait of local, politicized rhetorics," such as those professed by Raine at Berea (86).

Rich Lane invites readers to consider the far-reaching effects of how the academy configures rhetorical education by investigating rhetorical instruction provided to future secondary school teachers in English-education programs. After discussing curricula from several English-education programs, Lane concludes that a great percentage of secondary language arts classrooms are entrenched in nationalistic and aesthetically driven curricula as a result of what gets taught in English-education courses. Although the typical postsecondary curriculum "has undergone extensive discussion and reevaluation" in order to strengthen its rhetorical perspective, language-arts curricula remain focused on "canonical literature and literary analysis" (87). In response to this disjunction, Lane argues that English-education programs need to be infused with a more rhetorically based curriculum—a curriculum that might benefit future secondary school teachers and, in turn, their students.

With many of the essays in parts 1 and 2 suggesting that rhetorical education has effects that reach far beyond the academy, we suspect that our readers will also want to know more about how rhetorical education has functioned outside of official academic contexts. The essays in part 3 demonstrate that rhetorical education has never been limited to the classroom. Nan Johnson's essay, "Parlor Rhetoric and the Performance of Gender in Postbellum America," explores the important cultural work performed by the parlor rhetoric movement in the nineteenth century. This movement, she elaborates, "promised to put the skills of rhetorical influence into the hands of every American citizen who could read and could pay the price of an elocution or letter-writing manual" (107). Yet this promise, she explains, was heavily mediated by assumptions about gender and class. Despite its promises, the parlor rhetoric movement "reinscribed not the example of women's rhetorical advances into public life but rather a highly conservative construction of the American woman as a mother and wife who needed rhetorical skills only to perform those roles to greater effect" (107–08).

Through a detailed study of the Saratoga National Historical Park, S. Michael Halloran reminds us that rhetorical education need not come through textbooks or academically authorized teachers. Historical landmarks provide rhetorical education by instructing visitors about how to perceive and respond to historical artifacts. By creating a sense of shared identity among visitors, educational materials at such landmarks enable diverse individuals to engage in the rhetorical activities of shared public discourse. Through visits to landmarks such as the Saratoga battlefield, diverse groups of people come to share certain historical knowledge and national perspectives and become part of a discourse community of citizens. "These are sites of rhetorical education," Halloran asserts, "and the study of how [such historical sites] work to inform their visitors, and hence to form those visitors as citizens is a vast, inviting, largely unexplored, and deeply important field for rhetorical research" (144).

In an essay that serves as a companion piece to Halloran's, Gregory Clark studies "an instance of rhetorical education in America that is cultural rather than curricular" (145). Clark demonstrates how landscapes, particularly those mediated by institutions of national culture such as the National Parks Service, provide rhetorical education to a wide swath of the American public. Clark argues that when Americans gather in a landscape that has been rendered publicly symbolic of their nation, they are schooled in the experience of a common national identity—a fundamental part of American rhetorical education. This education in collective identity and national culture, Clark suggests, forms a basis for future instruction in theories and practices of public discourse.

Part 4 invites readers to discuss the past of rhetorical education in light of its future. More specifically, "Rhetorical Education: Back to the Future" encourages readers to consider how they might make use today of the information this collection provides about the different sites and purpose that have characterized rhetorical education in America. Given contemporary rhetorical situations, what can we learn from what we've done in the past? Which past pedagogical practices might we revive? Which current practices might we keep? What new practices must we develop?

In "(Re)Turning to Aristotle: Metaphor and the Rhetorical Education of Students," Sherry Booth and Susan Frisbie trace scholarly thinking about metaphor from Aristotle to Kenneth Burke and suggest that, by investigating the narratives buried within metaphors, teachers of rhetoric and composition can lead students to a richer understanding of how language shapes reality. Contemporary composition handbooks, Booth and Frisbie explain, present "a simplistic view [of metaphor] that urges teachers to help students avoid mixed or strained metaphors but does not address the role of metaphor in conveying and receiving—in constructing—meaning" (164). Yet the concept of metaphor, Booth and Frisbie contend, has a much richer history, one that considers metaphor "as a means to provide a new perspective or to persuade" and as a rhetorical strategy that "links language and psychology and spans the spectrum of human endeavor and inquiry" (177). Contemporary rhetorical education might draw on this history and enrich students' understandings of how language persuades.

The final essay in part 4, Laura Gurak's "Cyberliteracy: Toward a New

Rhetorical Consciousness," points to vast new territories for rhetorical education. Gurak traces historical configurations of literacy and suggests that the concept of literacy, as it informs the teaching of rhetoric, "must be reconfigured if it is to be a useful heuristic and critical tool for the sorts of discourse that will take place in the future" (180). The rhetorical curriculum of the twenty-first century, Gurak argues, will need to focus on the development of critical "cyberliteracy." After elaborating the promises and dangers of internet technology for rhetorical education, Gurak calls for a curriculum that helps students understand and critically evaluate the rhetorical features of digital communication.

As with all textual divisions, the "parts" of *Rhetorical Education in America* are rhetorical choices, and we intend them to highlight certain connections and conflicts among the essays. Other connections and conflicts will undoubtedly emerge for the reader across, and perhaps in resistance to, the divisions we have established. We hope that, in the end, readers come away from this collection not with all of their questions about rhetorical education in America answered, but with a desire to contribute to the unsettled yet vital conversations that surround the topic.

# Notes

1. By *America,* Margaret Lyday, Wendy Sharer, and I mean the United States of America. I wish to thank the other editors and Jessica Enoch, in particular, for their helpful comments on drafts of this introduction.

2. Malea Powell's scholarship on Native American oratory and writing provides keen insights into this problem.

3. Scholarship on historical definitions of literacy and historical developments of higher education abounds, some of the best being Harvey J. Graff's *The Legacies of Literacy* and *The Labyrinths of Literacy* as well as Bernard Bailyn's *Education in the Forming of American Society* and Karl Kaestle's *Pillars of the Republic.*

4. The scholarly contributions of John Brereton, Richard Bullock and John Trimbur, Robert Connors, Sharon Crowley, Keith Gilyard, Joseph Harris, Gail Hawisher and Cynthia Selfe, Susan Miller, Thomas Miller, Steven North, Robert Scholes, and Victor Villanueva—to mention a few others and omit far too many— constitute a body of research and reflection on the problems and solutions presented by rhetorical education in America.

# I
# The Implications of Rhetorical Education

# 1

# Rhetoric, the "Citizen-Orator," and the Revitalization of Civic Discourse in American Life

*William N. Denman*

The ancient links between rhetoric, civic life, and democracy are a part of the European heritage of rhetorical thought and practice. The history of rhetoric makes clear that the teaching of rhetoric was an instrumental part of the development of that civic persona, the "citizen-orator," whose skills were at the service of the community. The classical education that formed and trained the citizen-orator dominated much of higher education well through the eighteenth and into the early nineteenth century, particularly in American higher education. With the considerable changes that overtook American education in the nineteenth century, the neoclassical education that produced citizen-orators disappeared and took with it much of the relationship between education, rhetoric, and civic life. It can be argued that the disappearance of the old, neoclassical education was not a loss: higher education, in particular, became far more egalitarian and practical and was an integral force in national development. The counterargument can be made, however, that the disappearance of rhetorically based education was a significant loss to American civic life. The disappearance of the concept of "citizen-orator" from American education has deprived our students, and the citizens they become, of a central ability to function effectively in democratic life. It is necessary to trace how this disappearance came about, then consider why we should take action to resurrect it in our classrooms and discuss how we might go about doing so.

## Changes in Rhetorical Education

The rhetorical education received by the young men in American colonial colleges was based upon the precepts of classical rhetoric as interpreted by such British writers as George Campbell, Hugh Blair, and Richard Whately. One of the premises of this rhetorical education, derived from the ancients, was the linkage between the practice of rhetoric and its use in civic life. This concept of what came to be called the "citizen-orator" was embodied in the cultural ideal of the "good man speaking well" as educated in schools modeled after Quintilian's *Institutio Oratoria*.

Gregory Clark and S. Michael Halloran, in *Oratorical Culture in Nineteenth-Century America: Transformations in the Theory and Practice of Rhetoric,* point out that the discourse of the colonial period was based on "the neoclassical assumption that moral authority in a community is located in the public consensus of its members rather than in their individual private convictions." The discourse thus produced had as its consistent purpose "to form and sustain a public consensus, intellectual and moral, as the basis of civic action" (2). This was the discourse practiced by orators such as John Adams, Thomas Jefferson, John Witherspoon, Daniel Webster, and Edward Everett. This consensus-centered oratory did not long survive into the nineteenth century. Clark and Halloran take as their thesis the idea that "both the theory of rhetoric taught in the schools and the practice of public discourse sustained outside them were transformed during the nineteenth century from those of the neoclassical oratorical culture into those of the professional culture we see characterizing both colleges and communities by its end" (5–6).

A number of changes in American life had a great impact on the nature of rhetorical education and practice as we moved into the nineteenth century. Among those changes were a shift toward values that favored the individual, a shift in the economic structure of the growing nation that emphasized competition, the development of specializations in both occupations and in education, and most particularly, the rise of a culture of professionalism. To this list can be added changes in rhetorical and oratorical instruction: the growing influence of belles lettres and elocution. A development late in the century was the rise of popular oratory as a distinct type of oratory separate from political oratory. A final influence was the rise of writing and composition as forces in both education and society.

The first of these changes was a shift in values from what might be called a communitarian ethos to a greater consciousness of individual autonomy. The growth of individualism as a central cultural value meant that public life came to be seen as an arena for individual self-definition and action. American economic life in the nineteenth century saw rapid expansion both geographically and economically as the emergence of manufacturing changed the face of the nation. The nature of capitalistic competition brought a shift from an emphasis upon a society in which individuals saw themselves as a contributor to the public good to one in which the focus was upon their own economic survival (Clark and Halloran 11).

The emergence of manufacturing as a significant economic element brought with it the demand for a specialized work force, particularly a specialized and educated work force such as engineers. The creation of Rensselaer School, later Rensselaer Polytechnic Institute, in 1824 was in recognition of the need to move higher education away from the classical tradition. In 1827 Amherst College issued two reports, the first an inquiry into the deficiencies of the prevailing course of study, and the second a proposal to establish an additional program of study, parallel to the classical one, that would allow students to study other modern languages, agricultural chemistry, engineering, physics, and a range of courses in political science and history. These courses were established at the expense of Greek and Latin, but not at the expense of philosophy, rhetoric, and oratory (Rudolph 122–23). Clearly colleges were making some attempt to meet the changing needs of society.

With the rise of specialization in careers came the rise of what Burton Bledstein calls the culture of professionalism. The rise of a middle class in America brought with it a concern for individual achievement. The aspiring middle-class person sought to move, vertically, through levels of social and economic status. One of the ways this could be achieved was through the development of specific skills that moved the individual into a "professional" class as opposed to the laboring, trading, or artisan classes. Bledstein chronicles the rise of professionalism in nineteenth-century America and provides a picture of the rapid, almost manic, growth of professional culture. As he puts it: "Success in the middle class increasingly depended upon providing a service based on a skill, elevating the status of one's occupation by referring to it as a profession" (Bledstein 34). One of the ways in which an occupation could become a profession was through education. "[The] instrument of ambition and a vehicle to status in the occupational world" became a degree (Bledstein 34). The impulse to use education as the stepping-stone to occupational status had great implications for higher education. Indeed, the story of the American university is the story of the rise of academic specialization created to meet the specialized needs of the professional culture.

The rise of large institutions of higher education, particularly after the Civil War, had several effects upon the old, classical, oratorical education that furthered the demise of the "citizen-orator" in American life. Oral exercises, examinations, disputations, and the like gave way to written work. The greater numbers of students could be handled far more effectively with written examinations. Applicants to the universities could be evaluated more effectively by writing. The death of oratorical education was, in large part, the result of a need to move to writing as a primary instrument of education in the new universities as growth in enrollment drove the developing curriculum.

Two patterns were predominant in the teaching of oral communication skills in nineteenth-century American colleges. The first of these was belles lettres, with its emphasis upon word usage and style. The most popular text in use in American colleges in the first quarter of the nineteenth century was Hugh Blair's *Lectures on Rhetoric and Belles Lettres*. While Blair was influenced by the classical tradition, he "did not consider rhetoric merely to be concerned with oral persuasion. 'To speak or write perspicuously and agreeably, with purity, with grace and strength, are attainments of the utmost consequence to all who propose, either by speech or writing, to address the public'" (Hochmuth and Murphy 158).

A further example can be found in Samuel P. Newman's text, *A Practical System of Rhetoric* (APSR), which, first published in 1827, underwent sixty editions and was used in a number of colleges through the 1860s. According to Beth Hewett, "Primarily belletristic, APSR reveals Newman's synthesis of contemporary rhetorical theory as it bears on praxis; i.e., teaching thought as a foundation for good writing, general and literary taste, language usage skills, and style" (55). Halloran sums up the influence of belles lettres by pointing out that while belletristic rhetoric included a classical pedagogy based upon the use of models and imitation, it brought change: "the emphasis shifts somewhat, from persuasive to poetic discourse, and from the rhetorical virtue of *eloquence* to a new ideal of *taste*." He sees belletristic rhetoric as setting the stage for the elevation of interpretation and reading over invention and writing that would come to characterize English studies (Halloran, "From Rhetoric" 163).

Along with the emphasis upon style and language use, so prominent a part of the belles lettres tradition, came an interest in the quality of oral delivery. By the second decade of the century, criticism of the public performances of clergy, lawyers, and others in public affairs led to a concern for the teaching of proper delivery skills. In 1824 the Reverend Ebenezer Porter, the Bartlett Professor of Pulpit Eloquence at Andover College, published his text *Lectures on the Analysis of Vocal Inflection* followed by a second work on delivery. His *Rhetorical Reader* of 1831 underwent some three hundred printings by 1858. By the third quarter of the nineteenth century, elocution was a required subject in many colleges throughout the nation (Hochmuth and Murphy 162).

The last decades of the century saw the creation of a new mode of oratory that changed the old three-mode scheme. The four modes became judicial, deliberative, sacred, and popular oratory. The development of popular oratory was linked with the new prominence "that public lecturers and platform speakers had achieved by the latter part of the nineteenth century and the proliferation in nineteenth-century North American society of communal occasions at which platform speaking was a central activity" (N. Johnson, "Popularization" 156). All of these developments had gone a long way to removing the "citizen-orator" from civic life.

By the last quarter of the century, where rhetoric was taught it was primarily "in departments of English; oratory had a prominent position in colleges around the country but was losing vogue in some of the Eastern colleges; instruction was given in elocution in most of the colleges and was looked upon as an aid to students in their competitions for prizes in oratory." Debate as a pedagogical tool had become a part of the extracurriculum (Hochmuth and Murphy 169). The art of formalized debate had begun its long march to the margins of rhetorical training as an extracurricular activity limited to a few talented and interested students. Where rhetoric, as the art of creating messages, existed in any formal way it was primarily in the new departments of English.[1]

## Writing Instruction and Rhetoric

The final development that had influence on the demise of rhetoric's link with civic discourse was the rise of writing instruction. A revolution in writing technology occurred in the nineteenth century that had important consequences for the teaching of writing:

> Pens, ink, and pencils improved significantly, making it possible for people to write with less fuss and mess. . . . Paper decreased substantially in cost, making it economically feasible for people to write more, to use writing freely as a medium of exploration, to discard drafts and revise more extensively. (Halloran, "From Rhetoric" 169)

All of this, combined with dramatic increases in book and periodical publication, and with an increasingly efficient postal system, made it easier to conduct business and personal affairs in writing (Halloran, "From Rhetoric" 169). The physical nature of older writing instruments necessitated a two-step process of composing. The writer or speaker had to first think out very carefully what he wished to say and then write it down with care. In these circumstances the process of invention occurs in the mind. The shift in composing brought about by improved writing technology enabled writers or speakers to use writing to create and revise their work rather than as a way to record a finished work.

The emphasis placed upon writing in the second half of the nineteenth century might lead one to think that the new courses in composition that became a staple of instruction in departments of English would have a focus on rhetoric. To some extent, this was certainly true. What was lacking, however, was instruction in rhetoric that was linked with civic life. The composition course of the late nineteenth century "was an attempt to adapt rhetoric to the dramatically changed conditions both inside and outside the academy"—conditions that were influenced by the new middle-class and professional mores (Halloran, "From Rhetoric" 175). What resulted from this adaptation was a course that emphasized what came to be called "current-traditional rhetoric." This rhetoric placed

> emphasis on the written product rather than the process of composition or communication; classification of discourse into the four so-called modes (description, narration, exposition, argumentation); concentration on correctness of usage and certain stylistic qualities, without much reference to the invention of substance for discourse. (Halloran, "American College" 257)

Halloran sees the shift to current-traditional rhetoric occurring as the result of several of the influences mentioned earlier: the impact of belles lettres on pedagogy, the steady specialization of knowledge in the curriculum, and a shift in the focus of college curricula to an emphasis upon providing opportunities for individual advancement (Halloran, "American College" 262).

One significant factor of the current-traditional rhetoric taught in composition courses was the removal of persuasion from a place in forms of discourse. James Berlin discusses the texts by John Franklin Genung as typical of those used in the last decades of the nineteenth century. Genung treats persuasion in such a way that it removes it from the composition classroom. While seeing persuasion "as the apotheosis of rhetoric," Genung asserts that persuasion "cannot be undertaken without 'the close contact of personal presence.' It 'presupposes a speaker at close quarters with his audience.' This insistence on the oral act removes persuasion from a place in Genung's rhetoric, leaving to the composition class the scientific use of language" (Berlin, *Writing Instruction* 67). Another late-nineteenth-century text, *Principles of Rhetoric* by A. S. Hill, focuses on the four forms of discourse, description, narration, exposition, and argument. Argument is like exposition, according to Hill, in that it is addressed to the understanding, but it leads to belief rather than to understanding. James Berlin writes, "Persuasion is treated as a subclass of argument, differing from its source in that it 'is addressed not so much to the intellect as to the feelings.' It is relegated to the status of a 'useful adjunct,' and is presented briefly, almost as an afterthought, with little enthusiasm" (*Writing Instruction* 67–68).

Berlin reports that by the end of the century the typical composition textbook was largely devoted to the four forms of discourse and to stylistic matters. Correctness had become the most significant aspect of prose writing. It was a writing that was to serve the professional aspirations of the students, with an emphasis upon practicality. Courses were organized around actual writing and not the memorization of rhetorical principles. The emphasis was upon extensive writing of informal essays, including the daily theme or journal entry. Berlin concludes: "If textbooks told students anything about the stages of composing, they provided a mechanical model. The student was to select the subject, narrow it to a thesis, make an outline of the essay, write the essay, and edit it for correctness. They might also be given suggestions for introductions and conclusions." If an audience was to be considered, the model was an abstract one based upon the old faculty psychology and the forms of discourse (Berlin, *Writing Instruction* 73–74).

Halloran sums it up well: Much of great value was lost in the evolution from the neoclassical rhetoric of the late eighteenth century to the composition course of the late nineteenth. Heuristic theory and procedures virtually disappeared, and the sense of audience was narrowed. In place of a rich array of stylistic forms and techniques was the flat voice of mechanical correctness. The greatest loss was the sense of a large social purpose for writing, a social role for which rhetorical art was necessary equipment. The ideal of the citizen-orator was gone and little was offered in its place. "[T]he larger purpose of social leadership through discourse that had been both central to and explicit in neo-classical rhetoric had no equivalent in the rhetoric of English composition" (Halloran, "From Rhetoric" 176–77).

The concept of "citizen-orator" had a central role in the link between the teaching and practice of rhetoric both in ancient Greece and in colonial America. The idea that a well-educated citizen could, and should, be an active participant in the deliberations of the polis was important to the development of democracy. The loss of the "citizen-orator" as a goal of American higher education, due to changes that occurred in the nineteenth century, marked a significant change in the development of democracy in the United States. The practice of democracy—and politics—became a function of the newly emerging professional classes. This shift, perhaps the most important of all, has had serious effects on contemporary life. But if this ancient link between rhetoric and civic life largely disappeared from the study of writing, did it also disappear from the teaching of oral communication?

## Speech Communication and Rhetoric

The link between the teaching of public speaking and civic life was seen as an important element in the early years of the communication profession. Evidence of this concern can be found in textbooks used in public speaking courses. A survey of such textbooks from the 1920s until today shows that the need for oratorical training in a democracy was fairly consistently used as a justification for the teaching of public speaking. During World War II and after, many textbooks emphasized the need for public speaking in our democracy. The McCarthy period in the early 1950s and the civil unrest of the 1960s both prompted the authors of such textbooks to emphasize the link between oratory and democracy as the primary justification for learning speaking skills. This situation shifted somewhat in the late 1970s and 1980s when texts placed an emphasis upon personal and career goals as a primary reason for learning to speak well in public (Persi and Denman).

Certainly the teaching of rhetoric did not disappear from speech classrooms in the twentieth century. As Herman Cohen clearly demonstrates, rhetoric was, in the early years of the speech communication discipline, a central part of the curriculum and the focus of early writing in the discipline (Cohen 110–18). However, the broad expansion of the communication field, particularly after World War II, saw a growing emphasis upon social science aspects of the discipline, which often eclipsed rhetoric as an important part of the curricula. The varied nature of the basic or introductory courses taught around the country testify to the breadth of the discipline and to the extent to which there is considerable disagreement on what fundamental communication instruction college students should have. The most recent survey of basic oral communication courses in colleges and universities indicates that 55 percent of the courses are public speaking in nature and 30.1 percent are hybrid courses that include interpersonal and small group communication, along with some public speaking (Morreale, Hanna, Berko, Gibson 15).

## A Justification of Rhetoric in Basic Courses

Twenty-first-century life in the United States is clearly far more complex than life in Athens during the fifth century B.C.E. Yet our society, like that of the ancient Greeks, is a society concerned with power and its uses. If citizens today have strong feelings of disempowerment, one solution is empowerment. Clearly one source of power available to citizens is obtained through training in communication. Many of us may agree with Roderick Hart, a professor of communication and government at the University of Texas, when he asserts that communication is the most important subject taught in schools today and in the future. He returns us to Isocrates who "knew only three things: To become eloquent is to activate one's humanity, to apply the imagination, and to solve the practical problems of human living. When Isocrates taught rhetoric to his Greek schoolboys he empowered them; he helped them see avenues for making their minds count in the affairs of society" (Hart 101).

Teachers of communication, Hart argues, teach freedom, for "freedom goes to the articulate."

[I]f rhetorical power becomes decentralized, then it becomes in-
finitely more difficult for power blocs in society to practice economic, social, and political hegemony. When I, as a citizen, learn
to use the power of language successfully, I decrease my chances
of being victimized . . . when I learn how to speak the language of
power, then power becomes my inexorable ally and not my tormen-
tor. (Hart 102–03)

It is particularly essential that we give power to the voices of those
who have hitherto been voiceless in American life. The voiceless are those
who have historically been unheard, as well as those whose early education, upbringing, and cultural roots have discouraged active participation in civic life. Those whose rhetorical resources have been constrained
can find their voices through the practice of rhetoric and participation
in civic life as these things can be taught in communications classes. It
is time to bring the "citizen-orator"—and the "citizen-writer"—back into
the college curriculum.

## Some Solutions to the Problem

The "citizen-orator" can be reintegrated into our basic courses in a number of ways: first, not just by presenting rhetoric as the art of creating
messages for specific audiences but by presenting rhetoric as epistemic;
second, by restructuring the basic courses as a forum for civic participation; and finally, by emphasizing argument as a central element of persuasion.

James Berlin, in his volume on writing instruction in America in the
twentieth century, traces the development of epistemic rhetoric as it
emerged in the literature of composition studies from 1960 to 1975
(Berlin, *Rhetoric and Reality*). Berlin begins with a reference to Michael
Leff's 1978 *Central States Speech Journal* article "In Search of Ariadne's
Thread" where Leff explains that the distinguishing characteristic of the
epistemic view is "that rhetoric is a serious philosophical subject that
involves not only the transmission of knowledge, but also the generation
of knowledge." Berlin continues:

Rhetoric exists not merely so that truth may be communicated:
rhetoric exists so that truth may be discovered. The epistemic position implies that knowledge is not discovered by reason alone,

that cognitive and affective processes are not separate, that inter-subjectivity is a condition of all knowledge, and that the contact of minds affects knowledge. (Berlin, *Rhetoric and Reality* 165)

For example, a public speaking course that took the premise that rhetoric is epistemic could begin with consideration of the ways in which we use language through the process of communication to shape our views of reality. Instead of learning that knowledge—and truth or reality—are contained in electronic web pages, library card catalogs, or periodical guides, students would learn that they, too, can create knowledge for themselves and others through discourse. What they find in those library guides and web pages is merely evidence of the views of others about truth and reality—constructed knowledge that others see as valid but that is still open to a new dialectic. Students would still be presented with the basic structures of rhetorical practice, but within the context of classroom experiences that relate their newly created knowledge to the civic world in which they live.

A second way in which basic communication/composition courses can bring the concept of "citizen-orator" to life again is through a re-structuring of the courses themselves and of the textbooks used in the courses. This is one area where colleagues in composition are ahead of the speech communication discipline. Elizabeth Ervin discusses her solution to the question of how to encourage civic participation in first-year writing students. She begins with the premise that through the use of different textbooks she might refocus the work of her students toward civic participation. She details how the texts she examined and the one she first used, all "current-issues" writing textbooks, provided her students with opportunities to write about issues in class but did not lead them to writing about or acting upon those issues outside of class. After further work she developed a conceptual framework for implementing a "civic agenda" in her composition classrooms. Following the work of Robert Putnam she urges that we reimagine students as citizens who, even within the context of the classroom, can have that persona. Secondly, she urges that we reinvent the classroom as a "secondary association," one in which students see that "there is value . . . in participating in 'dense networks of interaction' *within* the classroom" (Ervin 395). Finally, she seeks to create opportunities for students to engage in authentic civic discourses. This pedagogical project entails rethinking the purposes of the writing assigned and the nature of the textbooks and other resources the students use. She concludes that the texts by Ann Watters and Marjorie Ford, *Writing for Change: A Community Reader* and *A Guide for Change: Resources for Implementing Community Service Writing*, move beyond the restrictions she found in other texts and provide the focus she desires.[2]

The third way in which we can bring civic discourse back into basic communication and composition courses is to emphasize persuasion and argument. The purpose is not to turn the basic courses into courses in argumentation and debate, but to provide much broader work in the uses of argument as the central factor in persuasion. One place to begin would be to focus on the role of public speaking as a vital element in civic life. The first edition of a recently published text used as a running theme the idea that the students enrolled in the course were going to function as opinion leaders in society. The text had a significant discussion of the nature of opinion leadership. A strong chapter on the rhetorical situation provided an extensive example of the founding of Mothers Against Drunk Driving as an example of how rhetoric can be used in a contemporary political setting. Later editions of that text almost eliminate that important emphasis, and the discussion of rhetorical situation becomes just a small part of a chapter on audience analysis.

Clearly, a textbook that placed emphasis upon the links between rhetoric, public speaking, and civic life could provide a foundation for a course so framed. Examining contemporary public speaking textbooks demonstrates, however, that such an approach would be at variance with current practice. Most public speaking texts used in basic courses place little emphasis upon public speaking and civic life, and those that make reference to it provide little in the way of concrete guidance on the role of rhetoric in public speaking. Indeed, the term *rhetoric* is often ignored.

In a brief examination of seven current public speaking texts, including several that are reported to be best-sellers, it was clear that the usual format is to provide at least one chapter on persuasive speeches and to refer, at least sketchily, to the use of argument as part of the persuasive process.[3] Some texts deal with argument, or reasoning, either as part of the broader chapter on persuasion or as a chapter unto itself. The discussion of argument varies from a discussion of deduction and induction to arguments from examples, cause, signs, analogy, and principles. Some texts make use of the Toulmin model, with discussion that covers anywhere from one page to several pages. Occasionally a text will discuss fallacies. In textbooks that range between 400 and 450 pages in length, no more than 20 pages in any one of the books deals with argument or reasoning.

Some serious suggestions about the teaching of argument have come from composition. Barbara Emmel, Paula Resch, and Deborah Tenney have edited a volume, *Argument Revisited; Argument Redefined: Negotiating Meaning in the Composition Classroom*, that is devoted to discussion of the teaching of argument. The editors view argument as a means of constructing contingent truth for those involved. Argument thus viewed is not hegemonic, supportive only of the status quo, but an instrument that can be used to further change. Furthermore, "when argument is misrepresented or excluded from the composition classroom, we deny composition a powerful system of literacy in which students engage in reflexive questioning of self and others and then progress to decision making and negotiations of meanings that grow out of that initial reflexivity" (xvii–xviii).

In a stimulating and possibly revolutionary chapter, "Classical Rhetoric: the Art of Argumentation," Jeanne Fahnestock and Marie Secor present a vision of a composition course built on classical concepts of argumentation. They begin with the assumption that most freshmen have little understanding of what it means to argue—to develop a position and support it with evidence. Their high school education has provided no such training. A 1992 national report concluded that students in the fourth, eighth, and twelfth grades perform poorly on persuasive writing tasks. Fahnestock and Secor believe that "[s]tudents clearly need more exposure to argumentative texts, need to learn how to read and evaluate them, and need to learn how to write them." This can be done, they argue, if students "acquire again the holistic vision, the 'big picture' provided by classical rhetoric" (99). Many current proposals and models are in use in composition for the teaching of argument, but what is needed is wide applicability. Classical rhetoric offers a complete art that takes the student from the initial stages of inquiry through to the final stages of dissemination. Fahnestock and Secor agree that much of what is taught in courses of "critical thinking" and in the Writing across the Curriculum movement (WAC) may be seen as teaching argument. Both these approaches have their weaknesses: critical thinking focuses largely on analysis of arguments, not on their creation. WAC courses see argument as discipline-specific, which often denies a general vocabulary for talking, and writing about, argument. They see classical rhetoric as an art that is complete and comprehensive in ways that cannot be matched by more modern approaches.

The use of classical rhetoric, as envisioned by Fahnestock and Secor, would emphasize seven elements: "the need for exigence, the stases as a way of sorting issues, the blending of the three appeals, a further explication of the topoi, the need to switch levels of argument, the restoration of narrative as a tactic of persuasion, and a deeper appreciation of the inventional possibilities offered by the figures of speech" (101). Their discussion of these seven elements is too long to be efficiently summarized here, but it is clear that they have conceived a course approach that is soundly grounded in the classical tradition while relating that tradition to the lives of contemporary students.

The authors recognize, too, the obstacles that can be placed in the path of such a proposal. First, of course, is the amount of training that teachers would require. To implement the changes they suggest might mean changes in the graduate education of composition teachers. The second obstacle they mention is an attitudinal one, the belief that all of this argument stuff is just archaic, or, to quote James Murphy: "Is this all just impractical antiquarian hogwash?" (121). Fahnestock and Secor clearly believe the answer is no.

More than thirty years of teaching basic communication courses, and particularly courses in public speaking, have led me to believe that those courses, valuable as they are to the students who take them, are failing in their broader purpose. I have also spent a good deal of time exploring and teaching rhetorical theory. As a result of that study I believe that our failure is not in teaching the essential skills of managing discourse, both in public speaking and composition courses. Our failure comes in not linking those skills to a wider goal: the betterment of civic life. I have tried to demonstrate how that failure came about in higher education and have indicated the central reason why I think we need to correct that failure: we need to teach communication as empowerment and rhetoric as the tool of empowerment. I have made some suggestions as to how we might correct our failure, for the ancient links between rhetoric and the development and maintenance of democracy are too important for us to continue to ignore in our basic courses.

## Notes

1. Nan Johnson, in her volume *Nineteenth-Century Rhetoric in North America,* indicates that textbooks of the later part of the century dealt with the qualities

that an orator needed in order to be successful, including the ancient concept of the good person speaking well. Oratory was seen, according to Johnson, as still necessary for the proper working of the political process. It is not clear, without a further examination of the texts of the time, if the authors were seeing rhetoric linked with citizen participation in civic life.

2. Carol J. Jablonski discusses much the same idea in her description of the public speaking class as a "deliberative community" in "A Reflection on Curricular Reform: A Challenge and a Role for Rhetorical Studies."

3. The texts examined were David Zarefsky, *Public Speaking: Strategies for Success;* Steven R. Brydon and Michael D. Scott, *Between One and Many: The Art and Science of Public Speaking;* J. Michael Sproule, *Speechmaking: Rhetorical Competency in a Postmodern World;* Stephen E. Lucas, *The Art of Public Speaking;* Michael Osborn and Suzanne Osborn, *Public Speaking;* George Rodman and Ronald B. Adler, *The New Public Speaker*. The most thorough discussion of rhetorical history and principles, with a chapter "Message Preparation: Invention" that includes topoi, is *An Introduction to Rhetorical Communication* by James McCroskey.

2

# Lest We Go the Way of Classics

## Toward a Rhetorical Future
## for English Departments

*Thomas P. Miller*

College English may go the way of classics if it continues to define its subject as solely the study of literature, at least that is the trajectory that Robert Scholes outlines in *The Rise and Fall of English*. Like classics before it lost its place as the foundation of liberal education, our learned language is "academic discourse"; we offer courses on great male writers; and we define our "work" as our research and scholarly writing, not our teaching. But the literary classics, the personal essay, and the modes of close reading taught in English classes might soon be succeeded by the digital literacies of the information economy. To make productive use of such assertions, I will discuss how college English has been shaped by the modern development of literacy, how the work of the discipline has changed along with broader developments in learning and the learned, and how the trajectory of study within English departments ought to change if we do not wish to go the way of classics.

The evolution of college English can be defined by historical changes in literacy. Literacy, as Paulo Freire taught us, includes the abilities of acting on the world and reflecting on the self through language. As such, literacy is a social praxis imbedded in history, complexly involved with the rhetorical process of negotiating received assumptions to address shared problems—a process that calls those assumptions into question when what is shared can no longer be assumed. A historical group experiences a literacy crisis when material and cultural changes destabilize the educational transmission of traditional values and privileged modes of transmitting them, as for example when communication technologies change within a generation, or when a dominant group is having trouble assimilating broader classes that do not share its values.

The history of college English is marked by a series of literacy crises associated with the evolution of print culture. Print is not what it was for Gutenberg, nor is reading what it was before television. The late-eighteenth-century transition from scribal to print literacies shaped the establishment of English composition, rhetoric, and belles lettres. The belles lettres were narrowed to a modern sense of literature a century later as the bourgeois reading public became a mass audience, creating a form of illiteracy that literary studies was established to eradicate. A century after that in the 1970s, the reduction of literature to classical fiction in English departments was called into question amidst the "culture wars" and the front-page crises over "why Johnny can't write" that shaped the emergence of composition and cultural studies.

One way to configure these historical developments in literacy and literacy studies is to define college English in terms of the technologies that do its work and the economies in which that work circulates and thereby gains value through use. The best historical example of a technology for producing and distributing knowledge I know of is the trivium—the formal methods for constituting the logical structures, grammatical conventions, and rhetorical purposes of educated discourse. College English began with the reformulation of the trivium during the Enlightenment. Knowledge was no longer to be acquired by deductions from traditional assumptions but by inductively generalizing from the individual experience. In a departure from the highly figured forms of Ciceronian rhetoric, knowledge was to be communicated in a plain style that served as a window on that experience. As the educated culture began to circulate in the language of common life, educated discourse had to be distinguished from the conventions of common people. Two of the first professors of English—George Campbell and Joseph Priestly—were the leading advocates of correcting English by inductively generalizing from educated usage, as well as being influential proponents of the "new" logic and rhetoric (see Howell). This reconception of the trivium reformulated the technologies of knowledge, creating the context in which modern history, political economy, psychology, science, and English entered the curriculum and eventually displaced classical languages and literatures.

The expansion of cheap print literacy transformed the trivium in ways that positioned the subject of college English in public education. The work of the discipline was first done by the belletristic essays of *The Spectator,* which were institutionalized as a standard of educated taste and usage in the first college English textbooks, most notably Hugh Blair's *Lectures on Rhetoric and Belles Lettres* (1783). Adam Smith's characterization of the "impartial spectator" has served as a pivotal point of reference for my analysis of the emergence of literary studies and social sciences out of rhetoric and moral philosophy. But rather than returning to the analyses I developed in *The Formation of College English,* I want to turn to the introduction of English into the colonial curriculum, and then review the professionalization of literary studies in the nineteenth century that ended up confining rhetoric to first-year composition courses. Some English departments are morphing from literary to cultural studies, and many others have expanded beyond literature to include rhetoric and composition, "creative" writing, English as a world language, women's studies, ethnic studies, media studies, and/or cultural studies. Nonetheless, reformers ranging from Elaine Showalter to Cary Nelson continue to ignore rhetoric and composition while appropriating work in the area to expand the market for professors of literature. A critical awareness of our institutional history may help clarify why rhetoric came to be ignored and how it can contribute to the practical skills, civic engagement, and critical awareness our students need in order to be effective and reflective in language.

## Rhetoricians Began Teaching College English (c. 1760)

When we begin our history with the introduction of English into marginal institutions that failed to perpetuate learned languages, we are challenged to look beyond the history of ideas contained within our discipline and assess the social sources and functions of the work we do. The first American professorship dedicated to teaching English was established in 1755 with the founding of the College of Philadelphia—a broad-based institution that combined a charity school for boys and girls with a grammar school and college. The second such professorship was established in 1784 when King's College was reorganized as Columbia College to break up the Anglican establishment in New York after the Revolution. These professorships marked basic changes in what professors taught and how students learned. Depending on whether one was an advocate of the new learning or a classicist, the introduction of English represented enlightened progress or a literacy crisis that threatened the foundations of the educated culture. Either way, our early history calls us to consider how American colleges have functioned as public institutions and how literacy studies have been shaped by the evolution of the modern reading public.

Unlike the English universities that they were reportedly modeled upon, American colleges have always been comparatively public institutions. While Oxbridge was closed to anyone who would not swear allegiance to the union of church and state, American colleges were governed by boards that included lay leaders, generally chosen from a range of sectarian backgrounds in order to ensure that the colleges would be seen as serving the public interest. Such perceptions were important because most colleges depended on intermittently enacted taxes and lotteries. Education was a public concern, according to Bernard Bailyn, because English colonists feared that succeeding generations would devolve into what Cotton Mather termed "the creolean degeneracy" (79). From the outset, colleges sought support by using rhetoric to teach Americans to speak as Englishmen. In the first description of an American college curriculum, *New England's First Fruits* (1642), exercises in English are mentioned, and rhetoric is advertised as the only subject other than divinity to be required from the first to the last years of study. English elocution was prominently displayed to the educated public to demonstrate what colleges offered. Historians have often emphasized the classicism of colonial colleges by citing requirements mandating the use of Latin, but the frequent reiteration of these mandates underlines the fact that students often do not learn what professors profess to teach.

The introduction of English was shaped by the transition from scribal to print literacies. Colonial New England was one of the most literate societies in the world, with literacy rates among adult white males that were 50 percent higher than those in England (60 percent and 40 percent respectively according to H. Graff, *Legacies* 163–65). Because they had few books, colonials read intensively but not extensively. Books were learned by heart, with literacy functioning as "a technology of the self" that imprinted the sacred text upon the consciousness through memorization (Warner 19–20). Richard Brown has characterized the information economy of colonial America as an "economy of scarcity" that followed "a hierarchical diffusion pattern" because information was transmitted orally from those with broader sources of information to those confined to the immediate community (19–20). This economy and the technologies that did its work were evident in the scholastic curriculum of the first two American colleges. Because of the lack of books, knowledge was transmitted orally—through declamations, recitations, commonplace "books," and compendia. Students reduced books and lectures to compendia organized schematically so that they could be memorized and recited to display their learning. In fact, a compendium, or "synopsis," was the original graduate thesis required of all M.A. candidates at Harvard. Such compendia were often cast in a syllogistic form. The syllogism was the primary instructional technology, and it inscribed the logic of a scribal information economy in the assumption that all that one needed to know could be deduced from shared traditions.

In the 1740s evangelical orators proclaimed a "Great Awakening" throughout the colonies, sparking debates in print and fostering support for educational reforms, including the founding of the colleges that helped introduce college English. The Great Awakening was a broad-based movement that popularized oratory but depended upon print for its broader impact. Benjamin Franklin's *American Magazine* (1741) and other magazines emerged to publish accounts of the oratory of itinerants along with debates on whether it was more important for preachers to be learned or inspired. Ministers were often the only college graduates in a town, and many frontier communities were left unchurched and uneducated because colleges were not keeping up with a population that was doubling every twenty-five years. Evangelical critics founded reading societies, schools, and academies, many of which evolved into high schools and colleges. Within twenty-five years, six colleges and dozens of academies were established by religious reformers and others dissatisfied with what Yale and Harvard provided. In New York City, Princeton, New Jersey, and Providence, Rhode Island, religious leaders founded colleges represented as public institutions rather than sectarian seminaries, and in Philadelphia, Franklin and his collaborators also positioned their new college as a more publicly useful alternative to the classical curriculum.

The introduction of college English studies was shaped both by the popular oratory of the time and by the transition from scribal to print literacy. Forensic debates of public controversies replaced the Latin disputations of scholastic metaphysics that had dominated higher education for centuries, but which disappeared in the decade after the American Revolution (see Potter). Literary societies emerged to provide students with opportunities to read, write, and speak about contemporary issues, and courses on English rhetoric and belles lettres were established. The only textbook to be published from the first English courses in America was John Witherspoon's *Lectures on Eloquence*. After graduating from Edinburgh alongside Hugh Blair, Witherspoon emigrated in 1768 to become president of the college that the evangelical "New Lights" had established at Princeton. Witherspoon's lectures on rhetoric and moral philosophy presented a politically engaged alternative to the subordination of rhetoric to taste that Hugh Blair's *Lectures on Rhetoric and Belles Lettres* helped institutionalize (see Halloran, "Rhetoric in the American College Curriculum"). A couple of innovations distinguish Witherspoon's "composition" course from those defined by scribal literacies. Witherspoon provided rules for "all sorts of writing" and listed readings for students, counseling them to read widely and avoid forming their style based on any single author (236, 238–39). Such recommendations became commonplace as students began to have more access to books. Witherspoon's predecessors and other college presidents had greatly expanded college libraries, and it is the wider availability of books that positions the emergence of composition at the origins of the print economy. While Witherspoon oversaw an extensive program of orations, he also assigned essays, and he was particularly attentive to correct spelling and grammar—the characteristic concerns of composition courses that assume the regularities of print as a model.

## Literature Became a Profession, while Composition Remained Simply Work (c. 1860s)

Witherspoon and his contemporaries have been characterized as the "preprofessional" era in Gerald Graff's history of the profession of literature. Advocates for that profession gained public support by proclaiming that professors of literature would eradicate the illiteracy of undergraduates, but, as the profession became established, the teaching of composition was dismissed as work that should have been done in high school. In this and other ways, the profession of literature institutionalized an alienation from the work of literacy. Clifford Siskin has argued that the modern categories of "disciplinarity, professionalism, and Literature" are key elements of the same historical formation (6). As part of an ideological substructure opposing "professional/amateur, discipline/avocation, [and] real/made up," the leisurely reading of fiction replaced the classics as part of what all educated people shared in common, whatever profession they worked in (6). Paralleling Siskin's argument, Terry Eagleton has examined how modern aesthetics was set in opposition to the world of work, with literature becoming a preserve for personal reflection in one's free time. The same alienation from work is evident within the teaching of composition, for as Sharon Crowley and others have argued, the belletristic rhetorics that institutionalized composition mystified the productive resources of discourse with doctrines of natural genius that dismissed invention as unteachable and concentrated instead on correcting taste and usage (*Composition in the University*). Such managerial theories of the composing process mirrored the ideology of professionalism, which assumes that the work of making things is unprofessional except as a process to be managed and that only those who are deficient have to labor at such work.

The institutional demarcation of the field of literature from the work of reading and writing can be dated from the literacy crisis that was manufactured to justify the expansion of the profession. A century ago a flurry of professional reports surveyed national trends and institutional practices, documenting that the majority of English courses were in composition while arguing that such work was too menial for professionals and really belonged to the schools. College English was publicized as a scholarly discipline in works such as *English in American Universities, by Professors in the English Departments of Twenty Representative Institutions* (1895) and other public commentaries that are reprinted by John Brereton and Gerald Graff and Michael Warner. In *PMLA* articles of the time, professors of English claimed "concessions" from "classicists" by representing literature as "an intellectual study for serious workers," free from the "desultory" pastimes that wasted "leisure hours" (qtd. Graff and Warner 42, 44). With stylistic criticism serving as a means to form character, English was institutionalized to teach Anglo-Saxon culture: "the study of English literature means the study of the great movement of English life and feeling, as it is reflected in the purest prose of representative men" (qtd. Graff and Warner 35). The literature of the English was used to teach the American middle class appropriate tastes, in part because the Anglo-Saxon character of the country was being called into question by rising waves of non-English-speaking immigrants (see Connors, *Composition-Rhetoric*). Once the field achieved public legitimacy, its major professional organization, MLA, promptly shut down its Pedagogical Section and ceased publishing any work on teaching (see Brereton 187).

With the professionalization of literature, rhetoric was reduced to teaching first-year composition. According to commentators of the time, the "bugbear" of "Freshman English" would disappear when literature was properly taught, because "efficient English teachers" would then be prepared to establish "a more serious attention to elementary English" (qtd. Graff and Warner 42–43, 45). Little was written about how teachers would be trained for this work. From its origins, the profession of literature avoided being distracted by its dependence on teaching composition. English professors promoted public concern by heralding a literacy crisis that arose when students failed the entrance exams established at Harvard and elsewhere at the end of the nineteenth century. This literacy crisis ensued in part because traditional technologies of instruction could not handle rising enrollments. The last of the Harvard reports in 1897 noted that "about the year 1870," enrollments increased "nearly fourfold," making the "oral method" of recitations impossible: "a system of lectures, with periodic written examinations, took its place, so that at last the whole college work was practically done in writing" (qtd. Brereton 112). Such accounts document that college English was established in response to changes in technologies and economies of literacy, and that with its establishment learning to write and writing to learn disappeared into work properly done elsewhere.

As professors of literature got serious about scholarship, composition ended up being taught by about the only instructors who could not claim a research basis for their work—former journalists, ministers, teachers of oratory, and faculty spouses whose work was to clean up students' language. Rhetoric did not become an area of research because the model for scholarly disciplines was imported from German universities. While completing their studies in Germany, aspiring Americans learned how to work in an educational economy segmented into specialized fields for faculty and free electives for students, an economy that valued research over teaching and graduate studies over liberal education. Rhetoric had disappeared from the German curriculum at the beginning of the century, and the two cultures of the modern American academy had no place for rhetoric either. It was not disinterested and methodical enough to be a science, and it was too mechanical and political to be an art. Failing to achieve the status of a modern art or science, rhetoric became confined to mere teaching, transmitted through the machinations of teacher-proof textbooks, which Robert Connors has described as "great steam-driven mass productions of ten and twenty thousand copies," circulating through "extensive sales and distribution networks" (*Composition-Rhetoric* 84). Making this massive enterprise invisible in scholarship on work in the field took concerted professional will, but it became much easier to divorce scholarship on literature from the teaching of reading and writing after the object of study was demarcated from nonliterary forms and political uses of discourse.

The alienation of literature from literacy is perhaps best characterized by the workings of the essay, which has been central to scholarship and teaching, but which itself has been the least studied of literary genres, as has been discussed by Susan Miller, Ross Winterowd, and other recent commentators. As a conversation with no one in particular for no political purpose or economic use, the essay effaces its social sources and institutional functions as peripheral to its unmediated representations of individual experience. In these and other ways, the essay serves as a paradigm for the culture of the book. According to John Trimbur's concept of "essayistic literacy," the idiosyncratic flow and personal voice of the essay divorce it from the conditions that produced it, enabling it to represent itself as a free form, thereby mystifying the disciplinary work it actually does on readers and writers. In opposition to Trimbur's characterization of the essay as the exemplar of the "rhetoric of deproduction," Kurt Spellmeyer has valued the dialogical elements of the essay—its ability to accommodate multiple voices, incongruities, and discontinuities. Spellmeyer usefully complicates Trimbur's analysis because "the essay" is actually a multitude of genres that can serve varied functions, depending upon how they are represented and taught. The conventions of personal essays and literary explications have ceased to seem natural as we move beyond the modern conceptions of free-form personal expression, but the belletristic essay has always been part of the work of the profession.

From its beginning, the teaching of English has been shaped by changes in literacy that have been represented as educational crises. One of the most influential eighteenth-century proponents actually represented the need for English instruction as an orality crisis. Thomas Sheridan justified teaching English by arguing that it would instill respect for established hierarchies by enabling the educated to speak eloquently for them. Sheridan's anxieties resound in more recent dictionaries of cultural literacy, encyclopedias of educated virtues, and defenses of the classics such as Allan Bloom's *The Closing of the American Mind* (1987). These works have more than mere similarities in title to the orality campaign that helped establish college English in Britain, Sheridan's *British Education: Or the Source of the Disorders of Great Britain; Being an Essay towards Proving, that the Immortality, Ignorance and False Taste, which so Generally prevail, are the Natural and Necessary Consequences of the Present Defective*

*Systems of Education* (1756). A form of cultural literacy is often codified and defended both when an educated culture is losing its currency and needs to be preserved, and when one is expanding to new groups and needs to be formalized and taught. The literacy campaign genre becomes historically important when an established culture enters a period of crisis and is called upon to explain itself in new ways or lose authority to a competing paradigm. The "culture wars" that began in the 1970s represented another such literacy crisis.

## Composition Was Disciplined, while Cultural Studies Went Interdisciplinary (c. 1970s)

The "interpretive turn" in the humanities and social sciences has become a benchmark for assessing how textual conventions became defined as ideological mediations. While theories of interpretation changed dramatically in the 1970s, literary studies retained an essentially interpretive stance. This point was made in 1980 in Jane Tompkins's "The Reader in History."

> What is most striking about reader-response criticism and its close relative, deconstructive criticism, is their failure to break out of the mold in which critical writing was cast by the formalist identification of criticism with explication. Interpretation reigns supreme both in teaching and in publication just as it did when New Criticism was in its heyday in the 1940s and 1950s. (224–25)

While the "locus of meaning" had moved from the "text to the reader," professors and students continued to "practice criticism as usual." Tompkins foresaw that the critical nexus was shifting toward the constitutive practices of discourse, and that this concern for "language as a form of power" would establish a place for critical theory that was "very similar to, if not the same as, that of the Greek rhetoricians for whom mastery of language meant mastery of the state" (226). Less than two decades later, J. Hillis Miller concluded "the future of criticism is a non-question" (xi). What had brought literary criticism to the end of its history, at least in the assessment of one of its leading practitioners? Rhetoric, composition, and cultural studies.

Cultural studies and composition emerged out of the same moment in the history of the culture of the book, with one following the interpretive turn through critical theory to focus on textualities, and the other representing a decidedly more utilitarian response to the changes in education and literacy that came with "open access." In the assumption that modern disciplines must be founded upon a research base, Steven North and others have dated "the birth of modern Composition, capital C to 1963," when research books began to appear (14). Like Composition, cultural studies emerged in comparatively broad-based institutions such as the Open University and Birmingham that were more accessible to broader classes of students, and apparently to new forms of scholarship as well. Composition and cultural studies represent parallel responses to the changes in the "information economy" that effaced the distinction between work and leisure. This distinction had been established as the modern reading public evolved into the "bourgeois public sphere." The erasure of these modern distinctions is refiguring the romantic alienation from labor that reduced English studies to literary studies by divorcing production from reception, demarcating creative and utilitarian texts, and valorizing works of genius as autonomous artifacts divorced from the social work that created them, the economic conditions governing their distribution, and the political purposes to which they are put.

In his last writings, especially his last book, *Rhetorics, Poetics, and Cultures: Refiguring College English Studies,* James Berlin integrated cultural studies with composition and rhetoric to redefine college English studies in postmodernist terms. Throughout his career, Berlin worked "dialectically" from the opposition of rhetoric and poetic, translating classical categories to make sense of the dichotomies that defined college English. For Berlin, cultural studies provided "methods for interpreting the cultural codes" that produce subjectivities (119). With these methods people can critique modes of representation and the hierarchies that govern them, including the hierarchies that defined literary studies: high/low, imaginative/functional, disinterested/political, aesthetic/objective. Berlin maintained that the transition from literary to cultural studies followed from the demand in the postmodern economy for information managers who can network to interpret changing situations for shifting purposes—lifelong learners who can be constantly retooled as markets change. Beneath this educated elite, production work is outsourced and temped, resulting in fewer decent-paying production jobs and more structural unemployment, as had occurred in college English itself with the reliance on part-timers to teach students how to produce discourse. In response to such trends, Berlin and Michael Vivion published curricular models and histories of institutional reforms. Unlike other popular anthologies of cultural studies, their collection emphasized teaching, a natural point of reference for work in composition but not cultural studies, which according to Henry Giroux has generally been indifferent "to the importance of pedagogy as a form of cultural practice" ("Beyond the Ivory Tower" 242).

This shortcoming is not surprising given intellectuals' tendency to devalue practical applications as unscholarly. Rhetoric's central concern with practical agency was excluded from college English studies when they were reduced to a modern sense of literature. This absence is evident in the traditional English major, which remains the staple of many departments, but which is beginning to undergo widespread reforms that promise to change the subject, in part by changing the subject position on just such points. At my own institution, general education courses have already been transformed under pressure from the administration to create a more standardized lower-division curriculum. In a manner that was not quite what was envisioned, surveys of literature are giving way to cultural studies courses that combine "readings" of popular films and the mass media along with literary classics, often organized around issues of race, class, and gender rather than traditional frameworks such as genres, periods, or masterworks. Because of reconfigurations in requirements, these courses have to compete for students in ways that general education surveys of literature did not. Such surveys remain the core of the English major, which also requires courses on Chaucer, Shakespeare, and Milton, but none on American literature, let alone literary theory, professional writing, or "literatures" of other disciplines. Traditional survey courses have confined literature to poetry, fiction, and plays, concentrating on a canon of masterworks used to teach students the crafts of close reading and of writing explications of primary texts, with history and theory of only secondary importance. These surveys had such obvious value within the culture of the book that they never really had to give a close accounting of what good they do because no one challenged the assumption that reading good books well is an end in itself. Such assumptions do not compute well in the sort of outcomes assessments that are becoming the means to assess the values of disciplines.

While such external pressures are beginning to focus English departments' attention on the work they do, cultural studies reforms of English department curricula often fail to attend to the crucial issue of practical agency. One of the most publicized examples has been at Syracuse University. According to his published accounts, Steven Mailloux attempted to revise the English major at Syracuse into a major in "English and Textual Studies." As chair at Syracuse in 1986, Mailloux proposed that "cultural rhetoric" become the guiding focus for the new major, which would be organized around a triangle comprised of "culture," "theory," and "rhetoric" on the three sides, with "reading" situated at the center of the triangle. His proposal was modified to define the three curricular areas as "history," "theory," and "politics," with "textual studies" replacing "cultural rhetoric" as the unifying focus. The purpose of the revised curriculum at Syracuse is "to make students aware of how knowledge is produced and how reading takes place" and "thus make them capable of playing an active and critical role in their society, enabling them to intervene in the dominant discourses of their culture" (*Reception Histories* 161). Mailloux characterizes the opposition to the reforms from the left and right as arising from an arhetorical stance that he traces back to the critiques of sophism by Plato and Aristotle. While Mailloux quite effectively depicts materialists and humanists as foundationalists, his critics raised crucial questions about how teaching students to criticize established ideologies will enable them to intervene purposefully in civic life (see Zavarzadeh and Morton). Too often even the most theoretically sophisticated reforms fail to attend to how critical interpretations will enable students to intervene in political institutions and economic affairs.

In the proposals for curricular reforms that conclude *The Rise and Fall of English,* Scholes sets out his guiding purpose in terms that speak to this need. To help students develop a "usable culture past" and an "active relationship with the cultural present," Scholes reenvisions college English studies in the form of a new trivium (104–37). "Grammar" courses on "Language and Human Subjectivity" and "Representation and Objectivity" replace "traditional composition courses." "Dialectic" courses will "study discourses that work at a high level of abstraction and systematization, in which texts are constructed not so much by representing objects as by abstracting from them their essential qualities or their principles of composition" (124). Finally, "rhetoric" is to be taught as "Persuasion and Mediation" by examining how purposes are mediated in all sorts of texts. Like Mailloux's proposals, Scholes's basic paradigm is coherent and well defined, yet open-ended in the way that heuristics for collaborative inquiry need to be. The challenge for enacting any such reformation of the English major will be to shift the perspective from the interpretive stance of the critical observer to the rhetorical stance of the practical agent involved in negotiations of received values to address practical needs. If this reorientation is to serve the purposes of oppositional politics, then civic philosophies of rhetoric will need to be redefined to move beyond the classical ideal of the individual citizen speaking for the common good, and take account of the theories of discourse that inform the proposals of Mailloux and Scholes. Work in cultural studies is redefining rhetorical theory along these lines, and broader trends are pressing the discipline to attend to the work it does and the practical purposes that work serves.

Partially as a result of the economic and institutional pressures that led to the reformation of the general education at my own university, the profession has recently become concerned with the shrinking market for its work and for the conditions employed in doing it. Such works as Michael Berube and Cary Nelson's *Higher Education Under Fire: Politics, Economics, and the Crisis of the Humanities* have focused on the economic dimensions of institutional work in a way that marks a new stage in the "culture wars." According to Berube and Nelson, the discipline has been invigorated with new theories, but progress has been limited by the reliance on part-timers and temps who have denied professional employment to the graduates of literature programs. Nelson and Berube have translated their criticisms of the "job system" into coalitions with graduate students within the MLA, and their criticisms have been answered by proposals from former president of the MLA Elaine Showalter to take the profession public by expanding the nonacademic market for literature graduates. Unfortunately, both the MLA and its critics seem to assume that turning composition jobs into tenure-track positions for literature graduates will enable the profession to continue business as usual. Berube and Nelson represent rhetoric and composition as nothing more than "instrumentalist" work concerned with the "'sorting' of the student body" (18–20), and they persist in equating English studies with literary studies in ways that suggest that they do not understand the teaching of literacy as more than mere service. While the economic phase of the cultural wars has brought working conditions into professional scholarship, the challenge for those seeking to make universities into institutions of public learning is to exploit the broader instabilities in institutional hierarchies that have raised these professional anxieties. The basic hierarchy of research, teaching, and service that is used to define academic work is losing its authority, and nowhere are its limitations more evident than in the assessing of the values of work in rhetoric and composition.

## Rhetoric at Work in College English

As our colleagues in English consider how to "go public," they should look to rhetoric and composition because we are already there. Unlike most English professors, many of us already collaborate with schools, community colleges, corporations, and agencies, and we do research on service learning, community literacies, workplace writing, political rhetoric, computers, and writing in the disciplines. Research, teaching, and service are indistinguishable in much of the work done in rhetoric and composition because we research teaching, write about our collaborations with schools, and assign our students to write about their work with social service agencies. These efforts speak to the duties of educational institutions, as outlined in John Dewey's *The Public and Its Problems,* to create a learning society that works collaboratively to challenge established assumptions in order to realize the potentials of public issues. The civic tradition in rhetoric presents many other sources that can be reinterpreted against changing conceptions of service, teaching, and research to make remediations of literacy central to the public mission of college English. I will conclude by sketching out the practical projects that follow from a civic commitment to going public that will involve us in redefining the purposes of college English.

A critical reassessment of our shared purposes should begin with service because that is how many of our most promising collaborations have been characterized by the institutions we work with. Public service provides an institutionalized category that can be appropriated to value civic engagements with social problems (see, for example, Lisman). Service learning is an established model that is becoming important in composition as activist research/teaching expands outward from participant/observer research on teaching and learning. Of course most English professors still identify with specialists across the country who work "in their area," while not considering the English teacher across the street as in any way involved in their work, other than as a scapegoat for their students' failures. This tendency is an extension of our tacit identification of our real work as scholarship rather than teaching. English professors need to spend more time in school, collaborating on teacher workshops and building the bridge programs for underrepresented groups that are essential if universities are really to be public institutions. Research and consulting on workplace writing have established other external relationships that are proving strategic as we establish the internships and courses for alternative English majors. Some of us are using collaborations on community literacies to develop coalitions with social service providers and government agencies, and these sorts of coalitions are crucial to creating networked English departments that can serve as resources for public problem solving, as is being done, for example, at Carnegie Mellon University through the Community Literacy Center. Linda Flower's efforts to formalize and teach genres that foster collaborative inquiry exemplify how broad-based service work can generate research that offers new models not just for teaching but for public discourse.

We also need to exploit the fact that we work with the first-year composition courses that are required of all undergraduates. The recent waves of reform proposals all cite the first two years of college as the most important. Reforms of general education began at my own university by assuming that integrating "skills" instruction into "content" courses would be the most efficient way to improve writing. We spent two years convincing administrators that students needed first-year composition courses *and* writing across the curriculum, not one or the other. We represented first-year composition as the place where students learn to analyze what they are reading and writing and thereby learn to think critically about how they are being disciplined. To show people our "student-centered curriculum," we gave them copies of the anthology of student writings that has been published here for more than twenty years. To show them that more can be done, we created an anthology of writings from across this university to represent the institution as a community of writers at work. Institutional reports, specialized research, "creative" writing, artwork, and service writings were brought together to create interdisciplinary symposia on public issues to provide students with a sense of the range and importance of the writing done at the university. To make composition the center of general education, we established forums where faculty speak across disciplines to public issues. Nobody talks about cutting composition anymore, and we have received funding to expand our work with computer-mediated literacies.

We need to rearticulate the centrality of rhetorics and poetics in civic philosophies of liberal education as we collaborate on general education reforms, because reformers often lack a coherent educational vision such as that provided by critical reinterpretations of civic humanism. In our research, as in our teaching and service, we need to learn more strategically—more rhetorically—from the institutional work we are doing. Those of us in rhetoric and composition have a stronger tradition of research on teaching than any other discipline outside education, and we are better connected to the workplace than any other area of the humanities. We are already expanding our research on community literacies, and this work is converging with historical scholarship on the rhetorical practices of varied traditions. This convergence is giving rise to courses that combine historical analysis, institutional critique, and service learning to teach the literacies of citizenship, and this convergence has the potential to revitalize rhetoric's traditional concern for the ethical and political concerns of moral or "practical" philosophy, a trend that may give new meaning to the historical relations of rhetorics, poetics, and civics.

We are already doing research on how higher education is organized and funded, as a result of the fact that composition specialists administer the largest programs in universities. However, we need to expand our institutional research to be more persuasive with other educators and to better serve our constituencies. We should be preparing graduate students to head general education programs, advise state legislatures, and do public work on educational policies ranging from school taxes to bilingual education. We also need to prepare graduates and undergraduates to do institutional research and advance institutional reforms in order to teach students how to use rhetoric as the art of deliberative action in nonacademic settings. Some of us are already doing activist research in communities (for example, Cushman and Flower), and other people in rhetoric and composition such as Richard Miller have argued for giving more value to our institutional efforts. Institutional research and activism are just beginning to be understood as intellectual work as humanists move beyond what Berube and Nelson have characterized as "a kind of idiot savant academic culture" that assumes any idiot can do administration and only an idiot incapable of scholarship would agree to do such menial work (24).

Those of us who administer composition programs, writing centers, or other "service units" are used to being treated as idiots as we struggle to explain our work to our colleagues and the public. The public generally assumes that English departments teach people how to read and write effectively. The "culture wars" were largely about what English departments teach people to read. As the debate shifts to institutional work, I hope that we can focus on what English departments teach people to do. If English departments are evolving from literary to literacy studies through the influence of cultural studies, rhetoric, and composition, then rhetoric can provide the focal point for a shift from an interpretive to an activist stance. Literacy involves not just interpretation but action, and our research, teaching, and service work on literacy need to attend to how citizens can act equitably on behalf of social justice. Critical reinterpretations of the civic tradition in rhetoric and moral philosophy can help us to define this project in ways that value the practical ability to mediate conflicts and speak to common problems. Such efforts can also help prevent us from becoming victims of the literacy crisis that continues to expand as our culture mediates the technological and cultural changes that are redefining the work of literacy.

# 3
# "To Get an Education and Teach My People"
## Rhetoric for Social Change
### Shirley Wilson Logan

Although established rhetoric and composition scholars routinely publish essays on the content of college writing classes, the truth is that graduate students provide the rhetorical education of most college freshmen. Courses with such titles as "Approaches to College Composition" and "Teaching Writing" go a long way toward preparing graduate students for this formidable task. What is often left out of such training, however, are discussions of the question, "Rhetorical education for what?" In this essay, I want to offer an exploratory response to the so-what question, a response that points in the direction of immediate and practical applications. Recognizing, at the same time, the institutional constraints under which most beginning writing courses are taught, I do not expect the ideas offered here to promote major curricular changes, but perhaps to generate changes in attitude and in approaches to a prescribed course of study among those who teach and those who supervise the teaching of college writing.

I want to suggest that, even in the information age, when it seems that everything is "time-sensitive," when few listen to extended speeches, and when participation in political affairs usually means watching televised presidential debates, an increased emphasis on rhetorical education would better serve those in marginalized communities than the current focus on technological training alone. The push to acquire computer skills all too frequently means that facility with oral and written language is neglected. In my own Washington, D.C., metropolitan community, for example, school-based literacy has taken a back seat to the proliferating "math and science summer academies" and "computer camps" for inner-city youth. University-based programs designed to prepare first generation college students for graduate school as a rule assign more value to research projects in the computer, mathematical, and physical sciences. Civic club volunteers spend hours totaling grocery store receipts to be submitted in exchange for computers. In 1999, Bill Gates, chairman of Microsoft Corporation, made a one-billion-dollar pledge in college scholarships for members of underrepresented groups out of a concern that "too many minority students are not reaching or finishing college— and in particular pursuing degrees in medicine, science and technology" (Sanchez). Such initiatives are all encouraging. We certainly do not need to add to the surplus of English majors. But we also do not need more computer scientists, engineers, or mathematicians unprepared to participate in public discourse.

Looking to the past for models and uses of rhetorical education, we recognize that social change has always been partially the result of rhetorical action, oral or written arguments crafted to elicit specific responses. Given that rhetorical action is initiated in response to mediated exigencies, few Americans have had a greater need to respond than have African Americans nor a greater desire to learn how to respond effectively.[1] From the perspective of a disenfranchised people, the exigencies appeared to be abundant.

Nineteenth-century African Americans first had to argue their entitlement to status as unenslaved human beings; thus the rhetoric of antislavery was necessary. Then blacks had to argue their rights to citizenship and to all the privileges and protections associated with it, and in response to these exigencies emerged antilynching and civil rights discourse. In the opening sentence of Frances Ellen Watkins Harper's 1891 speech to the National Council of Women, she both summarized these issues and incorporated arguments to support their implied claims.

> I deem it a privilege to present the negro, not as a mere dependent asking for Northern sympathy or Southern compassion, but as a member of the body politic who has a claim upon the nation for justice, simple justice, which is the right of every race, upon the government for protection, which is the rightful claim of every citizen, and upon our common Christianity for the best influences which can be exerted for peace on earth and good-will to man. ("Duty" 36)

While it may not be possible or even desirable to teach our students to produce the kind of balanced phrasing associated with Harper's grand style, we can use her discourse as an example of the application of rhetoric to social change. Not only serving to authenticate her as an intelligent and ethical speaker to what were usually skeptical audiences, Harper's classical oratory was appropriate to her time and her own rhetorical training as well. I am not then calling for a return to some sentimentalized good old days of oratory before computers and television and mass media, when children read. I do not experience the nostalgia expressed by David Blight, in his introduction to the bicentennial edition of the *Columbian Orator*.

> In an age when there is good reason to lament the decline of oratory and to fear for the future of the book in the face of the power of visual and electronic media, this elocution manual/reader lends us reassurance from the past. Like lost treasure, some old books can reemerge in the present and matter as much now as they did when they were new commodities in American classrooms. (xv)

As influential as the *Columbian Orator* may have been on Frederick Douglass's rhetorical education, which I discuss below, I do not long for its reappearance in writing classrooms. Nor am I promoting a belief in the "literacy myth," the notion that literacy leads to liberation or that literacy is superior to and separate from orality (H. Graff, *Labyrinths* 265). I am proposing that more attention be paid in composition classrooms—and in all classrooms—to the ways in which rhetorical competence influences and enables meaning and enhances the ability to manage human affairs. Given this old, yet new, rhetorical emphasis, disenfranchised communities (and I am aware that most members of such communities will not be in these composition classrooms) could benefit more fully from what E. O. Wilson calls consilience, which he defines as linking knowledge across disciplines in various relationships of intellectual synthesis (8). In other words, this is not an either language/or science proposition. More rhetorical training would offer a way to make sense of and act upon the convergence of knowledge, essential to effect social and political change. At the same time, this increased emphasis should not result in more isolated training in basic communicative skills; rather, this training should be linked to discussions of ways in which the confluence of knowledge, this discipline-rich pool of special topics, supports the first rhetorical canon, invention, and empowers those who respond daily to a wide range of social and political concerns. Sharon Crowley reminds us that "the instrumentalist or functionalist character of some strains of pragmatism (and of American liberalism itself) have made it possible for teachers of composition to forget Dewey's commitment to education as a primary means of bringing about social change" (*Composition* 17). Educators eager to teach the practical, the profitable, and the marketable should also ensure that this pedagogy is socially responsible.

In the following pages, I consider various contexts in which African Americans' rhetorical education and performance took place during the nineteenth century with two purposes in mind. First, these contexts and their inhabitants suggest ways in which we can prepare our students to enact a rhetoric of social change. Some of this past is usable. Thus the essay responds in part to Thomas Miller's call for teaching histories of rhetoric as a social praxis. He invokes Freire's notion of "loci of contradictions" as one way to help students understand such contemporary issues as health care, wherein our market economy bumps heads with our desire to provide every one with adequate health coverage. He writes that such "contradictions in the shared experience are the rhetorical situations that students need to learn to recognize and speak to" and argues that "[s]uch a reorientation will help students to view the history of rhetorical traditions from a rhetorical perspective, a perspective that is of considerable practical and philosophical importance in the study of composition" ("Teaching the Histories" 80). Second, I do this as part of a collective and ongoing effort to fill in "history in the spaces left," to appropriate the title of Jacqueline Royster and Jean C. Williams's recent *College Composition and Communication* essay. They point out that too often writers of rhetoric and composition history acknowledge the absence of African Americans in their narratives; that is, they create spaces for them, but do not actually fill these spaces or take black viewpoints into account (566). This essay aims to do both. I close by suggesting ways in which these past practices and practitioners chart a direction for current rhetorical education, a direction that would improve the quality of composition classes and the quality of social change.

## Contexts of Nineteenth-Century Black Rhetorical Education

Any discussion of the rhetorical education of blacks in post–Civil War America must be held within the frame set by several considerations. Most blacks acquired formal education in separate schools; this fact of segregation makes a discussion of black education both possible and needed. Further, it is the current resegregation, more than forty years after Brown vs. the Board of Education, that makes such a discussion possible and needed still—the difference today being that segregated schools are not called segregated or black schools; they are called inner-city schools. Addressing this state of affairs in a September 1999 letter to the University of Virginia, President John T. Casteen writes

> It is also a disgraceful reality that forty years after desegregation, the Virginia child most likely to attend an underfunded public school and least likely to encounter the AP courses and rigorous programs that prepare students to come here is an African-American child. And that child's parents and grandparents faced very much the same realities in their own schools.

Nonetheless, it is impossible to speak of black education as though it were uninfluenced by social and economic developments in American education generally. With steady determination, black people of all ages set about making up for years of legislated illiteracy in any way they could. With few exceptions, learning to read and write the language was the critical first step toward using it to persuade, but even these basic skills are acquired more easily by people who have something to understand and something to say. In many postbellum black educational institutions, administrators considered facility with language beyond the acquisition of basic literacy unnecessary if not pointless. Charles Stearnes, a teacher from the North, along with other white educators in the 1870s, held the opinion that "while black students excelled in oratory, they had no aptitude for mathematics" (McAfee 83). This alleged aptitude for oratory was considered natural rather than the consequence of any formal training. Such perceptions made educator Fanny Jackson Coppin even more determined to demonstrate proficiency in math to her Greek professor at Oberlin, "for I had always heard that my race was good in the languages, but stumbled when they came to mathematics" (15). Perhaps such perceptions account in part for the current emphasis on mathematics described above. We can imagine what additional limitations were placed on black learners by those who, unlike Stearnes, opposed a national integrated school system (McAfee 83). Believing that education was wasted on black students, these opponents feared their influence on white students in classrooms.

The first organized efforts to provide higher education for African Americans began well before the Civil War. These efforts unfolded in a number of contexts, not only in the schools supported by the Freedman's Bureau, the American Missionary Association, the American Baptist Home Mission Society, and the Board of Missions for the Freedmen of the Presbyterian Church in the U.S.A., but also and primarily as a result of the initiative of African Americans themselves. In fact, as one historian points out, during the antebellum period in Philadelphia alone, of the fifty-six black private schools, whites ran only twelve (Perkins 21). In Baltimore, black activists like the Reverend Daniel Coker, after teaching in the Sharp Street African Academy, established his own highly successful day school in 1802 (C. Phillips 163–64). Small free black communities in the South, e.g., in Augusta, Georgia, organized and supported schools before the Civil War. It is also the case that black church denominations, such as the African Methodist Episcopal Church, the Colored Methodist Episcopal Church, and the African Methodist Episcopal Zion Church, initiated the earliest efforts to educate the formerly enslaved. These denominations organized and controlled nearly all of the major colleges established by black organizations and shaped their educational policies. Blacks did not wait for benevolent white Northerners to educate them.

The Society of Friends, widely known for its antislavery and educational efforts throughout the nineteenth century, helped to establish schools for free blacks in the North. But even the Quakers did not always support formal education in those branches of knowledge where training in rhetoric would have been taught. Many of their institutions were conceived as "farm schools" for training in manual labor. A trade school established in Philadelphia in 1848 and named the Institute for Colored Youth (ICY) in 1852 offers one salient example: The students were apprenticed to black tradesmen who proposed that in the evening the boys would be schooled in the "higher branches" to include elocution, logic, and composition" (Perkins 21). Thus this push for more than basic literacy training also came from within black communities.

For thirty years, with Coppin at the helm, the ICY maintained a model academic reputation, with some proclaiming "the course of study equal to that of the average college" (Perkins 27). A captivating speaker who never used notes, Coppin, "purchased" out of slavery, was graduated from Rhode Island State Normal School[2] in Bristol in 1859 and from

Oberlin in 1865. In her 1913 book, *Reminiscences of School Life, and Hints on Teaching,* Coppin gives an account of her experiences, not specifically with respect to rhetorical education, but from it we receive the unique perspective of one former slave from both sides of the desk. Although Coppin enjoyed her early years at Newport, Rhode Island, she was compelled by other interests to move on.

> My life there was most happy, and I never would have left her [Mrs. Calvert, her employer], but it was in me to get an education and to teach my people. This idea was deep in my soul. Where it came from I cannot tell, for I had never had any exhortations, nor any lectures which influenced me to take this course. It must have been born in me. (17)

Suggestive of Quintilian's *Institutes of Oratory,* Coppin's *Reminiscences of School Life* is filled with advice on child rearing and discipline ("Of course, no cruel punishment should ever be allowed, and if whipping is to be done it is far better for the parent to do it, for his hand is restrained by love") and good manners and moral development ("However brilliant a person may be intellectually, however skillful in the arts and sciences, he must be reliable; he must be trustworthy"). It includes two chapters of practical advice on the teaching of English: "How to Teach Reading and Spelling" and "How to Teach Grammar." On audience accommodation, she notes, "Always avoid using what are called big words when writing on any topic, for they often do nothing but 'Darken counsel by words without knowledge.' Whereas the duty of the speaker or writer is to get before his hearers or his readers as clear an idea of his thoughts as he can" (75). And on practice in writing: "The only way to teach them to write correctly is to have them write. A good rule would be to have them write a little essay once a week, and have it corrected, seeing that all the rules of grammatical construction are properly observed" (80).

Among the faculty at the Institute for Colored Youth were Edward A. Bouchet, a black graduate of Yale, and Mary Jane Patterson, Coppin's schoolmate at Oberlin. No doubt these teachers, themselves trained at colleges offering classical training in rhetoric, incorporated this training into their teaching. But under the influence of Booker T. Washington and others who supported vocational training alone, the curriculum was changed in the 1890s. History and the Latin classics were eliminated and many science courses were consolidated. The school was moved twenty-five miles out of Philadelphia and out of the black community to a farm in Cheyney, Pennsylvania, where it was modeled after the more vocationally minded Hampton and Tuskegee Institutes (Perkins 21–40). This emphasis on vocational training, an emphasis of many post-Reconstruction schools, mirrors to some extent the current focus on technology over the humanities mentioned above. Still there were many schools that did not support the Hampton-Tuskegee Industrial model and maintained a more traditional curriculum that included rhetorical training. The commitment to racial uplift through education ("to get an education and to teach my people") that Coppin expressed here was shared by her peers throughout the century.

In the late 1860s, blacks established a number of combined high school and collegiate institutions. These institutions developed separately from institutions of higher education of Americans in general. For example, the Johnson C. Smith University was founded in Charlotte, North Carolina, as a collegiate and theological school in 1867. As one former president of the school pointed out, since few blacks in the area could read and even fewer could write, it may have seemed unreasonable to establish an institution for higher learning at that time, but the founders understood that funds could be more easily secured from the Freedman's Bureau and sympathetic Northerners then when concern for the cause was great (McCrorey 29–30). Rhetoric was included in the upper-level curriculum of such schools, as in schools generally during this period and well into the next century. One historian describing the English curriculum at black colleges in the 1930s wrote:

> With regard to the place in the curriculum of the required freshman course in rhetoric and composition, as it is commonly taught in American institutions, there seems to be at present no need for any radical change. The universality of the course attests to the high regard college English departments have for its teaching value. In only one Negro college, Claflin University, is instruction in rhetoric and composition relegated to the high school level. (Woodruff 2)

According to Woodruff, "reading an endless file of themes" and putting up with the indifference of faculty from other departments distracted from the main goals of the teacher of rhetoric and composition: accurate and precise oral and written expression and critical ability to judge the expressions of others (1).

## Past Practices

At a Galveston, Texas, meeting of black citizens to protest a violation of the 1875 Civil Rights Act, Norris Wright Cuney[3] reminded those gathered, "We must speak out when the occasion demands it, for by silence we invite oppression" (Winegarten 60). Black people, recognizing the consequences of silence, spoke out on numerous occasions.

If we consider those who employed rhetoric to some effect across the century, it is difficult to recover a clear picture of what those who received formal training in it were taught, and of course most received little. Rhetorical prowess was not a ticket to freedom, but it may have reduced the price for some. Perhaps the two best-known black rhetors of the nineteenth century, Sojourner Truth and Frederick Douglass, gained their freedom from slavery through direct, overt, physical action rather than through the dialectic of argument. As Steven Mailloux points out, reading sections of the *Columbian Orator* may have motivated Douglass to find the remedy, an act of rebellion, but that act was physical resistance to Covey, the slavebreaker, and physical removal from enslavement ("Misreading" 15–16). And while Truth demonstrated her rhetorical powers when she argued to a New York state grand jury against the illegal selling of her son Peter before hiring a lawyer to gain his release, this application of rhetorical power occurred after Truth herself had walked away from slavery by daylight. Both rhetors, through a physical act, "stole themselves." Nonetheless their verbal prowess—developed without formal rhetorical education—did enable action. Douglass delivered thousands of speeches and penned numerous articles arguing for social action, no doubt with immeasurable results. The lasting impressions of Truth's delivery were recorded by many who heard her speak, the 1851 "Ain't I a Woman" speech being, of course, the best known if, perhaps, the least reliably reported.

In the late eighteenth century Lucy Terry Prince, whose freedom was purchased by her husband, a former slave, used her natural rhetorical skills to bring a suit against a neighbor in Vermont who had encroached on her land. She eventually pleaded her case before Samuel Chase and the U.S. Supreme Court. The court ruled in her favor. During this same period, she also addressed the Williams College Board of Trustees for three hours, unsuccessfully arguing for her son's admittance to the school. She based her arguments on her family's military contribution (her husband had fought in the French and Indian War and two older sons had served in the Revolutionary War), and invoked the law, the Bible, and her friendship with a Colonel Williams, who bequeathed the land for the college.

Between the ages of five and fifteen, Maria W. Stewart, the first American woman to speech publicly on political matters, served as live-in help for a clergyman's family in Hartford, Connecticut. She took advantage of the family's library to augment the modest education she received in Sabbath school and elsewhere. In 1832, twenty-nine and widowed, Stewart spoke to the Afric-American Female Intelligence Society of Boston. Such organizations, also called literary societies, moral and mental improvement societies, lyceums, debating societies, and reading room societies, were formed among black men and women in the antebellum North between 1828 and 1846. These organizations engaged in political and social activities, which could be reported on in black newspapers and magazines. In part, their purposes were to establish and stock libraries, read and discuss books, and hold debates on current issues. These debates gave participants practice in public speaking. As Dorothy Porter argues, as a result of such activities, "free people of color, as a whole, owe some of their educational progress to the efforts of these societies" (563). It is likely that Stewart benefited from such affiliations.

Frances Ellen Watkins Harper attended her uncle William Watkins' Academy for Negro Youth in Baltimore until the age of thirteen. The Watkins family members were all involved in Baltimore politics, and William Watkins was known for his emphasis on precise language use. One former student mentions the use of Samuel Kirkham's *English Grammar in Familiar Lectures,* a popular early-nineteenth-century school book, along with Bingham's *Columbian Orator.* In the appendix, Kirkham wrote that "Grammar instructs us how to express our thoughts correctly. Rhetoric teaches us to express them with force and elegance" (219). Harper applied her training in rhetoric, elocution, and grammar to the work of abolition and civil rights from 1854 until her death in 1911. This highly motivated first generation of black rhetorical activists were mostly self-taught, though some had formal training. They began the transition among African Americans from language use for self-improvement to rhetorical education for action.

Postbellum social activists acquired some of their rhetorical education in schools established with the support of the Freedman's Bureau, various religious denominations, and generous endowments. For example, Ida Wells (1861–1931) attended Rust College in Holly Springs, Mississippi, founded by the Methodist Episcopal Church, North. In her autobiography, she writes of joining a lyceum in Memphis, where debates on public issues took place. As a journalist, she honed her rhetorical skills while critiquing the discourse surrounding mob violence. In 1892, the "Southern Horrors" antilynching speech launched her career as a public speaker. Many of the prominent black men and women leaders of the last decades of the nineteenth century traveled the same path from slavery to restricted freedom, to various forms of education and social action in one form or another.

Certain entries in *The Journals of Charles W. Chesnutt* provide an unusual record of the daily actualities of black schooling in the postbellum years. In one entry, Chesnutt, a fiction writer, essayist, and public speaker, mentions that he had been studying Quackenbos' *Composition and Rhetoric* and habitually writing practice essays. Few who knew him realized that Chesnutt had accomplished a great deal "largely through a strenuous self-education regimen" (*Essays and Speeches* xxv), assisted by access to a local citizen's well-stocked library. He never received a high school diploma, but at the age of sixteen became a teacher at the school he attended, the Fayetteville Colored Normal School, and its principal in 1880 at twenty-one. An October 1878 journal entry is actually a précis of lecture 10: "On Style—Perspicuity and Precision" of Hugh Blair's *Lectures on Rhetoric and Belles Lettres* (1783), a standard text in American schools in the eighteenth and nineteenth centuries. In an 1881 speech to the Normal Literary Society of Fayetteville, North Carolina, "Advantages of a Well-Conducted Literary Society," Chesnutt, then only twenty-three, stressed the importance of learning to speak coherently and convincingly through practice. He observed that one of the chief advantages of a literary society is that it teaches the rules of argument and helps one to develop the self-confidence to stand "without trepidation before a real audience, and discuss questions of public moment" (*Essays* 18), thereby linking rhetorical training to social action. Demonstrating a solid grounding in the classical tradition, he reminded his audience of Demosthenes' habit of writing his speeches over several times and memorizing them before delivery. Further, he recalled a British statesman's remark that on public matters it was no compliment to be thought to deliver speeches without preparation, adding, "I hold it criminal in a man to discuss great public measures without careful thought and study" (18). His address is filled with advice on speech making, the importance of preparation, and the role of oratory in a republic. He draws on his knowledge of Hugh Blair, emphasizing the usefulness of imitation. He also quotes from Levi Hedge's *Elements of Logick, or a Summary of the General Principles and Different Modes of Reasoning* (23). Chesnutt adds that oratory has never been an art practiced primarily for its own sake but is always associated with some cause, ending his speech with the rule that the goal of oratory is "truth, and not victory" (23).

Such comments from Chesnutt indicate the extent to which one prominent African American recognized the value of training in rhetoric, particularly for a disenfranchised people, and documents how he worked on his own to acquire it.

## Rhetorical Practices in Fiction

Fictionalized practices of rhetoric in novels by late-nineteenth-century black authors dramatize the high value placed upon facility with language. In Sutton Griggs's 1899 novel, *Imperium in Imperio,* he describes the lifelong friendship and rivalry of Belton Piedmont and Bernard Belgrave, one poor, one rich. On two occasions their rivalry culminated in rhetorical battles. The first competition was staged at their high school graduation where the "two oratorical gladiators" had both been asked to speak. Belton, the first speaker, addressed his class on the subject "The Contribution of the Anglo-Saxon to the Cause of Human Liberty." Bernard, rich, fair-skinned, and thus favored by the white judges, spoke last, delivering a panegyric to Robert Emmet, Irish nationalist leader. At the close of the novel, both men have united behind the Imperium, a black nation within a nation somewhere in Texas. Bernard, having been chosen president, delivers an address to the Congress of the Imperium in which he calls for rebellion ("The hour for wreaking vengeance for our multiplied wrongs has come"). Belton follows with a counterargument that the Imperium reveal itself to white Americans and work with the them for peaceful resolutions ("There is a weapon mightier than either of these [the sword and the ballot]. I speak of the pen. If denied the use of the ballot let us devote our attention to that mightier weapon, the pen."). His argument carries the day and the Imperium is dissolved. Following their performance Bernard congratulates Belton on his rhetoric:

"Belton, that was a masterly speech you made to-day. If orations are measured according to difficulties surmounted and results achieved, yours ought to rank as a masterpiece" (249). It's a curious novel, but of significance to this discussion is the extent to which most of the action centers on rhetorical rather than physical action. Much attention is paid to the rhetorical training both men received in preparation for their first ceremonial speeches and to the effect of their second speeches responding to fictionalized exigencies.

In contrast to the conversation constructed in Frances Harper's *Iola Leroy,* only men take part in the discussion of lynching during a heated meeting of the American Colored League, which Pauline Hopkins constructs in her 1900 novel, *Contending Forces.* Enraged black citizens of Boston have gathered to hear prominent citizens—including Luke Sawyer, who had experienced mob violence firsthand, and Will Smith, a DuBoisian type, who closes his speech with the following admonition: "My friends, it is going to take time to straighten out this problem; it will only be done by the formation of public opinion. Brute force will not accomplish anything" (273). In his words, we have again an appeal to reason ("the formation of public opinion") over "brute force."

## Conclusion: Rhetoric and Social Change

I am not holding up rhetorical education as the solution to all social ills. It never has been, as this selective narrative of nineteenth-century black rhetors demonstrates. For African people in America, it is difficult to speak of rhetorical education as a separate component of a larger universe of educational practices, particularly during a period when their right to an education was challenged and constrained on many fronts. Yet it is impossible to consider rhetorical education outside of this universe. We have to speak of privilege and opportunity first. And then we have to ask—if we can get through the tangle of oppression and denial to think about rhetorical education—rhetorical education for what? I have suggested in my title that it has been and might continue to be for social change, not in isolation, but in conjunction with other kinds of education.

For what purpose did Frederick Douglass, the nineteenth-century black speaker most often put forward as oratorical exemplar, use his self-acquired rhetorical education? Once he escaped from the peculiar institution of slavery, he applied his oratorical skills to shaping the opinions of Northern nonslaveholders. He did so first at the behest of William Lloyd Garrison and the antislavery movement but, ultimately, in response to his own need to articulate not only the conditions of slavery ("Tell your story, Fred" was Garrison's whispered advice) but also its moral and social implications. Recorded accounts of his performances suggest that he was an impressive speaker, but it is not clear to what extent his oratory benefited the cause and to what extent it merely benefited Douglass. For example, during a speaking tour in the British Isles, one of his hosts, a Reverend Campbell, summarized the audience's reaction marking the extent to which Douglass was no longer identified as a slave: "It only remains that we pass a resolution of thanks to Frederick Douglass. the slave that was, the man that is! He that was covered with chains, and that is now being covered with glory, and whom we will send back a gentleman." Consider, as well, these remarks from a local newspaper: "Socially, Douglass reaches upward, rather than outward to the laborers, one of whom he had been not so long ago" (McFeely 140).

Whether it was his intention or not, although much attention was attached to Douglass, it was not clear that it benefited the antislavery movement equally. At the end of one speech, the crowd was encouraged to purchase copies of Douglass's *Narrative* so that he might use the funds to move his family to England. It seems that Douglass's powerful oratory succeeded mainly in increasing admiration for himself. But perhaps that was the way some attitudes about slavery were changed: by recognition of the humanity of the enslaved, one person at a time. And if so, then Douglass's rhetoric did produce social change.

I could, of course, catalogue a long list of nineteenth-century black speakers who through formal training or self-instruction developed rhetorical competence within the oratorical culture of the time, addressing matters of social and political significance. And I could argue that their speaking did have some effect. But the times have changed. We no longer live in a culture that would attend to the extended rhetorical performances of the past. The rhetorical education I am arguing for would focus more on developing rhetorically critical ability—the ability to process the plethora of information bombarding us today in a way that reveals how language choices influence meaning. It would concentrate as much on evaluation and critical examination of contemporary discourse as upon its production. Those responsible for rhetorical education could, in fact, make this discourse the texts upon which class discussions are based. For example, students might use the text of a debate between two candidates for office as a starting point for a discussion of differences between deliberative and epideictic discourse. It would focus also on developing counterarguments against the discourse of difference and disdain embedded in much of today's public discourse. A clear choice today would be the heated debates surrounding affirmative action. A number of twentieth-century black public spokespersons, such as Martin Luther King, Jesse Jackson, Malcolm X, Louis Farrakhan, Barbara Jordan, Maxine Waters, Michael Dyson, Cornel West, Shirley Chisholm, Tavis Smiley, and Iyanla Vanzant, effectively articulate and respond to a range of concerns. But we also need to do more to train ordinary people, people who will never serve in Congress or march on Washington, or appear on Oprah or CNN, to engage in local discourse— to write letters to editors of printed publications, to television and movie producers, to their congressional representatives, to manufacturers of defective products, or to those reinforcing stereotypical beliefs, and to vocalize their concerns at PTA, community, and church meetings. Such initiatives should not be confused with functional literacy projects designed to teach people how to fill out job application forms or apply for a driver's license. The kind of education I am proposing here already takes place in various educational settings but is perhaps not as widely valued nor always recognized as rhetorical. It certainly has not received the community authentication essential for ongoing financial support. But that seems to be changing.

College service-learning projects often incorporate certain aspects of this kind of rhetorical training. According to the National Service-Learning Clearinghouse, almost two million students participate in service learning at four-year public and private institutions. Modeled on the community service requirements long established in many secondary schools, service learning is a teaching methodology that incorporates opportunities for students to use their skills and knowledge in service to and with the community. Composition classrooms are ideal sites for such collaborations, as in the case of one project where a business writing student in consultation with the restaurateur completely revised the printed menu for a popular local restaurant chain. Other projects bring the students more directly in contact with people in their communities. One service-learning web site includes the following language-rich examples of service-learning projects: cross-age tutoring with students at risk, intergenerational programs with an integrated reading and writing component to develop student literacy, community history projects where students use primary sources to establish and maintain historical exhibits, and civic studies projects that allow high school government students to learn firsthand about citizenship, democracy, and leadership (*Texas*). Other such projects include work with nonprofit organizations to create recruitment and information brochures and to write persuasive letters to local businesses, citizens, and the media. Another involved researching a neighborhood undergoing revitalization, interviewing residents and associations in the area, and developing profiles for a neighborhood newsletter and web site.[4]

Recently funded national initiatives also promise to reinforce the importance of rhetorical education. The Scholar/Practitioner Project is a collaboration among five universities and their surrounding communities. The project aims "to empower citizens to address issues arising as a consequence of state and local governments taking on responsibility for health and welfare programs." University scholars, local advocacy groups, and people in communities who are directly affected by this legislation will work together to develop strategies to influence policy changes. According to Ron Walters, project director, the people will be given "access to the kind of information needed to validate their expressions of concern to elected officials" ("Impact" 1). The project will draw on expertise across disciplines to gather and package this information, which can then be used to support welfare reform arguments. The University of Michigan, the Woodrow Wilson Foundation, and the White House Millennium Council have initiated a similar project, Imagining America: Artists and Scholars in Public Life. Project organizers "hope to encourage colleges and universities to work with community representatives on projects that draw on the strengths of the *arts and humanities*" (Franklin 6; emphasis added). Targeting issues of citizenship, literacy, and justice, this project has great potential for teaching and applying the results of rhetorical training, a strength of the arts and humanities.

Such collaborative projects as these, which combine the expertise of the academy with concrete community exigencies, share the need for effective rhetorical education and practice and expand upon Wilson's notion of consilience: "Win or lose, true reform will aim at the consilience of science with the social sciences and humanities in scholarship and teaching. Every college student should be able to answer the following questions: What is the relation between science and the humanities, and how is it important for human welfare?" (13)

A contemporary rhetorical education based on the ability to articulate the connections across branches of learning would produce a rhetoric of social change, truly essential to human welfare.

## Notes

1. I use the term *exigence* here to mean a way of viewing a set of social circumstances that when taken together imply some social corrective. I borrow this redefinition of one component of Lloyd Bitzer's rhetorical situation from Carolyn Miller, who writes that "[e]xigence is a form of social knowledge—a mutual constructing of objects, events, interests, and purposes that not only links them but also makes them what they are: an objectified social need" (157). In the nineteenth century, African Americans employed the socially acceptable vehicle of public address to articulate these needs.

2. The French adjective *normal* is derived from the Latin, which signifies a model, a pattern. The normal school proposed to teach not only the branches of knowledge, but also the processes by which the learning mind acquires that knowledge. Of course many of these "normal" schools fell short of this definition, concentrating primarily on content and in some instances on basic school work. See Salvatori, 167–231, for a discussion of the philosophy and curriculum of post–Civil War normal schools for freedmen. According to two different sources, she notes, there were as many as 56 colored normal schools in 1884 and nearly 150 in 1889 (178).

3. Cuney was a prominent politician and businessman and father of Maud Cuney Hare, a remarkable black Texas musician and writer in her own right.

4. See the NCTE's service learning web site (http://www.ncte.org/service/) for an annotated list of additional university-based service-learning projects.

# II
# Rhetorical Education in Diverse Classrooms

# 4
# Sew It Seams
## (A) Mending Civic Rhetorics for Our Classrooms and for Rhetorical History
### Jill Swiencicki

The book was wounded; it had stitches. I held in my hand an 1803 edition of Caleb Bingham's popular rhetoric handbook, *The Columbian Orator,* and fingered the wound the way I'd fingered my topographical atlas as a child. A torn page 232 was sewn together, producing what looked like a long, ragged scar on the side of a cheek. The edges of the page were burnt, the way my mother had burned the edges of her wedding announcement and then shellacked it onto a block of wood that hung in our front hall. Why the stitches? Could it be that, in putting out the flames that had crept up the edge of the page, the book's owner had accidentally torn 232 in half? Someone had sewn it together with what appears to be a medium-gauge twine. The seam of the needlework split in half a speech delivered to Congress in 1796 concerning a treaty with Great Britain; the words of the speech no longer matched up on either side of the twine: "tomahawk" became "tonawk," "I can fancy" became "I canancy" and, as if placed under a deconstructionist's erasure, the words "escape" and "power" were slashed through with a single stitch. Knots secured both ends of the needlework; the bottom knot was blackened, scorched. Might this suggest something other than my initial inference? Perhaps the fire happened after the page was torn and sewn? Was the owner twice careless: reading with a pipe or reading too close to the candlelight?

The book morphology indicates that at least two boys used this volume. Written four times on the title page was the phrase, "Woods Caperton, his book." Each of his lines experimented with varying degrees of flourish, as if the writer were relishing the performance of a new, public persona. Then, in neater, tighter script, the name "James Blythe Anderson" was written once, commandingly and steadily, above the table of contents. It seems *The Columbian Orator* allowed Woods a space in which to etch out a public persona that he was still practicing, to inscribe his desires within the ideological limits of the volume, and within the oratorical culture that gave this volume meaning. Woods repeatedly asserts the possessive "his book" while James signed his name just once, a masterful stroke that suggests he saw his own identity reflected back to him in the pages, a mimetic seal. Both signatures reminded me of my first year of college, of taking nervous, copious notes in the margins of my *Norton Anthology of American Literature,* trying to make the book's ideas mine.

I sat in my university's special collections archive with that early volume of *The Columbian Orator,* aware that my own hopes, fears, and desires guided my interpretation of the sewn page, the inscriptions, the contents themselves. That experience is a reminder that books, and the histories we write about and onto them, are associative sites: sites of unanswered questions, displaced identifications, negotiated subjectivities, and reflections of political, affective, and social relations. As such copious, varied repositories, they are sites that students and historians alike try to mend, amend, and care for. In the following essay I chart a few of the histories we have written onto this famous handbook as I write new ones onto it myself. I do this largely by exploring the approaches of the handbook's editor, Caleb Bingham, and the editor of the 1998 bicentennial edition of Bingham's book, David Blight. Using each editor's introductory essay to *The Columbian Orator,* along with analyses of selections from the handbook itself, I explore how the book is inscribed within eloquent traditions and practices, and institutional and cultural sites.[1] I first argue that the *Orator* expresses a tension between its hegemonic and transformative aims: between using instruction in "eloquence" to contain or assimilate social differences and a transformative space, expressed both in fresh conceptions of public discourse and in representations of physical violence, in which diverse subjects attempt to form themselves in relation to dominant notions of eloquent identity. I then explore how David Blight handles these tensions in his introduction to the 1998 bicentennial edition of Bingham's *Columbian Orator.* Blight's introduction frames the handbook through Frederick Douglass's experience with it.[2] I conclude by suggesting that recent associations between rhetoric and public-sphere theory offer a generative way to shift the associations we make with the *Orator* to keep such archival material an important part of rhetorical education now.

Exploring how the associations we make among texts, contexts, and readers express and mediate cultural anxieties offers a useful methodological approach for furthering new directions in the history of rhetorical education in America. John Schilb describes such a revisionist method as emphasizing "difference, displacements and disruptions." Such a method "enact[s] a process of reading marked by challenging questions about text and context."

> [It] will often involve sustained, even laborious confrontation with the intricacies of texts—with the word "texts" applying to so-called primary sources, other histories of rhetoric, and even the revisionary historian's own discourse. As the historian tracks back and forth between possible differences within texts and possible differences with the world outside them, with not even the historian's own work exempt from such determined oscillations, a revisionary history of rhetoric may indeed come to seem more the demonstration of a way of reading than the churning out of a readily usable product. (32)

This method describes a complex weave that stitches together past editors, readers, and rhetorical histories surrounding *The Columbian Orator* with present readers, contexts, and concerns. The process helps us see how we negotiate personal, cultural, and pedagogic values through books, addressing such questions as "What kind of history do we want to invent for rhetorical education in America?" "How do we inscribe its historical beginnings in North America—and around which texts?" "Whose body/bodies?" "What do we want rhetorical education in America to do?" "How do we want to connect these questions to the state of rhetoric in writing classrooms now?" Posing such questions is important as we excavate and reconstruct archives of knowledge in rhetorical education for, as Derrida argues, how an archive is constituted and interpreted signifies how political power is distributed in culture, which in turn signifies the measure of effective democratization.

## An Unruly Synthesis

First published in 1797 and recently republished in a 1998 bicentennial edition, *The Columbian Orator* is part of what Hortense Spillers calls our "national treasury of rhetorical wealth" (65). The handbook sold more than two hundred thousand copies in the first fifty years of its publication and claimed a place alongside the Bible and *The Farmer's Almanac* in American homes, influencing school boys and adults alike in using "the ornamental and useful art of eloquence" for upholding republican virtues (Blight xvii). Lawrence Buell confirms this assessment, citing *The Columbian Orator* as "the first American textbook on the art of speaking, one which occupied a central part of most educational curricula, especially in New England" (138). Kenneth Cmiel characterizes the book's social function as directly bolstering a republican nationalism and securing the neoclassical ideal of eloquent language as able to defend and reinforce liberty, virtue, and just governance (39). Similarly, Shelley Fisher-Fishkin and Carla Peterson read Bingham's text as "displaying the Enlightenment discourse of freedom and independence," instructing readers as to the optimal relationship between speaker and audience, and as to the goals of a successful orator, who is to speak "both out of a personal experience and on behalf of an entity larger than their individual 'I,' be it an entire nation, an oppressed group within the nation, or a broad principle such as freedom" (190). As each of these scholars suggests, *The Columbian Orator,* with its instruction on elocution, excerpts from famous speeches, and dialogues on such subjects as justice, virtue, and oppression, is a site for creating concord among individual differences and a larger, national, public collective. Instruction in "eloquence," or rousing, persuasive speech, is the ground on which this concord is forged.

But such treasures of rhetorical wealth are also sites of conflict. Artifacts such as rhetoric handbooks are places where our desires for coherent national, cultural, and political identities contend with the very differences that threaten to unravel seams of difference that are carefully stitched together. I see *The Columbian Orator*'s contents, arrangement, and instructional preface less as a coherent example of neoclassical civic rhetoric (one that could be transposed for contemporary critical pedagogy) and more as a conflicted statement about eloquence, social power, and public culture. The synthesis of moral, performative, and civic rhetorics contained in *The Columbian Orator* both enables and limits the critical education the handbook is prized for.

Caleb Bingham's *Columbian Orator* is a landmark in American rhetorical education in part because it uses the synthetic nature of post-Enlightenment rhetorical philosophy to contend with changes in the public sphere, especially rising linguistic, racial, and ethnic diversity. Bingham's editorial selections revise what and who constitute a public sphere in ways that are often more inclusive than what Jurgen Habermas himself defined as happening in eighteenth-century coffeehouses, periodicals, and salons. In the *Orator,* rational-critical debate happens in parliament, but also happens on mutinous ships, at the slave auction, and on the stoop outside the tenement. After the introduction on how to use the book, the *Orator* proceeds to provide, in anthology style, rhetorical genres, topics, and speakers that were decidedly accommodating of popular tastes and modes of discourse. For example, Bingham includes orations from Socrates and George Washington, speeches from Scottish members of parliament and American members of Congress, along with orations representing the "Indian chief" and the "small boy." The collection also contains dialogues between an "oppressive landlord" and his tenant, between a schoolteacher and his supervisory committee, and between "Slaves in Barbary" and their captors. Lectures are interspersed among these forms, offering advice on such matters as "the choice of business for life," and sentimental poetry and prose are intermingled with spicy dramas, like "The Tragedy of Tamerlane." In this heterogeneous intermingling of genres, subjects, and speakers, public participation emerges as "a complex array of discursive practices, including forms of writing, speech, and . . . performance, [that are] historically situated and contested" (S. Wells 328).

For its reflection of a spectrum of publics and discourses characteristic of the period, *The Columbian Orator* is an important touchstone for exploring the beginnings of civic rhetoric in American rhetorical education. Civic rhetoric is prized for its "concern for the social construction and practical applications of shared beliefs," for its political efforts "to teach citizens how to draw on received values to address public problems," and for its "dialectical engagement with how groups make sense of their past as they translate shared beliefs into practical action" (Miller and Bowdon 593). The *Orator* demonstrates these positive aspects of civic rhetoric through three editorial strategies. It does so first through its sampling of speeches relating to political domination by British, Scottish, French, and American statesmen, demonstrating rational-critical debates on matters of national urgency. Second, Bingham uses dialogue—between tenants and landlords, slaves and masters, aristocrats and publicans—to display the process of argument and how rhetoric can be used to resolve issues and promote action. In both these approaches Bingham allows institutions and individuals of unequal power to debate their positions in ways the social structure might prohibit. Fi-

nally, Bingham claims that randomly positioning the pieces in his handbook without regard to chronology or topic is important for an exciting
and "ennobling" reading experience. Bingham's interest in how position
creates meaning seems to heighten the effect of the mix of linguistic
styles he includes in the handbook. It also heightens the effects of the
representations of the varied class, racial, gender, and ethnic identities
that structured social relations in the United States. This attention to
the forms argument takes, to the spectrum of positions and locations of
argument, and to a larger purpose for those individual positions is what
endures about civic rhetoric and the pedagogies that promote it.

While the *Orator* offers readers a civic rhetoric, what often emerges in
the handbook is an anxious coexistence between hegemonic and transformative pedagogic authorities. Unlike hegemonic authority, which
"feels 'natural'; its operation . . . normalized within institutions like
schools," a "transformative authority, one calling for change in the fundamental order, calls attention to itself" (Jarratt, "Sapphic" 84) in part
by making "the formation of political consciousness the subject of literacy
education" (Jarratt, "Rhetorical" 37). In other words, while the content
of the handbook is critical and political, the pedagogies and moral philosophies that frame these texts threaten to limit such readings. If the
transformative spirit of the handbook occurs through its diverse representations of public discourse, its pedagogic framework—a synthesis of
neoclassicism, elocution, and moral philosophy—is less interested in
rhetoric that transforms power relations by inquiring into the social construction of ideas than one that is based in managing social difference
by reinvesting certain kinds of values, practices, and ideas with power.
In this way, education in eloquence becomes as much about acquiring
a privileged subjectivity as it is a guide to critical intervention into public
issues.

For example, in its "General Instructions for Speaking," the *Orator* opens with an anecdote extolling the virtues of techniques of self-
discipline that comprise the practice of elocution. The anecdote focuses
on Demosthenes' early rhetorical training and is meant to steel neophyte
orators as they begin their rhetorical education.

[Demosthenes] had both a weak voice, and likewise an impedi-
ment in his speech. . . . The former of which defects he conquered,
partly by speaking as loud as he could upon the shore . . . and
partly by pronouncing long periods as he walked up hill . . . and

he found means to render his pronunciation more clear and articulate, by the help of some little stones put under his tongue. . . . And because he had an ill custom of drawing up his shoulders when he spoke, to amend that, he used to place them under a sword, which hung over him with the point downward. (5–6)

Bingham uses Demosthenes' exercises to represent a program for training the body through techniques that create eloquent speech. His body is a site of discipline that needs to "conquer" its natural state through a series of discrete but rigorous corrections. Throughout these corrective exercises, Demosthenes is portrayed as the valiant romantic orator/ elocutionist: in the quote above he is howling at the waves, declaiming over hills, tongue-lashing stones, facing the sword. In the guise of conquering Nature, this orator actually conquers his own nature, and in turn submits to what is perceived as a correct eloquence. *The Columbian Orator* begins, then, not by foregrounding the transformative elements that I catalogued in the opening to this section, elements which make possible critical links with content and disposition and that make the practice of eloquence about developing diverse, agential publics and public discourses. It opens by personifying eloquence as a battle with self that takes place outside a recognizable civic space or discourse community.

That Bingham would open his introduction with this anecdote is significant in relation to Foucault's observation that the period of the late eighteenth century marks the shift between earlier systems of punishment and emergent forms of discipline. It is a historical moment when "the entire economy of punishment was redistributed" via law, custom, the organization of public and institutional space, and large-scale social reforms (Foucault, *Discipline* 7). Rhetoric at this time and into the nineteenth century participates in "a more refined mapping of the social body," its theories and practices creating new, discrete techniques of power that act on and shape bodies (*Discipline* 78). As a rhetoric manual for the middling social orders, Bingham's text evinces what Nan Johnson calls the "synthetic" nature of rhetoric in nineteenth-century America (*Rhetoric* 14–15), one offering a refined mapping of interweaving threads: a neoclassical rhetoric that values the cultivation of public, virtuous speakers who labor to activate the common, civic good through their uncommon eloquence; a belletristic insistence on imitation and critique of literature to help develop taste; a romantic ability to transport listeners by paying attention to affective response and description; a moral philosophy that provokes sensitivity to recognize eloquence, regulate one's own faculties to it, and seek out and produce a sympathetic correspondence between speaker and audience; and finally an overarching elocutionary focus on speech and gestures. This combination of rhetorical philosophies reconstituted power by regulating affective, psychological, and behavioral responses through sets of internal and external regulatory cues. But such disciplinary formations are not as neatly determined in practice as they appear in the description above; relations constituted through the exercise of rhetorical power "define innumerable points of confrontation, forces of instability, each of which has its own risks of conflict, of struggles, and of at least temporary inversions of the power relations" (Foucault, *Discipline* 27). In other words, in their uses and effects, this combination is an *unruly* synthesis of rhetorical theories and practices, one that exists in a tangled weave in *The Columbian Orator* both to secure hegemonic authority through pedagogy and also to enable transformative possibilities through its representations. I'll provide two examples: one in which this synthesis of rhetorical theories entrenches existing hegemonic formations and one in which it transforms power significantly.

"In order to render pronunciation distinct," Bingham argues in the introduction, "it is necessary, not only that each word and syllable should have its just and full sound, both as to time and accent, but likewise that every sentence, and part of a sentence, should be separated by its proper pause . . . for every one should speak in the same manner as he ought to read, if he could arrive at that exactness" (13). To make the cadence of reading the standard for effective prose is to normalize belletristic, mannered refinement and elocutionary exactness. Tom Miller finds that this synthesis of eighteenth-century rhetorical theories served as a forum to advance various social ends at a time when rhetoric had broader public engagements that made it an important site for the reorganization of the cultural hegemony (*Formation* 7). These rhetorics "project the authority of the educated into the public domain," soliciting students and readers to "adopt a set of values, values that in practice will tend to define who can speak and what is beyond question" (*Formation* 8). If the above example suggests the practices that signal proper speech, the following definition of eloquence featured in the *Orator* is an example of the moral values it recognizes: "To instruct, to persuade, to please; these are its objects. To scatter the clouds of ignorance and error from the atmosphere of reason; to remove the film of prejudice from the mental eye; and thus to irradiate the benighted mind with the cheering beams of truth, is at once the business and the glory of eloquence" (27). After this rousing description of the challenge eloquence offers citizens to enlighten themselves, Perkins ends, not by advocating action, but by advocating strenuous "imitation" of "above all Greek, above all Roman" eloquence (29). This neoclassicism is not so much revolutionary or critical as it is reproductive of dominant subjectivities. The discrepancy between the extensive codes for imitation and delivery and the polished samples of neoclassical civic eloquence in the anthology emphasize more than the expected differences between a readership and the eloquent performance of liberatory, revolutionary discourse they are meant to take up as good men speaking well. Here neoclassical rhetoric exists in an anxious synthesis with the discourses of elocution and moral philosophy, making education in eloquence more about the grooming of a specific subjectivity than enabling democratic practice.

The past few pages have addressed how a civic rhetoric is brought to readers, writers, and speakers as a course of action, observing the ways it is delivered through the pedagogies of elocutionary discipline, and ones that advise the imitation of certain moral attitudes and philosophies. If this kind of pedagogic authority counters the transformative elements of the handbook, it is also interesting to consider the representations of rhetorical insubordination that appear throughout the text. If the particular blend of rhetorical theories featured in *The Columbian Orator* uses moral philosophy to impart a set of values and beliefs, a different kind of transformative rhetoric emerges that is invested in circumventing this power formation. Because they present rhetorical engagement as disciplining subjects unjustly and failing to challenge power successfully, these rhetorics represent a desire for transformation in tropes of violence. For example, several of the antislavery entries in the *Orator* use violence as a rhetoric that will achieve ends and expedite matters of social justice that neoclassical rhetoric divorced from critique and action has not resolved. Just as systems of punishment persist within structures of discipline, acts of violence are not exactly outside the economy of the rhetorical. Indeed, representations of retaliatory violence in *The Columbian Orator* are sometimes used as threats against a rhetorical paradigm that fails to result in action and change. Consider the following moment from "Dialogue between Master and Slave," in which the slave, who in the course of the dialogue is freed by his interlocutor/master, enlightens his master on the reality of white "domination":

> I will tell you freely the condition in which you live. You are surrounded with implacable foes, who long for a safe opportunity to revenge upon you and the other planters all the miseries they have endured. The more generous their natures, the more indignant they feel against the cruel injustice which has dragged them hither, and doomed them to perpetual servitude. You can rely on no kindness on your part, to soften the obduracy of their resentment . . . superior force alone can give you security. As soon as that fails, you are at the mercy of the merciless. (1998, 211–12)

It can be argued that this dialogue, as well as the representations of violence that appear elsewhere in the handbook, could simply reflect a religious discourse that values "millennial violence" as a cleansing of moral corruption; or it could reflect the republican political ideology that values violence as part of the attainment of larger, more noble goals of liberty, democracy, and freedom. I see this reference to the threat of violence as invoking the hope for a transformative pedagogy that *The Columbian Orator* doesn't quite express. In this dialogue the slave speaks a "truth" of the master's condition that the master cannot see within the bounds of his reasonable dialogue. While Bingham stresses the importance of an awareness of the rhetorical situation, here the slave informs his white interlocutor of a rhetorical "condition" he was unaware of constructing. Further, Bingham stresses throughout the introduction to the handbook the importance of natural speech, of "follow[ing] nature" (10), of avoiding theatrical gestures and mannerisms (9), conveying the "truth" and "character" that comes from being a "good man" (7). But here the slave argues that artifice and duplicity represent the prudent rhetorical posture of the enslaved condition: one performs one's role in search of a fissure in the power dynamic. In fact, the slave assures the master that the more kind and submissive slaves act, the more the master can be assured that it is an act. What we are left with in this social contract is a social logic in which superior force is all that keeps power in place; this is the handbook's rhetoric of violence, one that substitutes for the critical, agential pedagogies that are absent from this text.

What ultimately makes this unruly synthesis of rhetorical theories and practices interesting is, as Steven Mailloux argues, how it expands the possibilities for ways of reading the anthology. For example, in his 1845 narrative, the dialogue between a master and his slave is the entry that Frederick Douglass singles out from *The Columbian Orator* as having a profound impact on his literacy development. In this we see that Douglass was influenced by the potential of rhetoric to show him that slavery was subject to argument and to the advocacy of abolitionism (a point I will discuss further in the next section). But in exploring the synthetic nature of the text, we can see how he may have been attracted to the text for other reasons. The book provided him the means to access and imitate a form of subjectivity—the eloquent speaker who is the central actant in an oratorical culture—which had extraordinary cultural power. This was a subjectivity that Douglass used to change the racist parameters of the culture he eventually gained access to as an orator, writer, and statesman. He may also have been interested in a combination of the two: the book's representations of violence that take up where the talk of rhetoric fails—ones in which slaves get revenge on masters, crews mutiny from ship captains, and a reverend at his pulpit begs "Africa" to be gentle at the day of judgment (Bingham 256–57), and the idea of eloquence as offering readers education in attaining a privileged subjectivity. As I argue in the next section, scholars have used Frederick Douglass to highlight the transformative authority embedded within the *Orator*. This association is a crucial one for rhetorical history; but it can obscure the complex nature of the text by allowing Douglass to stand in for its critical pedagogy. This approach allows scholars to avoid entering the pages of the *Orator* through analysis, sorting out its assumptions, pedagogies, and representations, and seeing the complicated and conflicted lessons someone like Douglass could take away from the handbook.

## New Editions

By all accounts, the impact of Bingham's book on Frederick Douglass was profound. In his 1845 narrative Douglass writes, "Every opportunity I got, I used to read this book" (51). He discusses the effects of two speeches in particular—a dialogue between a slaveholder and his slave, and a speech arguing for Catholic emancipation—saying that each "gave tongue to interesting thoughts of my own soul, which had frequently flashed through my mind, and died for want of utterance" (52). These essays, he says, "enabled me to utter my thoughts, and to meet arguments brought forward to sustain slavery" (52). In "My Bondage My Freedom" Douglass proclaims,

> that gem of a book, *The Columbian Orator,* with its eloquent orations and spicy dialogues, denouncing oppression and slavery—telling of what had been dared, done, and suffered by men, to obtain the inestimable boon of liberty—was still fresh in my memory, and whirled into the ranks of my speech with the aptitude of well trained soldiers, going through the drill. The fact is, I here began my public speaking. (305–06)

As Logan observes, "explicit statements of influence . . . from Douglass would seem to be the fulfillment of a rhetorical critic's dream" (1). Indeed, what Douglass gleaned from his reading of *The Columbian Orator* is nothing less than the ends of an education in rhetoric that combines the best from the classical period to the present moment: grappling with the notion of truth versus socially constructed meaning, valuing dialogue as a process of rational-critical debate on issues of civic urgency, learning diverse strategies for advancing a claim, negotiating social difference to democratic ends, and practicing eloquence as a form of action.

Although it was read by the likes of Abraham Lincoln, Ralph Waldo Emerson, and Harriet Beecher Stowe (Ganter 464), the *Orator* remains intriguing to contemporary rhetoricians, not because of these and other famous readers, but because someone like Douglass happened upon it. It has become synonymous with Douglass's rise to literacy and an emblem of the liberatory, critical potential of a rhetorical education. David Blight's introduction to the newly republished *Columbian Orator* reinforces the importance of this association. Titled "The Peculiar Dialogue between Caleb Bingham and Frederick Douglass," his introduction to Bingham's handbook has four aims: it documents Douglass's debt to *The Columbian Orator* through a review of Douglass's autobiographical statements; it speculates on the larger influence of the *Orator* on Douglass's career as a lecturer and public servant; it provides useful background on Caleb Bingham's career as an educator, reformer, author, bookseller, and civil servant; and it argues that the *Orator* is an important book to intervene in our present cultural moment. Blight's introduction takes on significance because of Blight's strong scholarly reputation and because of his essay's prime location; it is now the main critical statement on the *Orator* that students and teachers will read to understand the book's place in the history of rhetorical education. Since it had been stored in special collections rooms with little hope of escape, this new edition will be the one teachers use in speech, undergraduate rhetoric and American Studies courses, and graduate courses on histories of rhetoric in North America.

The associations Blight makes among Douglass's experience, antebellum cultural tensions over language use, and the history of the book itself create a profoundly useful method for uncovering the book's socially transformative potential. In one example of this approach, Blight places the *Orator* on a pedagogic trajectory with teachers as dissimilar as Sophia Auld, the white schoolboys who provided Douglass with a clandestine literacy community, and Charles Lawson, a freeman who taught Douglass "the spirit" behind the Bible's words (Blight xiv). In the midst of such diverse pedagogic and literacy experiences, Douglass read the *Orator*'s dialogues and saw that slavery was "subject to argument" and that there was "a world beyond his thralldom" (xiv). Placing the *Orator* in the context of these kinds of pedagogic moments, ones on the street, within the slave system, and within the discourse of religious conversion, helps us to better understand the complex ways in which the book's multiple and conflicted messages could be consumed with liberatory rather than hegemonic effects.

Blight's introduction creates a second dense network of associations, this time placing the *Orator* within the cultural tensions over language use that distinguished the period in which the handbook first appeared. At this time, tensions between democratic and aristocratic eloquence persisted, "where language grew as a conflicted melding of pressures from above and below, an emerging mixture of dignified, classical eloquence and the demands of democratic education" (xxii). Blight discusses how the handbook often defaults to classical, French, and British models for speech and behavior, but he highlights the way Bingham constructs the cultural tension over speech that most handbooks of the period avoid. Blight details Bingham's decision to commission his associate David Everett to author eleven dialogues for inclusion in the *Orator,* in which the speech is filled with dialects and colloquialisms, and the conclusions find "the underdogs outwit[ting] their oppressors" every time (xxi). Blight not only shows us the transformative cultural tensions in "education, ethnic pluralism, the nature of power and individual rights," but shows us how Bingham framed them within the handbook to make an argument for the power of reasoned debate (xxi). These linguistic tensions appear within the larger frame of Frederick Douglass's experience of mastering the oppressor's language traditions, showing how hegemonic rhetorical strains could be subverted even while they are seemingly faithfully executed. The associative links between cultural tensions over language use, Bingham's unusual intervention with Everett's dialogues, and Douglass's intervention into both create a dynamic and powerful method for reading this text. While my argument about the *Orator*'s unruly synthesis of rhetorical theories suggests something more haltingly transformative in its consideration of the handbook's pedagogic associations, Blight's consideration of its different associations suggests something more disruptive.

In his arguments for *The Columbian Orator*'s contemporary relevance, though, Blight's introduction shifts into a need to invest this rhetorical artifact with solutions for present-day fears about the moral and political function of rhetorical education. Blight feels passionate about the *Orator*'s relevance for our present moment, stating that "we live in a time at the end of the twentieth century when the goals of education and the texts employed have become the subject of intensive political debate. What should young readers study in multicultural America? Where should young readers find inspiration, the cadence, character, and meaning of language?" (xv). The following excerpt is his most detailed argument for why a late-eighteenth-century handbook can instruct and "improve" a late-twentieth-century audience:

In an age where there is good reason to lament the decline of oratory and to fear for the future of the book in the face of the power of visual and electronic media, this elocution manual/reader lends us reassurance from the past. Like lost treasure, some old books can reemerge in the present and matter as much now as they did when they were new commodities in American classrooms. The image of young Frederick Douglass hiding in his loft practicing reading and speaking from his *Columbian Orator* is far more inspiring than it is quaint. Indeed, those concerned in American society today with how young people garner and practice good habits and virtues in the face of so much popular culture vying for their attention might benefit from a slow examination of Bingham's reader. They might even wish to make the book talk by reading the dialogues and speeches out loud, as a family no doubt did in the previsual, preelectronic age of the early nineteenth century. As Douglass did, they will find both music and political meaning in the language. (xv–xvi)

Blight argues for the book's relevance by claiming it provides "reassurance from the past" for the present. It is read as a solution to an anxiety about waning eloquence, where a multiplicity of media powers prevail over what are perceived as more stable signifiers (the book, oratory), and which are seen as providing a single, unifying speech ideal and value system. A concern expressed in this binary is that the power differentials have shifted from an ideal oratorical culture whose purpose "was to form and sustain a public consensus, intellectual and moral, as the basis of civic action" (Clark and Halloran 2) to a mass media or popular culture in which information, subjects, and speech are characterized as heterogenous, decentered, and void of moral direction. The argument laments the decline of oratorical culture and fears the power of other cultural forms and discourse technologies that compete with it. This concern over cultural fragmentation has its origins in the nineteenth century and situates the *Orator,* and the form of eloquence it promotes, as a corrective for this supposed state of decline.

In order to make eloquence a cultural corrective to this state of decline, Blight situates *The Columbian Orator* in a moral economy, a system of exchange where the handbook becomes a "lost treasure" and "a new classroom commodity." The *Orator* is described as an alternative moral economy to the "popular culture" that "vies" for students' attention. In Blight's language, popular culture becomes an object—a commodity, like a book—that acts on subjects. In other words, popular culture is an entity separate from people instead of an expression of their vital, shifting, even conflicting beliefs, practices, and values. Here a virtuous consumption of *The Columbian Orator* and an illicit consumption of popular culture emerge in a battle for young people's attention. As if to escape this battle, the argument shifts into the private sphere, where a family gathers together to "make the book talk." This invocation of the family solidifies a withdrawal into a nostalgic, private sphere, one supposedly outside the system of exchange and opposed to the public, an answer for a late-twentieth-century public culture too fragmented to convey meaning.

In one aspect, Blight's argument for civic rhetoric is related to hegemonic assumptions about attaining cultural literacy: that there is a relatively stable, definable national discourse community; that there is a knowledge base that will enable people to share in the common language of this community; and that certain knowledge is best suited for defining that community (Bizzell 372–73). As Patricia Bizzell argues, if such a formation ever existed, "it may have owed its existence to historical circumstances that greatly limited the group of people who had access to it in terms of race, sex and social class" (373). Instead of seeing the knowledge and discourse technologies that emerge from new media forms and popular culture as different literacies that can be used to foster a critical literacy and engage different perspectives and value systems (which Blight forcefully argues for within the *Orator*'s historical moment), when he attempts to make the handbook relevant for today, Blight's argument maintains a particular neoclassical civic value system as an idealized rhetorical state. This assessment is affirmed when we ask where Douglass is in this argument for *The Columbian Orator*'s contemporary relevance. In the above quotation Douglass emerges in a single sentence in the middle of the argument, a sentence that breaks apart the connected thoughts on either side of it (that old rhetoric books matter because young people are in need of instruction in good habits and virtue). Douglass appears as hiding in his loft, reading and speaking from the *Orator,* providing what Toni Morrison might call a "metaphoric shortcut" (x) for Blight's idealized notion of civic pedagogy. Here Douglass is a location that stands in for the handbook's public virtues; this figure is "a location, a 'topic,' functioning as both a heightened example of public virtues or vices, and also as a prop for identification" (Wells 330).

Along with others, Rosa Eberly argues "that cultural texts [such as *The Columbian Orator*] have some role to play in reinvigorating participatory democratic practice" (Eberly 1). Toward these ends, Blight's introduction argues forcefully for a contemporary education in rhetoric that achieves profound cultural relevancies. His method, one that synthesizes Douglass's readerly contexts, contexts within the handbook, and larger cultural tensions, shows us a powerful convergence of textual, cultural, and personal associations. But in its argument for the book's relevance for today's classrooms, Blight's introduction upholds *The Columbian Orator*'s neoclassical civic foundation, which does little to further practical connections and associations. Joseph Harris makes a point that is relevant to this claim.

One of the central claims of public education in America . . . is that of working toward the forming of a nation-state that is not tied to any single ethnicity, of helping to create a public culture open to all individuals regardless of race, gender, or social rank. To invoke this sort of democratic culture is not to call for a return to a set of shared and communal values; rather, it is to call for a forum in which issues and concerns that go beyond the borders of particular communities of interest groups can be worked through collectively, debated, negotiated. (38)

Rhetoric handbooks and the theories they represent needn't be "solutions." As Harris suggests, and as Blight's larger argument suggests, we need them to be "forums" for assessing larger issues about the relationship between rhetoric, power, and subject formation.

The Columbian Orator is an example of the potentials and problems with a civic rhetoric that is at times divorced from a critical pedagogy. The frameworks of the Orator itself, as well as the frames imposed on it by historians, both enable and limit a pedagogy that fosters the transformative democratic change it claims to enable. Caleb Bingham himself would be surprised by my assessment. Not only was Bingham one of the most progressive education reformers, authors, booksellers, and civic officials of his time, but he was also an adherent of New Light Millennialism, a religious-inflected political radicalism that was opposed to the mannered elitism of Federalism, and that affirmed the capability of speech to change the course of history (Ganter 475). Granville Ganter argues that The Columbian Orator's insistence on "virtuous action" bears this idealistic position out in ways that other handbooks of the antebellum period do not. In making this argument, Ganter relies on the complex meaning of "pronunciation" in rhetorical history as signifying more than a valuing of elocution skills, but an instruction in elocution that makes delivery an action itself—that sets in motion change within audience members and within a culture.

For a critical perspective on this kind of "action," one that relates to how the connection between speaking and acting works in our composition and rhetoric classrooms, Elizabeth Ervin offers an important point. She posits that students need to understand "the profound difference between writing, [speaking, and reading] about issues in class and acting on them (in writing or otherwise) outside of class" (382). Her critique of the concept of action in rhetoric is useful for our purposes of reclaiming civic rhetoric for the classroom and for rhetorical history. Noting that "it is a tradition of liberal education to treat reading, writing, [and] discussing as actions" (385), she is wary of how this approach "might uncritically treat the classroom as a representative public" (386). Specifically, it "might convey tacit support for a voyeuristic relationship between students and their world, in which reading, analyzing, discussing, and writing in composition class are equivalent to intervening, acting, and participating in 'the real world'" (385). In promoting links between "literate and civic behavior," ones that reflect the general motive of pedagogy to enact social change, Ervin offers alternative paths for seeing "students as citizens and writing as an act of citizenship" (390, 393): modeling a participation in the world outside the classroom, writing for communities outside the classroom audience of teacher and students, and structuring social relations in the classroom as "dense networks of interaction" that are working toward "diverse publics outside the classroom to which they have an obligation" (395).

Another compositionist who is "realign[ing] rhetorical pedagogy to the public" is Susan Wells, who has made generative links among composition, rhetoric, and public-sphere theory. Her aim is to more carefully foreground what constitutes public discourse in making the connection between "readers, texts, and actions" (338). Wells argues that, in our discontinuous, fragmented civic spaces, "public speech is a performance in time, located at specific historical junctures, temporary and unstable, even though it is imagined as a location in space, always available, with secure and discernable borders" (327). She too offers ideas for how to actualize these observations about contemporary publics: conceptualizing the classroom as a version of a public sphere, analyzing texts produced in publics and counterpublics, producing student writing that creates a public, and working with the discourses of academic disciplines as they intervene in the public (338–39). In light of the observations of Ervin and Wells about public speech and public spheres, and in light of the transformative literacies that have emerged from the association between Frederick Douglass and *The Columbian Orator,* it seems that handbooks from the archives of rhetorical history are useful today in part for their ability to connect past and present cultural and pedagogic contexts, the aims and desires of particular readers, and writing that leads to action.

If "the civic tradition needs to be critically reexamined to access the limitations it imposed on public access and the rhetorical strategies that were used to overcome them," handbooks from the archives of rhetorical education are excellent places to begin that reexamination (Miller and Bowdon 594). Indeed, if the goal "of making students into certain kinds of human beings" has been a humanist goal of moral philosophy and neoclassical civic education since the late eighteenth century, then the present goal of rhetorical education is different: making the process of subject formation and knowledge production the very mode of inquiry for the course that above all promotes and enacts the excellent aims of civic rhetoric (Jarratt, "Rhetorical Power" 36); and moving a "self-reflexive practice directed at critique and self-consciousness" outward into "intervention," action, and "agency" (Wells 334). Using artifacts from the archives of rhetorical education as forums to engage students in redefining their role as participants in the present provides another way to open up the archive of rhetorical education for a critical dialogue about rhetoric, subject formation, and knowledge production—a dialogue that sees writing as action. We need to continue to (a)mend rhetorical history, not by resurrecting a version of civic rhetoric that reproduces its own limits and exclusions, but by realizing what it enables and associating these features with forward-thinking pedagogies from our own millennial moment.

## Notes

1. For Steven Mailloux, editing is "perhaps the best example of interpretive practice we have. It explicitly demonstrates several characteristics of the interpretive process: (1) its materiality; (2) its embeddedness in traditions of theory and practice; (3) its institutional and cultural locations; and (4) its involvement in rhetorical politics constituted by arguments over ideologies, professional and other" ("Reading Typos" 585, 586).

2. This is not an unusual linkage. Twentieth-century assessments of *The Columbian Orator* have largely taken place through an investigation of Frederick Douglass's association with the book, resulting in important scholarship in nineteenth-century literacy, rhetoric, and African American studies. For examples of such scholarship see Blight; Fisher-Fishkin and Peterson; Logan; Mailloux; Royer; Sisco; Wilken.

# 5
# Politics, Identity, and the Language of Appalachia

## James Watt Raine on "Mountain Speech and Song"

### Susan Kates

> If language is the mechanism through which we inherit history and culture, then each individual word functions as a type of gene, bearing with it a small piece of the specific information that makes us who we are and tells us where we have been.
>
> Tony Earley, "The Quare Gene," 1998

> The language of the Mountain People has been much maligned. It is neither careless nor degraded. Its difference from "United States English" does not indicate a corrupt falling away from modern speech, but rather a survival of the speech of an older day.
>
> James Watt Raine, *The Land of the Saddle-bags*, 1924

In the last decade, scholars in rhetoric and composition studies have begun to write the history of writing and speaking instruction in the United States as it emerged for students who, for the most part, did not attend traditional colleges and universities. Much of this scholarship examines the politicization of rhetoric curricula for white, middle-class women in the nineteenth century (K. K. Campbell; Conway); working class women in the early twentieth century (Greer; Hollis); and black students inside and outside of historically black colleges at the turn of the century (Kates; Zaluda). As Jane Greer explains, scholars have begun the historical work "that amplifies newly audible voices . . . and that insists on the value of the personal and the subjective" (248). Certainly many voices are yet to be recovered as we write histories of rhetorical education in America that are attentive to diverse student populations and the extracurriculum of composition studies. At this stage, significant gaps exist in our research because we have only begun to discover the community-specific modes of instruction that emerged for various groups of students of rhetoric in America in the late nineteenth and early twentieth centuries.

While scholars have begun to write the educational histories of women and African Americans, there is a notable silence on the region of Appalachia and the forms of rhetorical education that were developed to reach this group of students. Institutions such as Berea College in Berea, Kentucky, and Highlander Folk School in Monteagle, Tennessee, were founded for a particular student constituency—the students of Appalachia—and educators at these sites designed curricula built upon the study of Appalachian literature, art, and history. These institutions offered students from the region a sense of their cultural heritage, a heritage that was often stereotyped and characterized in a negative fashion in American popular culture.

Such depictions were criticized by James Watt Raine, a rhetoric professor at Berea College from 1906 to 1939. In his book, *The Land of the Saddle-bags: A Study of the Mountain People of Appalachia,* Raine mounts an articulate defense of the culture and, more specifically, the language of the people of the mountain region of Kentucky. He takes issue with the demeaning portrayals of their speech as those depictions appeared in literature and magazine cartoons. A chapter of Raine's text, "Mountain Speech and Song," provides a detailed overview of the history as well as richness of Appalachian language, urging those outside the community to take another view of it. Raine's defense is a particularly interesting one because much of what he has to say in his book has important implications for current debates raging in composition studies over the issue of language and identity.

My interest in the work of educators like Raine grows out of contemporary discussions about how we should address the linguistic differences of our students in the rhetoric classroom. Recently we have witnessed a number of events that have placed the subject of language and identity front and center in a host of educational debates. Consider, for example, the controversy surrounding Ebonics and the vigorous debate that ensued when, in 1996, the Oakland, California, school board voted to implement a new program giving Ebonics, or African American English, legitimate second language status in its schools. The assumption was that this practice would help African American students to learn standard English. Much to the school board's surprise, a national debate erupted, and the events surrounding the decision became so inflamed that the district was forced to drop all references to the word *Ebonics* and to implement the project by incorporating the ideas behind Ebonics without the controversial name. Parents and educational policy makers of many races feared that African American English would be taught at the exclusion of standard English, and this was perhaps the greatest misconception about Ebonics. The Oakland school board aimed to recognize the relationship between language, identity, and learning. The goal was to use Ebonics as a vehicle to other modes of communication and as a way to understand the value of different varieties of English in various contexts. These pedagogical ideas grew out of work by Geneva Smitherman, Sylvia Cunnigham, and others who contend that when black youth feel that they must make a choice between one variety of English and another, it becomes more likely that they may reject educational opportunites. The Oakland decision attempted to address the linguistic tension African American students may experience, and it became one of the most controversial language issues to erupt in public debates in decades.

Discussions such as those that have raged around the issue of Ebonics are overtly political, and there is no shortage of educators, administrators, or politicians who have an opinion on the subject. Yet few observe that a defense of regional language, such as Raine pursued in the early part of the twentieth century, is equally "political" insofar as it is tied up in the ways language and identity are connected. There is a close relationship between the argument implicit in Raine's text that I wish to discuss in this essay and the explicit description of the politics of language and language study that contemporary theorists such as Geneva Smitherman, Sylvia Cunnigham, Henry Giroux, and Paulo Freire describe in much of their work. I will discuss their contributions to the language/identity debate later in the essay. I want to begin, however, by stating my larger purpose in reading Raine's text: My goal is to use what Raine says about Appalachian language and identity to argue that present debates over language and culture, such as the Ebonics controversy, have a history, a history that can teach us just how important this issue is—and how it will persistently demand our attention if we do not observe it and address it in our pedagogies. The articles and books left to us by educators in the past, such as *The Land of the Saddle-bags* written by

Raine, do much to demonstrate that educators have long devoted significant attention to the issue of language and identity, to people's sense of their cultural worth and that of their neighbors. It is here, more than anywhere else, that the politics of language and of education becomes clear. By returning to the past—by recovering it—we can discover that our contemporary debates over the issue have an important history, one that we need to attend to if we wish to address this pedagogical dilemma more effectively.

## James Watt Raine: Background

Born to a Scottish family in London, England, Raine moved to the United States with his father and two brothers after his mother's death in 1869 when he was twelve years old. His family lived in West Virginia and later settled in Arkansas. Graduating from Oberlin College in 1893, Raine taught briefly at Oberlin and at Kansas State Agricultural College and served as pastor of two Congregational churches in New York and Ohio (Billings x–xi). He joined the faculty at Berea in 1906 and became a part of the community in which he lived and taught.

Raine's long tenure on the Berea College faculty in Berea, Kentucky— from 1906 to 1939—demonstrates his commitment to this Appalachian student constituency and to the institution founded to preserve and celebrate the culture of those individuals. Berea College is distinguished by its long history of service to students from its region, and its curriculum has long emphasized the study of Appalachian art, literature, and history. A college historically defined by its social activism, Berea was the first institution of higher education in the South to admit black and white students on an equal basis. It recruits students who have high ability but limited financial resources, serving Southern Appalachia by drawing 80 percent of its students from the area.[1]

After moving to Kentucky, Raine became a keen observer of mountain life, and his respect and affection for his community led him to work on a project that aimed to dispel stereotypes of the people of the southern mountain region. In 1924, after he had lived and worked in the area for nearly twenty years, Raine published a book celebrating Appalachian language and culture called *The Land of the Saddle-bags: A Study of the Mountain People of Appalachia*. (Recently this text has been reissued by the University Press of Kentucky.) In a chapter from the book entitled "Mountain Speech and Song," Raine argues that the roots of Appalachian English are in Elizabethan English; he traces many Appalachian words to Chaucer and Shakespeare and celebrates the ingenuity of many of the expressions used by the people of Kentucky. He attacks those, such as John Fox and other writers, who stereotype the language used in the region and depict a "drunken, slothful, gun-toting hillbilly prone to violence" in their work. In his analysis, Raine draws attention to the ways such depictions promote cultural stereotypes that are harmful to the people who live in the southern mountains.[2] His high regard for Appalachian language is significant because it asks us at least to consider the possibility that if Raine was willing to make such an overt defense of these modes of communication in his text, he may not have simply dismissed them as ignorant or incorrect in the writing and speaking courses he taught at Berea College.

Given the mission of the institution at which he taught most of his life and the book he wrote that celebrates the customs of Appalachian people, Raine was, at the very least, in a position to observe the pedagogical dilemma many of us face in our teaching of students who are members of other linguistic communities. Raine was not alone in these efforts. His work shares much with other Appalachian ethnographers such as Horace Kephart who published *Our Southern Highlanders* in 1913 and John C. Campbell who published *The Southern Highlander and His Homeland* in 1921. Like Raine, these scholars worked to elevate the image of a group of Americans who had been, in their estimation, largely misunderstood and unfairly characterized in popular culture. Unlike other writers across the country who were all too willing to disparage the customs and the language of the people of Appalachia in stereotypical fashion, Raine sought to draw attention to the inaccuracies and the cultural denigration in their work.

## The Land of the Saddle-bags (1924)

Raine begins his chapter on "Mountain Speech and Song" with the words I quoted at the beginning of this essay, calling attention to the ways in which the language of the Appalachian people has been denigrated by authors such as Fox, who made his literary reputation on the negative portraits he created of those in the southern mountain region in works such as *The Kentuckians*. Raine works to resist Fox's linguistic depictions by drawing attention to misconceptions about Appalachian English and the ways in which those misconceptions create cultural misunderstanding. In suggesting that the differences in Appalachian language from "United States English" do not "indicate a corrupt falling away from modern speech, but rather a survival of the speech of an older day," Raine minces no words in this overt defense of this regional variety of English. His criticism of stereotypical depictions of Appalachian language in literature and popular culture, as well as his attention to the ways that it differs from "United States English," indicates his awareness of what is at stake in such negative characterizations. Raine's insistence that Appalachian language is "neither careless nor degraded" is a particularly interesting defense by a rhetoric teacher of this historical moment, or any moment, for that matter, given the reputation of those who teach writing and speaking as the "guardians of correct usage."

Working strategically to elevate the status of the language utilized by the inhabitants of his region, Raine links it to the forms of English present in Spenser and Chaucer, arguing that what some would characterize as a mongrel jargon in American literature is really a language descended from Elizabethan England. "Our magazine writers," Raine writes,

> usually overdo the dialect in stories of Mountain life. They make
> their characters speak in a mongrel jargon. It is true that Mountain
> speech is a development from Elizabethan English, in which an
> unusually large number of the old words have survived. (96)

Raine argues that so many old words have survived because the surroundings and habits of thought of the mountaineers are largely the same as they were in Shakespeare's day (96). Suggesting a kind of fossilized linguistic community existed in the mountains because few roads brought change, linguistic or otherwise, to the towns of Appalachia, Raine works to combat negative characterizations of Appalachian language by giving them Elizabethan credibility. He connects certain pronunciations by the people of Appalachia to those of another day:

> They say fur with Sir Philip Sidney, and furder with Lord Bacon
> (which is, of course, as correct as murder, from murther). They
> go back to Chaucer and form plurals by adding es, especially in
> words ending in st; as postes, beastes, frostes, joistes (or jystes),
> waistes, nestes, ghostes, in which cases the es forms a second syl-
> lable. With this habit of making plurals, they treat new words with

similar thoroughness: "I tell ye, man trustes is wrong." The habit transfers occasionally to verbs, "Hit costes a lot." "The rope twistes all up." (97)

Raine attempts to give regional language historical credibility because in tracing this form of regional English to another time and place, he hoped to provide a cultural integrity to the Appalachian people, a cultural integrity that outsiders who wrote about the region were not interested in preserving. By linking the usage of certain terms to Sir Philip Sidney and Lord Bacon, Raine attempts to create a cultural barrier against such assaults by those writing about the regional speech of the inhabitants of Kentucky.

This linking of terms to another historical moment was not uncommon at the time Raine was writing; certainly his view of Appalachia as a linguistic community descended from an Elizabethan one is consistent with the scholarship of his day. As I mentioned earlier, he based his work on that of Kephart and Campbell who advocated a similar reevaluation of the language of southern mountaineers based on this understanding. It is a view of the language of the southern mountain region that was disseminated as late as 1936 by H. L. Mencken, in his book *The American Language.* "The dialect of Appalachia," Mencken writes,

> is based primarily upon the Southern English of the late Seventeenth Century, but it has been considerably modified by the Northern English brought in by the Scotch-Irish. The mountain folk are fond of thinking of themselves as the only carriers of pure Anglo-Saxon blood in America, but as a matter of fact many of them are Celts, as an examination of their surnames quickly shows. (358)

While Mencken resists the assertion that the language of the Appalachian people is descended solely from the Anglo-Saxons, he adds that there was a strong Celt influence, like Raine, and he advances the notion that the versions of mountain English spoken in the region of Appalachia grow out of the legacy of Southern English of the late seventeenth century. This is an assertion that Appalachian studies scholars modified in later years.

For example, in his foreword to the reissued version of *The Land of the Saddle-bags,* Dwight Billings underscores why the understanding of language advanced by Campbell, Kephart, Mencken, and Raine is essentialist and problematic, given what we know about the ethnic make-up of the region. Billings explains that

> half of the coal-mining workforce in the central Appalachian coalfields of southern West Virginia were European immigrants and one-fourth were African American at the very moment in time when folk song collectors were searching for traditional British ballads in the region's most remote areas. This ethnic distribution challenges the essentialistic images of mountain people as Anglo-Saxon or Anglo-Celtic folk, frozen in time, such as those that flourished in the era of *The Land of the Saddle-bags.* (xxxiii)

Like Billings, J. L. Dillard notes that while some linguists may rely occasionally on this characterization of the speech of the southern mountains as Elizabethan or Shakespearean English, most current linguists show the picture to be much more complex with both linguistic retentions and innovations (77). In other words, contemporary linguists resist the notion that any form of American English could have preserved the language of the sixteenth century without any transformations whatsoever.

Raine's characterization of a fossilized linguistic community is also problematic in its failure to distinguish between the number of linguistic communities in the area referred to as Appalachia. His work begs the question of how other regions of the country might differ from the region of Kentucky he designates when he uses the term *Appalachia* and what he implies by his use of the term. Generally the region of Appalachia is considered to be the eastern portions of Kentucky and Tennessee, the western portions of North Carolina and Virginia, and the mid and southern region of West Virginia. Construed in this way, Appalachia is a rather vast section of the country and has historically been home to a diverse group of people. Raine, unfortunately, does not account for the diversity of the region in his portrait of the people of Appalachia. His ethnic distribution of the area in *The Land of the Saddle-bags* is far too homogeneous, and, consequently, his linguistic depiction of the region is limited by this point of view. Even so, Raine's text is important to those of us interested in the history of rhetorical education in the United

States because it illustrates that educators have often understood the relationship between language and identity and the pedagogical hazards that denying this relationship could have on the teaching of writing and speaking.

Moreover, Raine's text represents an important acknowledgment of the culturally induced ways in which we come to understand and make judgments about regional language and those who speak it as "other." Throughout his chapter on "Mountain Speech and Song," Raine does more than defend Appalachian modes of communication as legitimate forms of English. He goes so far as to celebrate the ingenious aspects of the language spoken by the people of this region. He explores, for instance, inventiveness that characterizes the language use of Appalachian people, challenging the stereotypes of outsiders who have failed to observe the linguistic creativity possessed by members of this culture:

The magazine writers charge the Mountain People with being slow and rather stupid, with a very limited vocabulary. Of course the vocabulary of invention and machinery is lacking because mechanical contrivances for sale elsewhere are not commonly found in the Mountains. But the fact is that the Mountain People are, unconsciously of course, unusually skilled with language. They have one gift that modern speech has largely lost, the ability to make phrases and even words to fit the needs of the occasion; to express the fresh thought or feeling while it is fluttering over their minds. (101)

Raine's characterization of the modes of expression outside of Appalachia as "mechanical contrivances" is an interesting hierarchical shift of language value: he emphasizes the creative and spontaneous use of language by Appalachians in a way that suggests the unpolluted and uncorrupted nature of the community. However, the form of linguistic isolation Raine suggests is unlikely, as Dillard and other linguists have pointed out. Even so, the celebration of the linguistic ingenuity of Appalachians who can create a new word or phrase for a particular occasion, who can "express the fresh thought or feeling while it is fluttering over their minds," is a fine and unusual tribute to people of this region at this time.

## Language and Identity Concerns: Past and Present

I want to move from Raine's work on language and the culture of Appalachia in the early part of the twentieth century to more recent attention to the issue. Geneva Smitherman argues in the fiftieth-anniversary issue of *CCC* that the subject of language and identity has an important history, one that needs more press and more discussion in educational circles where so many policies that affect students' lives are made. In "CCCC's Role in the Struggle for Language Rights," Smitherman recounts the long struggle for the Students' Right to Their Own Language declaration of the early 1970s. She reminds us of that important portion of the background document that states:

> We need to discover whether our attitudes toward "educated English" are based on some inherent superiority of the dialect itself or on the social prestige of those who use it. We need to ask ourselves whether our rejection of students who do not adopt the dialect most familiar to us is based on any real merit in our dialect or whether we are actually rejecting the students themselves, rejecting them because of their racial, social, and cultural origins. . . . Our major emphasis has been on uniformity, in both speech and writing; would we accomplish more, both educationally and ethically, if we shifted that emphasis to precise, effective, and appropriate communication in diverse ways, whatever the dialect? (qtd. in Smitherman 360)

Smitherman's attention to this important declaration emphasizes the ethical dimensions of our work in the rhetoric classroom. While her work focuses primarily on African American vernacular, current debates have an even broader history than we have acknowledged, and that history includes the struggle over class and regional issues of language use. Her article, tracing the ups and downs of the struggle to acknowledge students' language rights, emphasizes the importance of this history in our field and makes clear that it is an issue that has reemerged with intensity over time.

We might ask, however, why it is that debates over the teaching of standard English generate so much controversy whenever they emerge. Perhaps it is because they underscore the politics of language instruction and the cultural vulnerabilities of students who study and learn standard English uncritically, without the benefit of understanding what is at stake in this practice of cultural and linguistic assimilation. In the following statement about language, identity, and politics, Giroux explains that present debates are so controversial because they concern the ways that language conditions a sense of self. "It is through language," he writes,

> that we come to consciousness and negotiate a sense of identity, since language does not merely reflect reality but plays an active role in constructing it. As language constructs meaning, it shapes our world, informs our identities, and provides the cultural codes for perceiving and classifying the world. (*Schooling and the Struggle* 46)

Giroux's understanding of the ways that language constructs a sense of identity echoes Paulo Freire and others who emphasize that the teaching of writing and speaking is controversial for the very reasons that Giroux describes—because the word is tied directly to self. Language, in other words, conditions whatever sense of selfhood we possess and makes the contemplation of self possible. But what if the language that conditions self is outlawed and denigrated? In *Pedagogy of the Oppressed*, Paulo Freire emphasizes the mediating power of language and the critical relationship between epistemology and the word. Freire writes, "Dialogue is the encounter between men, mediated by the world, in order to name the world and those who do not wish this naming—between those who deny others the right to speak their word" (69). This mediating feature of language, as Freire makes clear, is the way that language conditions identity, and it has a great deal to do with why the issue continues to generate such heated responses in contemporary educational debates. For when educators fail to consider with their students the political dimensions of writing and speaking instruction, they uncritically promote standard English in ways that, as Freire observes, may "deny others the right to speak their word."

The emerging histories of rhetorical education in America suggest that many educators who taught diverse student populations understood the concerns that Smitherman, Cunnigham, Giroux, and Freire describe. Many of them wrote about this feature of their teaching in the textbooks they authored or in articles they published. Like Raine, they came face to face with the issue of language and its relationship to identity politics. How could they fail to do so, given the fact that so many of them taught students in separatist institutions—students who could not or did not attend many of the more elite colleges in America—and whose devotion to communal language practices could be observed in the rhetoric classroom? As a result of their experiences with specific student constituencies, Raine and other educators acknowledged, as Earley does, that language "functions as a type of gene, bearing with it a small piece of the specific information that makes us who we are and tells us where we have been." And they understood, as so many of us do today, that for students who may come from communities where their own language, like that of the mountain people described by Raine, "has been much maligned," taking on standard English involves a complex negotiation with cultural identity. Thus, if those of us who teach writing and speaking are not sensitive to what this negotiation means to the cultural/ communal worth of these students, we may participate in the denigration of the discourse of those communities to which those students belong, and may, in some instances, alienate some students from academic culture altogether.

Raine's efforts to cast new light on the ways and words of the people of Appalachia was indeed an admirable goal for a rhetoric professor in 1924. The intense and detailed exploration of his defense must cause us to wonder how he might have gone about the business of teaching writing and speaking to Appalachian students. Raine's orientation toward Appalachian language and culture in *The Land of the Saddle-bags* allows us to imagine a rhetoric professor who would try to bring that same integrity to considerations of regional language in the rhetoric classroom, thus allowing students to see their language as part of their cultural heritage. It seems quite possible that a rhetoric professor such as Raine who sought to understand regional language in all its complexity might have helped students to understand that complexity as well.

In the midst of contemporary educational debates over Ebonics, rhetoric scholars have a duty to understand how similar debates emerged in other historical moments and to reflect further on how the issue of language and identity plays out in our own writing classrooms. Whether we consider African American English, the regional language of students in Appalachia, gendered discourse, or other varieties of English, the concerns over language and identity that have emerged recently have a long history that rhetoric historians have not yet adequately researched nor acknowledged in their work. Certainly we have a responsibility to recover more pedagogical materials, educational treatises, and books like Raine's that will help us to understand how educators approached language and identity in the rhetoric classroom of the past as we continue to find ways to honor the various ways of speaking and writing that students bring to our classrooms. A more complete portrait of local, politicized rhetorics can only aid us in this endeavor as we give our attention to a matter that has such important pedagogical consequences for our students.

# Notes

1. For a detailed history of Berea College, see *Berea's First 125 Years: 1855–1980* by Emily Ann Smith and Elizabeth Peck.

2. Allen Batteau argues that most cultural myths about Appalachia grow out of the urban imagination. Batteau explains that "whether in movies about a coal miner's daughter or in the use of rural themes of merchandising," these themes draw "on the imagery and motivations" that have captivated an affluent, urban society (1). In *The Invention of Appalachia*, Batteau provides a detailed cultural exploration of these stereotypes by literary activists such as Theodore Dreiser and John Dos Passos and by journalists such as Charles Kuralt.

# 6

# A "Forgotten" Location
## A Rhetorical Curriculum in English Education
### *Rich Lane*

The current state of English-education curricula in our universities and, by default, the curricula in a great percentage of secondary language-arts classrooms remains deeply entrenched in chronological, nationalistic, and aesthetic content—in other words, canonical literature and literary analysis. This is the case despite the fact that in the past twenty years, the structure of English studies at the postsecondary level has undergone extensive discussion and reevaluation, with the influence of postmodernism, the cultural-studies movement, and the rise of rhetoric and composition as a discipline. One form of this reevaluation of curricula includes what Fredric Jameson terms the "linguistic turn"—an effort to "recover the tools of rhetoric in discussing the material effects of language in the conduct of human affairs" (Berlin, *Rhetoric, Poetics* xvii). Scholars, particularly in rhetoric and composition, have posed a return to a rhetorical approach to English studies in the classical and epistemic sense of the term *rhetoric* in order to displace the defining role that literary texts and literary analysis have held in English departments. A form of this rhetorical approach studies not only the analysis, but also the production, use, and consumption of discourse in its various rhetorical textual forms. More importantly, the goals of a rhetorical approach are specifically and concretely linked to civic responsibility and service to the community. However, the education of our secondary teachers has been virtually absent from this discussion. Here, I offer English education as a key location for the implementation of a more comprehensive, rhetorically based education for students at both the secondary and postsecondary levels. Furthermore, this often "forgotten" location needs to gain the attention of both graduate programs in rhetoric and composition and the discipline as a whole as an initial starting point for any larger curricular changes at both the secondary and postsecondary levels.

Although significant movement has been made within many English departments toward expanding the objects of study and establishing diverse attitudes toward the study of texts,[1] English-education courses have remained committed to preparing teachers to carry on the status quo in the content of curricula, a literary-analysis based program of study. Many teacher preparation courses attempt to use texts that challenge the nationalist, literature-based content of teaching English at the secondary level, yet most fall short of offering the strategies and philosophies needed to prepare teachers to implement more-rhetorical approaches. Thus, a literature-based strategy continues to reinforce national and local standards movements that these teacher education programs and the NCTE seem to oppose. Even though new pedagogies— with emphases on writing practices and cooperative learning—have dominated discussions of secondary English courses in the last ten years, the content and overarching philosophy of these courses remain tied directly to literary analysis. When we in the academic world discuss questions of where a rhetorical education should be located, implemented, and how it should be structured in American education, we must begin with our future secondary teachers.

## The "State" of English Education and Secondary Curricula

Recently, the English community has witnessed an increase in scholarly research on English education in the form of studies of "methods" courses and collections of teaching narratives.[2] Although this type of research has always been present within English studies, the recent increase in articles and books in this area indicates a renewed concern for English education. This concern is perhaps due to the recent emphasis from the MLA given to teaching practices.[3] It is also due to the rising number of English teaching majors entering English departments. Both factors make scholarship in this area important in understanding the role English education will play in the future of English departments. The number of secondary teachers scheduled to retire, along with the shortages already occurring in several states, makes teacher education a crucial issue both economically and ideologically for English departments.

Two publications offer insight into the current state of English education at universities and colleges: Peter Smagorinsky and Melissa E. Whiting's study, *How English Teachers Get Taught*, and H. Thomas McCracken and Richard L. Larson's collection of reflective stories, *Teaching College English and English Education*. My observations concerning the current "state" of English education also rely on my experiences teaching English education and writing at four universities, teaching at three secondary schools, and my conversations with and observations of secondary teachers.

## Locations

The location(s) of English-education programs within English studies varies in the current departmental structures. I use the term "location" as Adrienne Rich employs it in "Notes toward a Politics of Location," where she discusses the responsibility and importance of tracing the personal backgrounds of both authors and readers. As Rich points out, it is equally important to trace the personal and ideological positions of programs within departments in order to understand their construction and subjectivity (210). There is little uniformity in the way English-education programs are placed. Some departments have chosen to "take back" their secondary methods preparation courses and to house them in English departments, while leaving certification and student teaching requirements to education departments; the Smagorinsky study illustrates that this configuration is most common (156). Other English departments have taken on the observational and student teaching duties in conjunction with education departments. Still other English-education programs are housed exclusively within education departments —the English department being responsible for the "content" learning of the preparation process. In all these physical locations, English education holds an ideologically subordinate position to that of traditional literary studies—a location similar to one held by rhetoric and composition programs. The subordination of rhetoric and composition as a discipline has been well documented by James Berlin and Susan Miller as being a subordination taking the form of feminization (Miller's term) and/or being in the subordinate role of "service" to the traditional English department curriculum. In addition, universitywide, first-year writing courses have taken on the role of an all-encompassing preparation for academic writing throughout a student's university career. Often these courses are viewed as remediation for the ills of secondary preparation.

While the specifics of English education's subordinate status differ (the feminization of English education is clear, as female undergraduates are more encouraged to pursue teaching, while their male counterparts are encouraged toward graduate school), the models of "service" and remediation in English education negatively drive the curriculum. Due to the methodological nature of many of the courses in the English-education curriculum, the students and faculty are viewed as "practitioners" in much the same way as are writing teachers. Thus, these programs are primarily seen as providing a "service," which appears in opposition to the more "difficult" tasks of theory-building and literary analysis. A common perception of English-studies faculty is that English-education majors are somehow "dumbed-down" versions of those English majors going on to graduate school. An ironic contrast in these perceptions is that English-education majors are often required by state-mandated standards to hold a higher GPA than traditional English majors. This perception may also carry over to attitudes about English-education faculty. Recently, a colleague commented that English faculty on search committees found English educators to be less qualified in their research abilities than those trained in literary analysis for jobs in departments requiring various teaching duties. While many of the duties of English-education programs are service oriented, the binary of service as opposed to theory created here is clearly false. In this binary, service is often perceived as not intellectual, as undertheorized, or as "common." Thus, service is often seen in opposition to the higher aesthetic goals of literature within the university.

English education is also seen as remedial or, at least, as preparing to teach the remedial (secondary students). The curriculum is viewed as supplemental to the content of literary studies. One question to be asked by departments could be: as the number of English-education majors has increased over the past twenty years, have college classrooms addressed the needs of these students in employing literary content in their future classrooms? From the construction of current secondary curricula, it is clear that students continue to carry over the heavy emphasis on literary analysis to the very different audience of a secondary classroom. Many students, in fact, actively resist efforts made in methods courses to challenge this assumption of prominence.

Thus, English educators, as well as the students they prepare, hold precarious locations within contemporary English departments. They are recognized as useful, even fruitful, for English departments; yet the negative service status of English-education programs positions them and their faculty as either subordinate to or apart from greater curricular changes. A second question for this discussion invites English educators to embrace the service status they embody and to ask themselves and English departments: Whom are we serving? If we are serving an elite group of soon-to-be graduate students, then certainly the current curricula of university and secondary schools should continue in its presentation. However, if by the term *service* we mean the better preparation of our students and future teachers in developing communicative skills that will contribute to public/civic activity, then we need to embrace service and begin to restructure curriculum as one that is more rhetorically based.

## "Methods" Courses

The study by Peter Smagorinsky and Melissa Whiting is one of few surveys devoted to what is actually being done in courses designed to prepare students for careers as secondary language-arts teachers. The authors studied the syllabi of a large number of "methods" courses from across the country in order to provide insight into the approaches, assignments, and strategies that are employed within the methods classrooms and the theories and issues represented in methods classrooms. The study gives an objective, although admittedly limited, account of the variety of approaches, the activities and assessments, and the theories and issues represented across the country.

Smagorinsky and Whiting illustrate that trends in English education are toward "student-centered" classrooms. They also demonstrate movements toward holistic learning and assessments, the need for field-based experiences, and the essential need for inquiry-based experiences for English-education students, both in the field and in their reading (100–11). Yet, an important element seemingly overlooked in this study is a discussion of the content of the secondary courses as advocated in the methods classroom. In other words, what, not just how, are we teaching teachers to teach?

While the study of syllabi reveals changes in the strategies and approaches to teaching from more traditional lectures and question-answer-bound assessment to student-centered, collaborative, and responsive pedagogies, the form and content of the texts is most often, if not always, a "given." Berlin and others have traced the emphasis on reading and analyzing literature in English studies to two factors originating in the late nineteenth century. The first was a desire to establish a "national" literature that would be distinct from the English literary tradition. The second is what Berlin calls the "shift from the citizenry [for decision making in practical and political matters] to university-trained professionals" (*Rhetorics, Poetics* xiv). Both factors drove secondary curricula throughout the twentieth century and produced classrooms where both English and American literature became the primary class content. For a great portion of the twentieth century, in fact, writing in different rhetorical situations, with the exceptions of literary analysis and grammatical competence, was virtually invisible.

In Smagorinsky's study, the curriculum that is implied in the syllabi bears out Berlin's assertions. One piece of data that is mentioned in the concluding chapters of the study illustrates the great continuity in the "methods" courses, demonstrated by the fact that a good number of older texts were still used on a regular basis. These texts include books such as Hook and Evans's *The Teaching of High School English,* originally published in 1950 with the most recent edition in 1982 (101). Texts such as this one rely heavily on the assumption that literature and literary analysis are the foundations of any English course. Classical (more recently, "multicultural") literature is virtually always the text behind journal writing, peer group work, and "writing as process" approaches. In fact, while there seemed to be great diversity with the approaches being introduced, there is very little mention of any sort of rhetorical content outside of analysis of literature and writing expository/academic prose (51–99). There are nods to reader-response approaches, to analysis of media texts, and to creative writing in the syllabi, but little attention is paid to student production of media texts, poetry, short stories, or nonfiction prose. In fact, creative writing is most often segregated from other language-arts courses and perceived as both advanced and extracurricular. As Terry Eagleton has pointed out, textual interpretation was important to rhetoric before the late eighteenth century, but it was markedly subordinate to textual production (Berlin, *Rhetorics, Poetics* xvi). In today's secondary curriculum the reverse is the status quo. There is also little if any mention of the production, consumption, or analysis of other forms of discourse: nonfiction prose, media texts, technology-oriented rhetoric, political speech and discourse, or, perhaps most importantly, the discourse of the "everyday"—how we express ourselves in various textual daily forms. It seems while we, as English-education instructors, are ready to radically alter the ways in which secondary students are taught, the bulk of what the students are taught remains virtually unchallenged.

## NCTE Statements and Standards

Although the heavy emphasis on literature is not difficult to understand, this approach to content is in distinct contrast to latest NCTE standards. The guidelines written in 1996 for both language arts in general and for the preparation of teachers advocate "students reading a wide range of print and non-print texts" (Smagorinsky viii). They also advocate "developing an understanding of and respect for diversity in language use," and fostering the use of "spoken, written and visual language to accomplish their own purposes" (viii). In fact, "Principles of Content Knowledge" in the *Guidelines for the Preparation of Teachers of Language Arts* goes even further than the general guidelines: "composing is a practice that covers a wide range of . . . rhetorical situations . . . [teachers should] display a broad view of what constitutes text" (qtd. in Smagorinsky 8). For several years, the NCTE has advocated a type of rhetorical education—the interpretation and production of a variety of texts and the use of both literary and "everyday" content for the study of language arts. Yet, despite these guidelines, the actual classrooms of our secondary schools continue to use anthologies and other texts almost exclusively literary. More than one secondary teacher summarizes this approach as being "*Beowulf* to Virginia Woolf."

The contrast between the general standards and the guidelines for teacher preparation is also curious. In the *Guidelines* English educators and their students are strongly encouraged to view language arts as not simply an exercise in literary analysis, but rather a study of literature and other texts in the context of a secondary language-arts classroom: "the curricula must include not only a knowledge of literature, language, and the process of composing suitable for majors in English, but also a specialized knowledge appropriate for teachers of the subject" (14). Yet, the general standards are not nearly as assertive. The question is, of course, if the NCTE is strongly in favor of opening the discipline and pedagogy of secondary education, why has this content not come into our schools in serious ways?

One answer can be found in the NCTE general guidelines themselves. Although the twelve standards advocate a more rhetorically based program, they also continue to separate literature from the rest of the discussion: "Students read a wide range of literature from many periods in many genres to build an understanding of the many dimensions of human experience" (viii). Why, after discussing a wide range of print and nonprint texts, does the NCTE undercut this goal by separating, and thus prioritizing, literature (and using the term "literature" instead of text). Another answer to the question of why other texts have not been employed is that the training of secondary teachers remains primarily literary in nature. As has been shown, outside of learning methods for teaching writing, English-education students are not often exposed to types of writing (either in consumption or production) other than literary/theoretical.

Despite the inconsistencies, the research gathered from studies of the syllabi and the NCTE guidelines still provide a good foundation for the possibility of change in our curricula. There have been significant changes in pedagogy, the guidelines have advocated a move to a type of rhetorical education in language arts, and English departments, even if only for economic reasons, have begun to recognize the important utility their English-education majors provide. All these factors make the time ripe for the move to a more rhetorically based education—a "truer" language arts. But the movement must come from "below" as well as "above"—from within our English departments, our future teachers in particular, and, as a result, the curriculum of our secondary schools.

## Rhetoric, Rhetorical Education, and Rhetoric Authority

Before going more specifically into how a rhetorical education would look within our English-education programs and secondary schools, some definitions of rhetoric and rhetorical education are in order. My definitions derive from the influences of sophistic, social epistemic, and feminist models of rhetoric. At the center of these definitions is the foundation of rhetoric in the Aristotelian sense of rhetoric as "argument." In all the elaborate definitions and various strategies one employs to discuss rhetoric, we are always essentially arguing—arguing in a sophistic and dialogic sense, as opposed to the more modern connotations of two opposing sides producing winners and losers. All the discourses covered and explored within a rhetorical experience are based in arguing for something, for taking a stance, whether one is arguing purely to entertain, to inspire, or simply to present relevant information.

Returning to sophistic models of rhetorical education for contemporary classrooms is useful, because these models hold many similarities to the ideas of language associated with postmodern and feminist discourses and hold prominent the idea that service is an essential part of such an education. These perspectives "reveal language to be a set of terministic screens . . . that construct rather than record the signified" (Berlin, *Rhetorics, Poetics* xvii). Thus, a return is useful first because the Sophists reinforced the idea that practice cannot be divorced from theory or philosophy. They believed that each informed the other in crucial ways that produced informed and persuasive civic arguments. Second, sophistic rhetoric illustrates the importance of pedagogy, as they were primarily teachers. For the Greeks, particularly the Sophists, the rhetoric teacher's intent was to produce students who were to be "good men speaking well." As Sharon Crowley points out:

> the central focus of this educational system was to produce students who were not only highly literate, but who were conscious of the power and responsibility, conferred on them by their mastery of linguistic and discursive skills . . . the practice of rhetoric entailed deep concern about important ethical, political, historical, and legal questions." ("A Plea" 318).

As Protagoras argued, civilizations rest on the fact of each citizen's inherent possession of the "capacity for intelligent political decisions" (Jarratt, "Rhetorical" 39). Sophists also believed that truth is a relative type of knowledge that is produced by the process of argument through language. Sophists do not deny that there may be objective or ideal realities, but they assert that if they exist, they can never be known definitively— we can only grasp the truths through our own historical and cultural experiences.

These ideas, adopted in a rhetorical secondary school curriculum, hold important consequences in terms of the choice of texts studied and the approaches taught for the interpretation of these texts. First, the sophists practiced teaching methods and encouraged student interpretations that were dynamic rather than static. The major pedagogical method was a combination of dialogic conversation and modeling.

While not fully equal in terms of authority, teacher and student learned from the other. The goal was the production of "located" truths or the discovery of new insights: "The Sophists thought teachers should be active participants in bringing about change in these arenas" (Crowley, "A Plea" 329). Like many modern writing teachers, this model advocates the study of discursive practices, rather than searches for truths, formulas of certain success, or universal themes. It also views the individual "both as a location of a separate mind perceiving distinctive visual and aural stimuli and as a member of a group of like-minded individuals with responsibility to participate in the democracy" (Jarratt, *Rereading* 92). The model for English education and for secondary teachers is one where students are prepared not only for aesthetic appreciation but also for civic action.

This epistemic view of rhetoric demands a unique relation between teachers and students. Influenced by sophistic and feminist practices, Susan Jarratt advocates a relation of authority between student and teacher that offers a model for secondary teachers and teacher educators where the teacher acts as what she terms a "rhetorical authority" ("Rhetorical" 35). In this relation, power and authority are not denied, or made invisible. Teachers become authorities who are explicit in their positioning within the classrooms and institutions both politically and ethically. Teachers establish themselves as people who are in different locations than those of their students, perhaps with more expertise in various areas, a wider range of knowledge and experience, and, ultimately, in positions that ask them to evaluate and judge students. The relationships between students and teachers are not value-free relationships, but ones where students are encouraged to become critical citizens, gaining a sense of social as well as rhetorical authorities; a key for teachers is in encouraging, even demanding that students locate themselves both socially and historically. As Jarratt illustrates: "Motivating students to locate themselves socially and historically in relation to the subject of the class can mediate institutional (teacher) authority and create the possibility for counter-authority to emerge within students' own discourses" ("Rhetorical" 36). In other words, the relation between teachers and students attempts to minimize the coercive elements of the discourse by making it an explicit and discussed part of the relation itself. Both teachers and students reveal their positioning and recognize it as provisional and dialogic, in order to begin the processes of continually negating, consuming, and contradicting these positions. This type of relation counters the coercive confessional relation found in approaches where the speaker is posed as the agent, and the listener as the passive recipient. In a more rhetorical approach, both teachers and students act as speakers and listeners, entertaining many other voices and creating a dialogic engagement that includes the teacher in a "collective activity through which we are all constantly engaged in processes of semiotic transformation" (Jarratt, "Rhetorical" 37).

How do sophistic concepts of a rhetorical education translate to strategies for curriculum in language arts for our English-education programs and in our secondary language-arts classrooms? Why is it important to drastically reconstitute the ways in which our teachers teach and students learn at the secondary level? In the twenty-first century, the missions, the technologies, and the needs of the students are clearly different. The historical precedence of the literary approach will be hard to penetrate. Yet, we can begin in English education to advocate a new process, one that presents a type of language arts that explores the power and agency of language in many arenas. Stephen Tchudi and Paul J. Morris points out in *The New Literacy: Moving Beyond the 3Rs* that we need to begin to teach our teachers ways to present various textual and communicative forms, to interrogate different discourse communities, and to deal with both the consumption and production of these texts. Additionally, Berlin asserts: "Our historicist perspective on current English Studies hierarchies enables us to regard all manners of discourse as worthy of investigation, including film, television, video, and popular music" (*Rhetorics, Poetics* xvi). I would add to the list explorations of everyday discourse. It seems not only important in our media-saturated culture that students are able to both interpret and produce discourse in these forms, but also an essential and ethical part of a language-arts education. Preparation in the production and interpretation of all of these texts, intertwined with an appreciation and understanding of literature, seems paramount in our changing society.

The expansion of texts in the content of courses and curricula is also important, because as the "discourse of the everyday" is studied, so too can the ethical, political, and social effects of these discourses. Teachers must be equipped with an overall structure of language arts, the goals of which are linked to civic participation and responsibility. An epistemic view of rhetoric stresses the power and agency of discourse in ways that challenge students and teachers to think about the results of their speech. It is vital that teachers begin to deal with issues of media responsibility and its ties to rhetoric—that students in secondary schools are exposed to the ways media language is used to argue, to persuade, to manipulate.

Part of this concept of rhetorical education within language arts needs to include methods and content from service-learning pedagogies. Preparing students to become more-participatory citizens involves exposing them to different cultures and social situations through service to and with their communities. Students need to practice the powers of language and to view just how this power is illustrated throughout various cultural circumstances. The blurring of texts and discourses in a rhetorical approach to language arts makes the ultimate goal civic rather than appreciative or aesthetic. Yet, as we have seen with the infusion of "multicultural" texts into secondary curricula, the "add and stir" approach is not effective. Our teachers are still trained in literary analysis. Our textbooks are still, by and large, literary anthologies. The people of our country are still under the myth of literary elitism. We need to begin, then, with our future teachers of secondary, even elementary schools, in order to begin to view differently—to truly "revise," "re-vision"—both the content and strategy of our approaches.

## Drafting a Plan for Re-vision

As this discussion has illustrated, key locations for moving to more rhetorical forms of education are our teacher-education programs across the disciplines. To tinker with the curriculum at the university level in writing programs or even across disciplines seems to be employing the same "top-down" approach that has been used for a century. Increasingly since the 1960s, universities have become locations of mass education much like secondary schools, so the need for the more rhetorical approaches of the nineteenth century have once again become needed at the postsecondary level. However, if our secondary curriculum remains one where critical thinking is translated as literary analysis and where writing means only academic forms of written expression, then postsecondary education will continue to experience the failures of recent years in engaging and preparing students for the future. If change is really in the wind, it will be crucial to develop a program that truly employs rhetoric as its guiding methodology. During this development, we must be attentive in using various rhetorical situations, in exploring the diversity of literacies that exist for our students today, and, finally and most important, in integrating the practice of service with the consumption and production of texts.

Tchudi and Morris offer a working definition of rhetoric, similar to those already discussed, which can be employed effectively in our Eng- lish- education methods courses: "Rhetoric, at its best, is the study of dis- course—language—and how it operates in a variety of contexts. Rheto- ric thus subsumes the work and the language of the scientist and the mathematician; it examines the words and methods of the historian" (33). What is advocated here is the study of rhetoric, of language arts, truly as the study of language, of discourse. Future teachers need expo- sure to and practice in the interpretation and production of a variety of textual and rhetorical situations. The study of these discourses should come alongside literature, with the emphasis being on reading, writing, listening, speaking, and viewing practices within these various dis- courses. Critics will say that adding discourses will only complicate teach- ers' missions in their future secondary classrooms, but in my own classes I see the teachers becoming clearer about their missions.

Often, teachers are unclear on the value of teaching a literature-based curriculum and are unable to answer the student question: why are we doing this? In our age, this is an important, if not *the* important ques- tion to be able to answer for students and for the teachers themselves. By using literature as just one of the chosen components in a language- arts curriculum, teachers can more accurately place the crucial location of literature within the language practices of American and global cul- tures. At the same time, teachers can explore and celebrate the value of discourses of other disciplines, other media, and other rhetorical situa- tions. This type of change in the content begins to appreciate different ways of speaking, viewing, and expressing oneself both for the individual and community and to prepare students to better understand and pro- duce communication in their daily lives.

To achieve these goals, content such as the study of discourse analysis, in its broad sense, is crucial for future teachers. As we have witnessed in the media coverage of the shootings at Columbine High School, the un- derstanding of discourse is crucially important in understanding events, as well as, perhaps, in preventing events like the Columbine shooting. It is clear that the discourse of groups such as the "trenchcoat mafia" or the "jocks" needs to be explored both for what they communicate and for the types of miscommunication they create for students, faculty, the community, and our nation.

We need to prepare our teachers to re-vision, re-see, language arts as a rhetorical study. The content of this curriculum needs to include explorations of media, technology, political rhetoric, academic rhetoric, and other cultural texts. Perhaps, most importantly, the exploration of everyday rhetoric that reinforces and reshapes our ideas about gender, race, class, and sexual orientation among other locations must be addressed in order to help students become more critically aware of the power and effects of language practices. This study of discourse analysis can be achieved through a variety of texts, including literature. The reading of essays concerning discourse, as well as research by the students in which they collect and analyze data from their own situations and experiences, is essential to this type of study and to the idea that our discourse has power in our lives.

The expansion of our definitions of text within the language-arts classroom is another step toward looking more closely at developing students' various rhetorical literacies, instead of being bound to the literary as a vehicle for literacy. Particularly within our English-education classes, we need to stress that developing a diverse set of literacies should be our guiding objective. Carol Pope, after studying various national reports on the goal of literacy, has identified five areas of proficiency needed by those who will join the workforce: the ability to communicate and work collaboratively, the ability to work effectively in a multicultural society and workforce, the ability to adapt, the ability to think critically, and the ability to use available technology (qtd. in Tchudi and Morris 32). Tchudi and Morris add one more to the list: the ability to think creatively and imaginatively (32).

Increasingly, "those who join the world of work" are students who have completed at least some postsecondary education. Therefore, as many might imagine, Pope is not talking about masses of high school graduates. Students need to become more developed in multiple literacies in order to participate in their communities. The idea of literacy as reading and writing must begin to give way to the multiple ways people communicate and become literate. An understanding of this concept helps students begin to question, assert, and reassert what it means to be a literate citizen—to become active in the process of obtaining and defining their own literacies.

Finally, and perhaps most importantly, we must reestablish our future teachers as agents of change in their communities. Not only should they prepare students to become more active participants in their communities and our nation, but also they must feel that they are making an impact on society. In recent years, largely due to legal considerations, teachers have been trained to mute the role they play in the community and in students' lives. Many of my own students repeat advice they hear in their education programs that tell them to be very careful of their involvement with students, parents, and communities. The future teachers have become so paranoid from this advice that they begin to see themselves as production workers, responsible for but alienated from the products, the students, and their communities. For these reasons, and because literacy can be learned more effectively by experience with multiple types of literacy, service-learning approaches need to be integrated more consistently into our rhetorical curriculum.

Service learning can mean many things to many people. It is most often defined as a pedagogical technique for combining authentic community service with integrated academic outcomes (Erickson and Anderson 1). At its core, a service-learning approach advocates having teachers and students experience learning through service to the communities in which they live. The approach shares the concern of classical rhetorical education for community and civic agency in that "field-based experience aimed at addressing the common good characterizes much of the theoretical basis of service-learning" (Erickson and Anderson 2). This type of learning experience is a key component that is often missing both from the education of our future teachers and from our secondary curriculum. Through service learning, teachers can, by example, become agents of change in their communities, as well as become guides for students in service-learning projects that both enhance student learning and contribute to civic needs.

In language-arts education, service learning can be used as both a pedagogy for learning about literacy practices and as a method in itself of teaching language arts to secondary students. One example of service-learning pedagogy in teacher education is Joseph Keating's course in secondary education. Keating, a professor at California State University at San Marcos, assists his San Diego secondary-education students in critically examining important social issues through self-selected community service projects. The project includes such activities as tutoring in non-English-speaking communities, leading to students broadening the scope and focus of lesson plans in both English and Spanish classrooms (Erickson and Anderson 2). My own courses, along with the courses of my colleague Janet Kaufman, have employed service-learning approaches and have taught these approaches as strategies for secondary classrooms. Currently, our upper-level methods classes have created and are now staffing a family literacy center in collaboration with a local high school and its community. In creating the center, students in our classes have learned how to evaluate community needs, to work with administrators, teachers, and community leaders, and to assess the needs of students in that particular community. Our students begin to connect and employ the teaching methods learned in the classroom to the project and, thus, are better able to envision their own teaching and use of service learning. More importantly, these types of projects create teachers with classrooms that will be active in impacting communities. The teachers truly begin to learn about the power of the concept of language and literacy and the cultural and global implications of their work as teachers of language arts.

## So . . .

The "forgotten" location of English education within English departments can be instrumental in the development of more rhetorically based education curricula, because the impact these programs have is at two levels. Most obviously, requiring a more rhetorically based preparation program will affect the contents and the ways our future teachers teach at the secondary level. This type of preparation, however, can also motivate English departments to reevaluate their own programs and curricula. If teachers are prepared rhetorically, postsecondary students will be versed in a variety of discourse situations and will demand that this type of civic education continue. Departments also have to come to terms with the number of teaching majors they are producing. Curriculum will have to address the needs of these majors and, perhaps, become more rhetorically based.

At the secondary level, teachers and administrators must begin to see this type of rhetorical education as "the basics." The public demand for better reading and writing skills can be better dealt with under a rubric that deals directly with effective presentation and persuasive skills in a variety of areas. A rhetorical education such as the one described here will produce students better able to read and write critically in the broadest sense of reading and writing. They will also become more active participants in their work and their communities—an outcome that can only increase the quality of academic work done at the university level and serve the common good of the greater community.

# Notes

1. The English departments at Syracuse University, University of Pittsburgh, and Carnegie Mellon University are programs that integrate various textual areas within English studies.

2. Some additional recent collections include Ira Hayes's *Great Beginnings* and Jim Burke and Mary Frances Claggett's *The English Teacher's Companion*.

3. See Franklin, Laurence, and Welles, *Preparing a Nation's Teachers: Models for English and Foreign Language Programs*.

# III
# Rhetorical Education beyond the Classroom

# 7
# Parlor Rhetoric and the Performance of Gender in Postbellum America

*Nan Johnson*

I want to presume in this discussion that a feminist reading of the history of rhetoric necessarily means that the complicated relationship between rhetoric, power, and the inscription of cultural norms must be addressed as we revisit or uncover rhetorical texts and pedagogical programs of the past. In particular, I want to read the nature and influence of the American parlor rhetoric movement of the late nineteenth century as a tradition that allows us to map how a rhetorical tradition participates in cultural work or the working out of a cultural problem. I want to suggest that we can read in the parlor rhetoric movement signs that the struggle of American culture with the "Woman Question" was ongoing in the postbellum period and that the institutional power of rhetorical pedagogy was implicated in that struggle.

The parlor rhetoric movement promised to put the skills of rhetorical influence into the hands of every American citizen who could read and could pay the price of an elocution or letter-writing manual.[1] However, in ideological terms, this promise concealed as much as it offered. Heavily biased along gender lines, parlor rhetorics reinscribed relatively separate and distinctly unequal rhetorical spheres for the sexes. Despite the fact that middle-class white women in the latter decades of the nineteenth century were securing work and education outside the home in ever increasing numbers, and despite the prominence of notable women such as Frances Willard and Elizabeth Cady Stanton, whose rhetorical powers were widely known and admired, the parlor rhetoric movement reinscribed not the example of women's rhetorical advances into public life but rather a highly conservative construction of the American woman as a mother and wife who needed rhetorical skills only to perform those roles to greater effect. Phenomenally appealing to a culture convinced that speech reflected character and intelligence, parlor rhetorics exerted a significant ideological presence in the middle-class American home. The conservative gender agenda of the parlor rhetoric movement testifies to a deep ambivalence in postbellum America toward women's rights and their claims to rhetorical space that remained unresolved in American life even at the turn of the century. The role of parlor rhetoric and its pedagogies in sustaining this ambivalence reminds us that the cultural impact of rhetorical performance cannot be understood fully unless we recognize the institutional status of rhetoric and the ways in which rhetorical pedagogies and the practices these promote can reinforce, and be reinforced by, normative ideologies that enjoy the status of cultural capital.

In the chaotic decades after the Civil War, Americans were weary and disheartened. Postbellum America sought to heal wounds that ran deep by reconstructing a foundation for American life that prized the eternal values of education, progress, expansion, and the stability of the family. In this era of suppressed desperation, cultural energy moved in a myriad of ways to reinforce social values and habits of behavior that enshrined, among other icons, the American woman as a central player in a drama of recovery and the American home as the single best foundation on which the health of the nation could be rebuilt.

Characterized as that necessary angel whose moral influence in the home would reflect upon the whole nation, the American woman was reinstructed as to her proper sphere of influence at every opportunity in the popular press and in a variety of culturally significant discourses that shaped public opinion. Influenced by this confluence of discourses, the public's view of the rhetorical role of women as public figures was mixed. The great cause of abolition, which had propelled so many women to take to the lectern and to take pen in hand, had passed and the rhetorical role of women was by no means secure. With the passing of abolition went American women's most prominent hold on the rhetorical climate of the nation, a nation that in the latter decades of the century was far from accepting the causes of female suffrage or temperance as equally righteous issues. The tension in the land over the "Woman Question" was palpable and very much on the public's mind. In an era in which the American public sought the redrawing of a conservative social landscape, the persistent efforts of determined women to challenge traditional boundaries curtailing their lives was met with similarly determined efforts to reinscribe those boundaries. Nowhere is this suppressive energy more clear than in the influential discourses about the etiquette of rhetorical performance: how to speak, whom to speak to, and what to speak about.

Between the end of the Civil War and the turn of the century, the controversy in American life about who women were and ought to be played itself out in popular rhetorical manuals of the day that offered condensed versions of academic rhetorical theories of elocution, oratory, and composition. The public's general interest in education could be satisfied by several types of educational materials for home use. Encyclopedias, conduct manuals, and rhetoric handbooks promised a complete home education in subjects ranging from math and English to bookkeeping and dancing. Rhetorical training was given top priority in this curriculum for the home learner. Letter writing, public speaking, and composition were typical entries in tables of contents not only of rhetoric manuals but also of encyclopedias and etiquette handbooks that focused on general information as well as lessons for leading a happy and useful life. That rhetorical skills were so prized tells us just how institutionalized rhetoric was in nineteenth-century American life. Rhetorical training was marketed as tantamount to an advanced formal education which, in the last decades of the nineteenth century, most Americans did not pursue. The parlor rhetoric movement did the cultural work of promoting rhetorical literacy while simultaneously reinscribing a cultural agenda to limit the rhetorical space of women's lives.

The pedagogical effort at work in postbellum parlor rhetorics to restrict women from rhetorical spaces of power drew upon an existing context of institutionalized efforts to confine women to "feminine" rhetorical roles. Scholarship has long established the fact that nineteenth-century academic rhetoric served the interests of a dominant class consisting of educated, white males and that women's access to formal academic instruction in the most valued forms of rhetoric was systematically restricted before the Civil War.[2] As prominent speaker on women's rights and abolition during the antebellum period Lucy Stone reports, although Oberlin College admitted women, an education in the art of public speaking was denied to her. According to Stone, "I was never in a place where women were so rigidly taught that they must not speak in public" (qtd. in Blackwell 64). Stone was allowed to join formal classes in rhetoric only on the condition that she remain silent. As the work of key scholars such as Lillian O'Connor and Karlyn Kohrs Campbell has made irrefutably clear, the experience of Lucy Stone was far from singular.[3] Even women like Stone who secured a college education when few American women did faced the repercussions of a cultural anxiety about the possibility of women moving into the rhetorical arenas in which cultural power was brokered. Those forms of literacy denied to Stone and nineteenth-century women in general were the very modes of rhetoric through which social, political, and cultural power were disseminated: the arts of argumentation and public speaking. The denial of rhetorics of power to women was rationalized by leading nineteenth-century educators, social commentators, and many rhetoricians who consistently reiterated familiar objections in various prominent cultural dialogues in the decades preceding the Civil War. The most popular arguments asserted that women were intellectually incapable of the analytical skills on which the logic and development of argumentation and oratory depended, and that women lacked the emotional and moral force to convince others of their ideas.

These assumptions reveal themselves rather obviously in the prefaces to antebellum rhetoric manuals designed for use in female academies and colleges in which authors frequently emphasize the fact that only certain material is suited for the female students. One representative author, T. S. Pinneo, stresses that delicacy of the female mind had been a "prominent consideration" in the compiling of *The Herman's Reader for Female Schools* (1847): "Every article has been carefully studied with reference to . . . its appropriateness . . . to the cultivation of the female mind and heart, the development of correct sentiments and taste, the encouragement of gentle and amiable feelings, and the regulating and maturing of the social affections" (5). The gender link between rhetorical material and the development of the feminine "sensibility," emphasized by Pinneo, stands in contrast to the general principle at work in such antebellum rhetoric treatises written for male students as Samuel P. Newman's text, *A Practical System of Rhetoric* (1842), which is based on Newman's lectures at Bowdoin College and Amherst. Writers of rhetoric manuals designed for young women stressed feminine delicacy. Newman, on the other hand, makes it clear that his pedagogical program is intended to develop intellectual judgment and forceful expression: "It is a received maxim that to write well we must think well. To think well implies extensive knowledge and well disciplined intellectual powers" (16). The principle of selectivity governing Newman's choice of material focuses on the relationship between the study of exemplary models of writing and oratory and the development of the ability to produce successful public discourse. One of the most popular rhetoric treatises circulating in the period between 1820 and the Civil War, *A Practical System of Rhetoric* represents the male orientation of influential antebellum academic rhetorics, which addressed readers as those young men who would soon enter public life.[4]

My purpose in rehearsing the well-documented bias against women receiving the same kind of rhetorical education routinely offered to men is to remind us of the status such views enjoyed in antebellum America and to make the point that this suppressive agenda for rhetorical education had forged a link of propriety between rhetorical performance and gender in the popular mind well before the Civil War. Parlor rhetoric manuals marketed to the general public in the latter decades of the century reinscribe exactly this same restricted definition of rhetorical behavior for women. To understand how significant it is that parlor rhetorics persistently discourage women from aspiring to rhetorical roles of leadership, we should remind ourselves of the cultural power of rhetorical education before and after the Civil War. The nineteenth-century academic tradition in rhetoric fostered the view that eloquent speech was the mark of the well-educated and thoughtful citizen. Prominent postbellum rhetoricians like G. P. Quackenbos and John Franklin Genung, whose treatises circulated widely in nineteenth-century colleges and universities, defined oratory as the rhetorical art that contributes the most toward the proper workings of the political process, the disposition of justice, and the maintenance of the public welfare and social conscience.[5] These rhetoricians persistently defined the rhetorician as male, and they discussed the ethics and epistemology of rhetoric with the male as the universal prototype. As Quackenbos observes in his treatise, *Advanced Course of Composition and Rhetoric* (1879), "spoken language" is "employed by man alone" and that language use in general is the sole province of "men" because "men alone possess reason" (13). Quackenbos's assumption that ontological links between reason and language use are gendered is clear also in his explanation of argumentative discourse: "The Writer should select such arguments only as he feels to be solid and convincing. He must not expect to impose on the world by mere arts of language; but placing himself in the situation of a reader should think how he would be affected by the reasoning which he proposes to use for the persuasion of others" (388). Quackenbos's gendered attention to the relationship between reasoning and persuasion is echoed in Genung's *Practical Elements of Rhetoric* (1886).

> In order to persuade men, the speaker must make them tacitly recognize him as one to be trusted. . . . Of such trust and respect the initiative must be taken by the speaker. Not with cringing or flattery, not with any brow-beating air of superiority, but with a manly, self-respecting frankness, he is to approach his audience as men occupying a common ground with himself. (449)

The distinctly gendered construction of character Genung outlines is underscored by his representation of male speakers as exemplars, including Daniel Webster, Edmund Burke, Thomas Macaulay, Henry Ward Beecher, Patrick Henry, and Abraham Lincoln (450–69). The creation of a canon of male exemplars is even more significant when we note that both Quackenbos's and Genung's influential academic treatises were published in the postbellum period following an era when prominent women abolitionists and women's rights advocates such as Lucretia Mott and Elizabeth Cady Stanton had traveled the country widely and had their speeches avidly reviewed in the popular press. Yet, given the ostensible opportunity to include such women as notable exemplars of persuasive public speakers, Quackenbos and Genung do not cite them.[6]

While it is not surprising a century before the feminist critique of sexist language that the ideal orator is characterized by Quackenbos and Genung as "he," we cannot underestimate the significance of the fact that, within the most prestigious discourses on rhetoric in nineteenth-century culture, the effective and powerful public speaker was always characterized as male. We cannot say then that the use of "he" or the references to "men" simply reflect stylistic features of the conventional discourses of the time. We know enough about the constructive force of the relationship between words and ideology to recognize that not writing women into this picture was the same move as writing them out. From Newman to Quackenbos to Genung, before the Civil War and after, the rhetoricians who structured rhetoric courses at prominent and emerging colleges across the country fused the concepts of "the great orator" and the "American man" into such a seamless amalgam that, from the beginning of the century to its end, the aspirations of women to move into the sphere of influential rhetorical space were characterized as aberrations. The nineteenth-century view of the great orator was so essentialized that the conspicuous examples of brilliant female speakers and writers such as Frances Willard or Susan B. Anthony did little to revise the dominant construction that women in general had no appropriate claim to the discourses of power.

Among parlor rhetorics of the postbellum era, which included elocution manuals and letter-writing handbooks, the gender markings in elocution readers, often titled "Speakers," are particularly conspicuous. Unlike elocution manuals, which were also marketed to the "home learner" and provided detailed explanations of the principles of elocution, "Speakers" included only highly abridged explanations of standard rules for delivery about voice and gesture.[7] Usually comprising only one introductory chapter or preface, discussions of rhetorical theory in "Speakers" took up far less space in these hefty texts than did extensive selections for study, practice, and performance. Imitating loosely the belletristic orientation of academic elocution manuals, which defined texts according to rhetorical aim, "Speakers" group selections under widely recognizable genre categories such as "Patriotic Recitations," "Holiday Readings and Recitations," "Descriptive Readings," "Pathetic Selections," "Humorous Recitations," and "Historical Poems and Orations" (Lumm, *Home School Speaker* 18–19).[8] The range of selections in "Speakers" reflects the assumption of authors and publishers that rhetorical performance was a central activity in the home and community. Advertising its contents in terms that were by that time familiar to a readership expecting to gain a rhetorical education in the home and put it to use, *The American Star Speaker* (1902) presents itself as

a manual of vocal and physical culture [and] elocution . . . with appropriate selections for Readings and Recitals, both public and private embracing the serious, comic, patriotic, heroic, sublime, humorous, descriptive, didactic and ridiculous. Suitable for Home, School, Church, Lodge, Club, Literary Societies, and Public and Private Recitals with a variety of selections for use at all Holiday and Special Day Celebrations. (1)

"Speakers" were extremely popular in the 1880s and 1890s and many were reprinted or revised between 1900 and 1920. Promising "something for every one," texts like Emma Griffith Lumm's *The New American Speaker* (1898) and Charles Walter Brown's *The American Star Speaker*

(1902) slipped onto the sideboards and into the bookcases of the middle-class American home (Lumm, *New American Speaker,* preface). Contextualized theoretically by the academic discipline of rhetoric that promoted rhetorical training as the mark of the well-educated and contextualized ideologically by the gender bias of that same discipline, the "Speaker" tradition reinscribed the conservative inclinations of nineteenth-century rhetorical pedagogy in the late decades of the century and also carried that conservatism over into the early twentieth century. The status of these widely circulating texts tells us that popularized pedagogies of rhetorical performance were powerful agents in the inscription of the cultural idea that rhetorical literacy was essential. This position as a prestige discourse also had its ideological consequences for the construction of female identity. By affirming conservative definitions of gender while promoting rhetorical skills for one and all, the "Speaker" tradition enacted the widely held cultural ambivalence regarding what roles women should have in rhetorical space.

Like manuals used in the academy, parlor "Speakers" promoted the notion that training in vocal expression should be sought in all settings, private and public. The editor of the collection *The American Star Speaker* puts it this way,

> The power to charm the heart and steal away the senses; to divert the mind from its own devising and hold an audience in breathless spell as the orator paints the rosy tints of heavenly longings, or leads the imagination down through the labyrinths of wonderland, or depicts with lightning tongue and thunder tones the horrors of the doomed, comes not by nature, but by work, work, work. (Brown 20)

The message here seems to be that everyone, in every setting, can and should acquire formal elocutionary skills. On the surface, such advertisements seem to transform an academic view of what constitutes ideal public speech into practical instructions for private and home use. But if we look at the introductions to these parlor rhetorics more closely, we notice that "the orator" whose skills are so highly regarded is not the inclusive category it first appears to be. The editor of *The New American Speaker* (1898) makes this quite clear when she describes the skill of oratory as a male attribute in these words: "The gift of speaking, of being able to make people listen to what you say, of inspiring men with ideals and convincing them of truths, is the most superb power a man can possess" (Lumm 28). Although parlor rhetorics seemingly were designed to provide the opportunity for improvement in speaking for the general public, there is a not-so-subtle indication here that definitions of rhetorical genre and performance are linked to gender in these texts. This becomes even clearer when we notice that selections marked for performance by women can be differentiated in subject and genre from those intended for performance by men. A range of subtle evidence suggests that rhetorical genres such as orations, serious literary poems, and essays on intellectual and political issues were considered the province of men, while descriptive poetry and poems about marriage, children, or traditional female duties and virtues were considered appropriate for women to perform in the home and at community occasions.

One of the most revealing internal inconsistencies in "Speakers" is the contrast between their claim to a genderless interest in preparing the home learner for public life and the number of textual features that make the opposite case that men's and women's rhetorical performances should be viewed differently. It is quite typical of the compilers of "Speakers" to imply that anyone could hope to be a great speaker through study and practice. For example, Josephine W. Stratton and Jeannette M. Stratton, compilers of *The New Select Speaker* (1902), encourage all of their readers to think of themselves as prospective public speakers.

A great demand exists for just such a book as this Popular Speaker. We are all interested in oratory, eloquence, public school and all other kinds of entertainment. Every person holding a public position is expected to be a speaker, one who is able to address an audience on popular questions and furnish information in a convincing and pleasing manner, such as will enlighten the people and form the basis of action. To this end it is necessary that young persons should be instructed in elocution and they should be furnished with books for this purpose. The trembling boy or girl who timidly appears before a public assembly may yet become renowned as an orator, which, all will agree, is one of the noblest uses to which intellect and genius can be devoted. (iv)

The framing here of the prospective orator as either boy or girl would seem to imply that the gendering of rhetorical space has been overcome by 1900. However, a close reading of *The New Select Speaker* and other texts like it reveals that the discursive and pictorial force of the "Speaker" tradition tended to keep in place the cultural icon of the ideal orator as male and subtly, perhaps even unconsciously, define the rhetorical roles of women in domestic terms.

As the reader turns the first pages of *The New Select Speaker,* before reaching the exuberant title page on which Stratton and Stratton promise "directions for expressing written thought in a correct and pleasing manner," two illustrations appear back to front. In the first, "Recitation at an Evening Entertainment," a tall, dignified man in evening attire is addressing a salon gathering of attentive men and women who generally seem to be hanging on his every word. Following this black-and-white drawing is a photograph collage of four small pictures depicting a woman performing the poem "She Would Be a Mason." The young woman is dressed in a long, loose fitting gown with neoclassical lines. The juxtaposition of the male orator on the previous page with the woman in what would strike any turn-of-the-century reader as an "acting" pose sets up in bold imagery a disparity between the kinds of rhetorical roles parlor rhetorics were willing to support (see figures 1 and 2). What we must recognize is what any of the Strattons' readers would have understood about "She Would Be a Mason." As an anti–women's rights poem with the explicit subtext that women should keep to their own sphere, "She Would Be a Mason" is intended to be funny and is included by the Strattons under the generic heading "Humorous Recitations." The photograph of the woman reciting the poem with rather melodramatic overtones is intended to illustrate how the poem should be performed. It is certain that the Strattons' readers would get the "joke" of the poem, which mocks "the ridiculous Mrs. Byrde" who wanted to be a Mason. Referred to in the body of the poem as "ridiculous," "inquisitive," "nabbing" [nagging], and "teasing," "poor Mrs. Byrde's" efforts to join a traditionally male organization are lampooned mercilessly.

> The funniest story I ever heard,
> The funniest thing that ever occurred,
> Is the story of Mrs. Mehitable Byrde
> Who wanted to be a Mason.
>
> Her husband, Tom Byrde, is a Mason true,
> As good a Mason as any of you;

1. "Recitation at an Evening Entertainment," Stratton and Stratton, *The New Select Speaker*, 1902.

He is tyler of lodge Ceruliean Blue,
And tyles and delivers the summons due,
And she wanted to be a Mason too
This ridiculous Mrs. Byrde. (275)

By positioning the performance photograph of "She Would Be a Mason" following the commanding male speaker illustration and by representing a photograph of an actual performance of a woman presenting "She Would Be a Mason" as a humorous joke on a woman's temerity, the Strattons undercut their promise to educate one and all for public life. The images of performing bodies collectively make the opposite case: the young man should study the arts of expression and plan to claim the serious attention of his peers, and the young woman can expect to put on costumes and embody the "in" joke that women make fools of themselves when they try to move out of their proper spheres. That the Strattons would be the last to see how this pair of gendered images compromises their ideological claims to be offering an enabling

And she wanted to be a mason too—

He consented at last to admit her

The candidate begged 'im to let him go home,

Then came a pause—A pair of paws Reached through the floor.

2. "She Would Be a Mason," Stratton and Stratton, *The New Select Speaker,* 1902.

pedagogy regardless of gender goes without saying. The contradiction is so obvious that it has to be read as one of those moments when the grip of normative ideology is so strong that it reasserts its presence at the level of subtext no matter what the ostensible surface conversation might be. In all of the 464 pages of *The New Select Speaker,* there is not a single illustration of a woman giving a speech. Instead, women are shown in a series of several photographs presenting dramatic readings of emotionally stirring poems or showing their elocutionary talents in acting out emotions with gestures and facial expressions. In poses evocative of statues, women are represented acting out emotions such as "Fear," "Hope," "Mirth," and "Lamentation"; the women in these "tableaux" appear not to be using their voices nor to be representing these emotions in the service of any intellectual argument or persuasive political effort.

The subtext of ideological imagery in *The New Select Speaker* is the rule and not the exception in the "Speaker" tradition. One of the consistent generic features of these texts is their use of photographs and drawings to represent performance styles and topics. Functioning in much the same way as pictorial representations of women in the periodical literature of the time, the visual images in "Speaker" manuals present women as the embodiment of "the ideology of domesticity, maternal instruction, and the power of sentiment."[9] A set of illustrations appearing side by side in Henry Davenport Northrop's collection *The Ideal Speaker and Entertainer* (1890) provides another vivid and representative example of how this ideological subtext regarding gender constructs a "serious" rhetorical role for men and a "sentimental" or frivolous one for women. In illustrations appearing across from one another in *The Ideal Speaker and Entertainer,* a young boy in a suit poses seriously as if about to begin a speech. This photograph is entitled "The Boy Orator." Across the page is "The Gypsy Tambourine Girl," a smiling young girl dressed in "gypsy" clothing and holding flowers and a tambourine in her hand (see figures 3 and 4). The young girl is presented as an entertainer in costume, performing a selection as a "gypsy girl," while the young man is presented as an intent apprentice of oratory. In a culture in which oratory was viewed as a major form of cultural influence, this pairing of images is highly revealing. Like the ideological argument made by the juxtaposition of the illustration of the elegant male speaker with the photograph of "poor Mrs. Byrde" in *The New Select Speaker,* the visual rhetoric of the pairing of the boy orator with the gypsy girl reinscribes explicitly that men and women operate in different rhetorical spheres.

The persistent inclusion of illustrations like "The Gypsy Tambourine Girl" and the critical absence of any female equivalent of photographs like "The Boy Orator" in *The Ideal Speaker* and other texts like it reminded the reading public that women needed only to acquire those rhetorical skills that corroborated their roles as wives, mothers, or lighthearted entertainers.

The representation of women in the "Speaker" tradition is further complicated by the fact that illustrations depict women performing material from only certain genres of readings. By looking closely at the relationship between the titles of illustrations and the selections being performed, it becomes obvious that women are being encouraged to associate themselves with types of subject matter such as "exercises with musical accompaniment," "holiday readings," and "the pathetic and homelike." The titles of illustrations, typically first lines of poems, give us some indication of the associations being encoded between gender, genre, and rhetorical space. Even a cursory review of illustration titles from a cross section of "Speakers" makes the case that the cultural message promoted by parlor rhetorics is that women should be associated primarily with the performance of sentimentality. For example, note common titles such as "Breaking hearts without regret, a winsome, sparkling, gay, coquette" from a photograph of a smiling, flirtatious young woman in street wear in *The Ideal Speaker and Entertainer* (80); or "I'm Sitting Alone by the Fire Dressed just as I Came from the Dance," a photograph of a sad young woman holding her head in a pensive pose in Lumm's(1899) [63]. A particularly striking example of a woman performing gender appropriately is "Alike to Those We Love, and Those We Hate," from Lumm's *Home School Speaker and Elocutionist* (1898), in which a young woman strikes a gracious pose after seemingly just having read a letter (see figure 5). The title to this photograph also contains in parenthesis, "See Poem, 'Goodbye.'" Included under the generic heading "Pathetic Selections," the poem "Goodbye" is a sentimental poem focusing on an idealized emotional response to a loved one's final departure. The selection of the line "Alike to Those We Love, and Those We Hate," as a heading for the performance photograph stresses what a postbellum readership would interpret as an ideal woman's emotional generosity in the face of personal grief.

> We say it for an hour or for years,
> We say it smiling, say it choked with tears. . . .

3. "The Boy Orator," Northrop, *The Ideal Speaker and Entertainer,* 1910.

4. "The Gypsy Tambourine Girl," Northrop, *The Ideal Speaker and Entertainer,* 1910.

5. "Alike to Those We Love, and Those We Hate," Lumm, *The Home School Speaker and Elocutionist*, 1899.

We have no dearer word for our heart's friend,
For him who journeys to the world's far end
And sears our soul with going; this we say,
As unto him who steps but o'er the way,
"Goodbye."

Alike to those we love, and those we hate.
We say no more at parting at life's gate,
To him who passes out beyond earth's slight,
We cry, as to the wanderer for the night, "Goodbye." (193)

In the photograph, the softly dressed and carefully turned out young woman looks sad but composed. Such an image confirms the idealization of the nineteenth-century woman as a being of deep feeling but also someone who characteristically is strong and wise in the face of life's emotional trials. Although this illustration stresses the "best" of the nineteenth-century woman, the space in which these virtues are enacted is clearly the home, and the occasion being depicted, receiving news of the death of a lover, brother, husband, father, or friend, falls into the sphere of domestic life. Although admirable and serious, unlike "poor Mrs. Byrde" or "The Gypsy Tambourine Girl," this idealized image shows a young woman performing gender appropriately.

The ideological assertion in "Speakers" between gender and rhetorical genre is reinforced by the fact that illustrations of women are not typically linked to the performance of selections from anthologized genre headings such as "Patriotic Recitations," the "Heroic and Warlike," "Historical Poems and Orations," or the "Religious and Sublime." These more intellectually significant genres are directly linked to men through illustrations featuring them in formal evening attire or occasionally in costume. Across the pictorial record of the "Speaker" tradition, men are presented in costume far less frequently than women. In those rare instances in which men are depicted in costume, they are shown as famous Shakespearean characters such as Lear or Mark Anthony or are photographed in biblical garb acting out scenes from poems with religious or philosophical themes.

The manner in which "Speakers" treat the performance categories the "Pathetic and Homelike" and "Tableaux" also makes this distinction between rhetorical roles and rhetorical spaces. The "Pathetic and Homelike" explicitly focuses on domestic and maternal themes and is one of the most obviously female-marked genres in these collections. The assumption lying behind the inclusion of such a category is that the performance by women of selections dealing with the themes of filial devotion, motherhood, and the care of children will universally touch the heart. In the performance of such themes, women would present themselves at the apex of their social significance. However, when we review typical titles from this category, we find that the sentimentalization of the role of women and mothers only calls attention to the ways in which women's influence is limited by their social sphere. Consider the relentlessness of domestic and maternal themes in these selections from the "pathetic" category: "Rock Me to Sleep Mother," "The Preacher's Mother," "Only the Baby Cried for Lorraine," "Just Two Wee Shoes," "A Child's Dream of a Star," "How Tim's Prayer Was Answered," "The Gambler's Wife," and "Saving Mother."[10] Performances by women would be certain to touch the heart and affect the emotions. In contrast, men could plan to change minds and affect moral responses through their persuasive rendering of selections with powerful patriotic or religious themes such as "Liberty and Union, One and Inseparable," "Patriotism Assures Public Faith," and "The Crucifixion" (Hoyle, *The World's Speaker* 22).

In addition "Speakers" encouraged women to act out feminine themes in tableaux performances. One of the most pictorially gendered of the rhetorical genres anthologized in speaker manuals, tableaux (also defined as "statuary") consists of acting out famous scenes from history, events from widely known dramas or poems, images from paintings, and various lessons from life. Subjects for tableaux vary in nature, ranging from the enactment by male performers of famous historical events (such as Lee's surrender to Grant at Appomattox and the major battles of the Revolutionary War) to the portrayal by women of typical domestic scenes (such as the preparation for a party or the care of children). "Speakers" taught women to identify with tableaux selections covering topics such as "Hope" and "Mirth," as illustrated in *The New Select Speaker* (92), or "Forgiveness," as illustrated in a performance photograph from *The American Orator* (see figure 6). In this tableaux, the two women strike an idealized pose of one woman obviously dispensing "forgiveness" to another. The tone of this illustration is one of gentle kindliness, a quality nineteenth-century readers would associate with the ideal woman. In many tableaux selections depicted in photographs, women are shown saying nothing but embodying feminine virtues. Both men and women are shown enacting tableaux of domestic scenes under titles such as "Courtship under Difficulties," described as "For Two Males and One Female"; "A Family Jar," a selection depicted in a photograph showing a mother-in-law and a young couple with the caption "Too Much Mother-in-law"; and "My Feelings Are Hurt beyond Measure," in which a man seems to be attempting to console a woman who is distressed (Hoyle, *The Complete Speaker* 351, 428). The gendering of this type of rhetorical performance is conventional in all respects; men are shown in these domestic tableaux acting out their roles as suitors and husbands. In other pictorial representations, men are shown performing historical, literary, or biblical male characters (e.g., "Washington Irving and His Literary Friends"; "Mercutio, the Friend of Romeo") or decisive men of action. For example, in a tableaux photograph entitled "Let It Be Patriotism First—Then Love," an older man in a Union uniform is seen urging a younger soldier to put love of country ahead of his love for the lady in question, who stands with her arms beckoning to the young man (see figure 7). The placement in this tableaux of the Union officer center stage with the two young people on either side of him centralizes his moral authority in this scene and adds emphasis to his argument that the woman's importance is not equal to that of the noble male task at hand (*The Home School Speaker and Elocutionist* 155).

What we can observe in these performance photographs of tableaux is yet another instance of how the "Speaker" tradition allocated rhetorical categories along the lines of gender. Women were encouraged to involve themselves in acquiring rhetorical skills for the kinds of performances that rank lowest on a scale of rhetorical power. Instead of being given access to rhetorical power in any real sense, women are encouraged to affirm their roles as guardians of domestic morality by perfecting the rhetorical skills of enacting tender, humorous, or domestic sentiments. Although parlor rhetorics often advertised their offerings as a "golden cargo" and represented the study and practice of speaking and reading aloud as a precious opportunity to better oneself, the invitation offered to women by these manuals was, in fact, an invitation to remain in their place. As the author of *The International Speaker* explains, "Reading aloud with propriety and grace is an accomplishment worthy of acquisition. . . . It is peculiarly valuable to [the female] sex because it so often gives them an opportunity of imparting pleasure and improvement to an assembled family during the winter evening or the protracted storm" (35). While parlor rhetorics performed the service of extending the range of formal rhetorical education by transforming academic training into popular pedagogy, there is a troublesome move here. By characterizing parlor rhetoric as a necessary form of literacy while simultaneously gendering certain genres, popular rhetoricians left most women stranded in the parlor, earnestly, even movingly, reciting poems and striking poses while ever greater numbers of men received the training to have the conversations and arguments that shaped intellectual, political, and cultural life.

If we ask ourselves the question, "What cultural work did popular rhetorical pedagogy perform in postbellum America?" we get a complex answer. What the example of the gendering of rhetorical space by parlor rhetorics makes discomfortingly clear is that informal rhetorical pedagogies had institutional status in nineteenth-century America and that the power of that institutional status was wielded in the service of a highly conservative agenda of gendered behavior. The very traditional rhetori-

6. "Forgiveness," *The American Orator*, 1901.

7. "Let It Be Patriotism First—Then Love," Lumm, *The Home School Speaker and Elocutionist*, 1899.

cal spaces defined for women by the parlor rhetoric movement in post-bellum America indicate that while the boundaries of the so-called woman's sphere stretched a little, the debate about what rhetorical roles a woman could perform was far from over. In particular, the rhetorical construction of the white middle-class woman continued to be a complex and ambiguous one as the century ended. To look directly at the role that rhetorical pedagogies played in the construction of gender identities and to weigh the complicated ways that rhetoric dispensed power is to read the history of nineteenth-century rhetoric as a multi-layered text.

# Notes

1. For information about the range of parlor rhetorics see Nan Johnson, "The Popularization of Nineteenth-Century Rhetoric: Elocution and the Private Learner," in Clark and Halloran.

2. Our understanding of the rhetorical progress of nineteenth-century American women has been broadened by a number of recent works by such scholars as Jacqueline Royster, Anne Ruggles Gere, Carol Mattingly, Martha Watson, Shirley Wilson Logan, and Jane Donawerth.

3. The history of nineteenth-century American women and their rhetorical challenges and accomplishments owes a great deal to the groundbreaking scholarship of Lillian O'Connor and Karlyn Kohrs Campbell. Their work provides an analysis of the rhetorical careers of numerous notable women who broke gender and racial barriers to proceed to the platform, including Angelina Grimke, Lucy Stone, Elizabeth Cady Stanton, Lucretia Coffin Mott, Sojourner Truth, Susan B. Anthony, Frances E. Willard, Ida B. Wells, and Mary Church Terrell.

4. For other explorations of the gendering of nineteenth-century rhetoric see Tonkovich and Brody.

5. For details on the theoretical foundations and pedagogical orientation of nineteenth-century academic rhetoric see Nan Johnson, *Nineteenth-Century Rhetoric in North America*. See in particular "Habits of Eloquence," 227–47.

6. In the late postbellum period and at the turn of the century, Genung's texts *Practical Elements of Rhetoric* (1886), *Handbook of Rhetorical Analysis* (1888), and *Working Principles of Rhetoric* (1900) were the most widely used texts in American colleges. Quackenbos's text, *Advanced Course of Composition and Rhetoric,* was the most widely used and circulated American academic rhetoric manual between 1850 and 1880.

7. Academic elocution manuals typically covered the following topics in detail: articulation, inflection, accent, emphasis, pause, force, pace, pitch, attitude of the body or stance, gestures of the hands, gestures of the arm, position of the

feet and legs, and expressions of the face and eyes. The early-nineteenth-century American prototype for elocution manuals was Ebenezer Porter's *Analysis of the Principles of Rhetorical Delivery* (1827). Porter's text was widely used at American colleges between 1827 and the 1880s.

8. In the 1880s and 1890s, "Speaker" manuals varied little in their contents or organization favoring these genre titles for grouping selections for study and performance.

9. See Lehuu. Lehuu observes that sentimental "visual texts came to serve as medium and midwife for the dissemination of the culture of sentiment in antebellum periodicals" (91).

10. Titles like these appear regularly under the "pathetic" category. Often certain poems were anthologized in several manuals creating a kind of domestic canon for women performers. See for example the inclusion of Dickens's "The Death of Little Nell," in *The Ideal Speaker and Entertainer* (194) and *The Complete Speaker Reciter* (174), and "A Child's Dream of a Star," appearing under the "pathetic" in both *The Twentieth Century Speaker* (191) and *The International Speaker and Popular Elocutionist* (243).

# 8

# Writing History on the Landscape

## The Tour Road at
## the Saratoga Battlefield as Text

### S. Michael Halloran

I have some vague memory of a long-ago family picnic at the Saratoga
Battlefield—a log blockhouse meant to evoke the time when American patriots fought to stop the British advance toward Albany, and a
curious stone monument with a high-relief carving of a man's booted
leg. My mother explained that it commemorated the bravery of an
American general named Benedict Arnold who helped win the battle of
Saratoga but then became a traitor. She told me that the monument was
meant to honor the one honorable part of the man, the leg in which he
was, as the inscription on the back of the monument said, "desperately
wounded" in a bold charge against the British.

In recent years I have returned often to the Saratoga Battlefield,
officially the Saratoga National Historical Park. The boot monument is
still there, but the blockhouse was removed in 1975. New York State
Route 32A, along which my father found a picnic area convenient to the
blockhouse, is also gone, but I've managed to discover a trace of it. The
public thoroughfares that ran through the fields on which the battle of
Saratoga was fought, together with most other postrevolutionary structures, were razed to make way for a closed-circuit road designed to tell
the story of the battle. The ersatz blockhouse sat for more than two
decades in a field to which it was "temporarily" removed on its way to
the nearby village of Stillwater, where it was finally reinstalled as a visitors' center during summer 1999.

The Saratoga National Historical Park is a place for having what Greg
Clark elsewhere in this volume calls a "public experience." It is home to
no one individually, but in coming together there with others we can

transcend our differences to experience a common identity that makes this place a home to all of us collectively. Such an experience is a form of rhetorical education in that the collective identity enacted is what makes it possible for us to become a public, and hence to engage in public discourse. As in the classrooms that we associate more readily with the project of education, the first and most crucial fact is simply being together in a place that evokes a certain decorum and calls upon us to attend together to some object of common interest.

At Saratoga the main object of common interest is, as in a traditional classroom, a text. Through signs and other interpretive materials, the tour road tells the story of a crucial Revolutionary War engagement and projects it upon the landscape. The narrative is rhetorical in that it foregrounds particular characters and events; it invites us to identify with the heroes, to relive their strivings and inhabit their passions, to become consubstantial, in Kenneth Burke's sense of that term, with the people who fought at Saratoga. It tells of ideals that motivated our political forebears to fight and die there, to shed blood and transform the picturesque countryside into a sacred place. The story told by the tour road inculcates shared ideals that can become the stuff of ethos and enthymemes, the common ground that allows us to argue our differences in public discourse.

A standard against which we might try to measure the tour road at the Saratoga Battlefield is what Frederick Antczak calls "popularization." In *Thought and Character*, Antczak analyzes the public-lecture circuit that emerged during the Jacksonian political era as a site of "democratic education." Its social purpose according to Antczak was to transform ordinary people into citizens qualified to assume the responsibility of a more widely available franchise. Focusing on the problem of how to bring disciplined understanding to popular audiences, and invoking Plato as theoretical precedent, Antczak posits a hierarchy of rhetorics practiced on the lyceum and Chautauqua circuits.

> The *indulgence* of the democratic audience played shamelessly to the audience's commonplaces for purposes of the speaker's gain. . . . *Vulgarization* of ideas at least tried to change the audience's mind about something, but only about a particular conclusion. . . . Finally, some few lecturers . . . tried to reconstitute their audiences intellectually. They aimed at the training and improvement of their

listeners' thought and character, and they were not deflected by the possibility that such reconstitution might be unwelcome. (9)

This highest form of democratic education Antczak calls *popularization,* and he develops extended analyses of the public lecturing of Ralph Waldo Emerson, Mark Twain, and William James as examples. In the vocabulary of this volume, Antczak's work is a study of rhetorical education at nonacademic sites where people learned to engage in public discourse.

If we view a public historical site such as the Saratoga Battlefield in the terms developed by Antczak, we can ask: to what extent does it attempt to "reconstitute" its audience, to engage their passions without pandering, to expand their consciousness without indulging their prejudices? Historian Michael Kammen suggests the difficulty of any such project (213–25). He writes of the paradoxical coexistence in our time of a pervasive fascination with "heritage," as indicated by the widespread popularity of historical sites of many kinds, and "an alarming degree of ignorance and apathy" about history. The desire to claim a heritage that purports to help us understand who "we" are seems greater now than ever before. "Heritage tourism" has become big business. Yet much of the heritage phenomenon reduces to what Kammen calls a "cultural amnesia" that substitutes a sanitized and oversimplified fairy tale for the complexities of real history. (For an extended example see Tony Horwitz's *Confederates in the Attic: Dispatches from the Unfinished Civil War,* which documents the tendency of some Southern heritage enthusiasts to sanitize history.)

Without public knowledge of the past we may remain ignorant of who "we" are and hence be unable to engage with each other in public discourse. Popularizing historical knowledge at nonacademic sites like the Saratoga Battlefield is thus an important mode of rhetorical education. This essay is an analysis of one sustained effort at this kind of rhetorical education. It is motivated by my long-term interest in the complex interrelationships of place, discourse, and community identity, an interest I share with Greg Clark.[1] But my fascination with the Saratoga Battlefield is also the expression of a personal yen to recover one small piece of the golden age of my childhood. My project is thus susceptible to the snares of heritage. I hope my work contributes to the task of developing a rhetoric of popular history that would meet Antczak's criterion of engaging the audience in "the search for intellectual and moral reconstitution" (8). Yet I must acknowledge at the outset my own membership in a public that simultaneously seeks and resists reconstitution.

## A Battlefield Becomes a Park

The Saratoga National Historical Park is the site of two battles fought in mid-September and early October 1777 between British forces under the command of General John Burgoyne and American colonial forces under General Horatio Gates. Burgoyne had led a powerful force down Lake Champlain, Lake George, and the upper Hudson River toward Albany, where his plan was to converge with the armies of General William Howe and Colonel Barry St. Leger. The grand strategy was to cut the colonies in two, and if it had succeeded, the American Revolution might well have ended as a minor uprising. But St. Leger's eastward march along the Mohawk was stopped at Fort Stanwix, Howe turned his attentions toward Philadelphia rather than Albany, and Burgoyne was defeated by the American forces who had fortified high ground on the western shore of the Hudson at Bemis Heights, about thirty miles north of Albany and just south of a village then known as Saratoga and now called Schuylerville.[2]

On-site commemorations at the Saratoga Battlefield started before the conclusion of the Revolutionary War and continued through the nineteenth century. Around the centennial of the battles a number of stone monuments were placed by a group called the Saratoga Monument Association, and in 1923 another group formed the Saratoga Battlefield Association, Inc., to promote acquisition of the land for public use. On the urging of the association, the State of New York acquired a significant part of the battlefield and established it as a state historical park, which passed to the federal government in the late 1930s and became a national historical park in the 1940s.

As governor of New York, Franklin Roosevelt was an enthusiastic supporter of the newly established state park, and during a visit there in 1929 gave expression to the educational purpose it would serve: "on a battlefield like this at Saratoga, we should be able to visualize the history which was made here. We should have some central spot from which anyone with no knowledge whatever of military science should be able to understand it" ("Remarks"). Later, as president of the United States, Roosevelt took a keen interest in Saratoga's development as a national park. During an October 1940 visit, he chose the site for a visitors' center that would serve as the "central spot" from which ordinary citizens could gain an understanding of the battles (Wilshin, "Narrative Report" 10). A file labeled "The Roosevelts and the Park" in the NPS archive at the battlefield contains numerous letters and memoranda documenting FDR's ongoing involvement. In a 1939 memo to the secretary of the interior, for example, he states his view of the qualifications that should be required of the park superintendent: "He should (a) be absolutely accurate in his historical research and data and (b) he should have outstanding imagination as to how to dramatize the historical facts in kindergarten language and signs and restoration work so that the average tourist can understand through his eyes what the whole thing is about" (memorandum to Ebert K. Burlew).[3]

Many of the early visitors to the battlefield had themselves fought there or were kin to men who had. The monuments that were placed around the 100th anniversary of the battles include several that are inscribed as given in honor of grandfathers and great-grandfathers who had fought at Saratoga. Other monuments signify ethnic or sectional ties to the battles. In 1913 the Saratoga chapter of the Ancient Order of Hibernians erected a monument to Tim Murphy, a marksman credited with shooting the British field commander Simon Fraser. The State of New Hampshire placed a monument in 1927 to honor the New Hampshire militiamen who fought at Saratoga. In 1936 a coalition of Polish-American societies erected a monument to Thadeus Koszyusco, the Polish military engineer who designed and supervised the construction of American fortifications at Saratoga and other sites during the Revolutionary War. Members of the Fraser clan placed a memorial to General Simon Fraser as recently as 1986. The nearly two dozen monuments scattered across the landscape of the battlefield speak eloquently of familial and group pride in what happened there.

But advocates of a public park at the battlefield recognized that it would serve a different population, as Franklin Roosevelt's view of the need for "kindergarten language" in interpretive materials rather ungraciously suggests. The massive wave of immigration in decades leading up to the 1920s was a matter of deep concern to the elites who promoted establishment of the battlefield as a park—so much so that laws drastically restricting immigration had been enacted just three years prior to establishment of the New York State Park at the battlefield. Increased wages, shorter working hours, and the development of affordable automobiles meant that working people would have access to places like the Saratoga Battlefield. The stated purpose of the Saratoga Battlefield Association—"To stimulate and promote patriotism in all who owe allegiance to, or dwell within the confines of the United States" (Articles of Incorporation, as quoted in Michael Phillips)—suggests that its members were keenly aware of the increasing diversity and mobility of the population.[4]

## Reading the Tour Road as an Educational Text

As early as 1930, Rev. Delos E. Sprague wrote a guidebook explicitly designed for use by motor tourists to Saratoga, which was published by an organization calling itself "The Battlefield Publishing Company." In 1939, planners for the National Park Service envisioned an auto tour road that would be dedicated to the specific purpose of "allow[ing] the complete story of the battle to be told" (Appleman). First among the functions of such a road would be to provide "access to the chief points of historic interest where a clear, comprehensive interpretation of the area may be given" (Wilshin, "Narrative"). The plan was finally realized in the 1960s with the construction of the ten-mile tour road that exists today. In contrast to the public roads used by earlier visitors, the tour road was designed for an explicitly educational purpose. It exists solely to project a narrative of the battles on the landscape and instruct citizens in how to experience the landscape as what Franklin Roosevelt called "a shrine" of the national culture. The tour road is thus akin to the oratory in which Pericles memorialized the heroes of the Battle of Marathon and Abraham Lincoln the soldiers who fought at Gettysburg. Perelman and Olbrechts-Tyteca make the point that there is a strong connection between epideictic discourse and education, in that establishing and strengthening adherence to common values and assumptions is a function of both (47–54). In the case of the tour road, responsibility for articulating the narrative, and hence for establishing the values it celebrates, has been assumed by an agency of the national government, a bureaucratic custodian of what John Bodnar calls "official culture." With the development of the tour road and its associated interpretive materials, the National Park Service has assumed the role of educator and visitors to the park become its pupils.

The road is open to autos and bicycles. A sign announces "No in-line skating"—a safety measure no doubt, but perhaps also a matter of classroom decorum. The verge of the paved road is closely mowed grass. The central areas and the walkways at the stops are similarly either paved roads or mowed grass, but the park generally has the character of minimally tended woodland marked by frequent open spaces. Deer, songbirds, and other wild animals are abundant. The views include panoramic vistas of the Hudson River and the Green Mountains of Vermont to the east and of the Adirondack foothills to the north. Many park visitors come just to enjoy the scenery, to picnic or bike or hike, or to ski cross-country. The tour road moves through countryside that seems on its surface untouched by either modern life or the bloodshed of the battles that took place there in 1777. On a clear day, riding the tour road can feel like a visit to a pastoral, premodern Eden complete with picnic tables.

The overview film shown at the visitors' center makes explicit the contrast between the tranquil beauty of the landscape and the grim realities of what happened there. It includes a sequence of colorful autumn scenery accompanied by a voice-over reading passages from the diary of a soldier who speaks of wolves howling in the night as they dug up and tore at the corpses of soldiers who had been hastily buried in mass graves after the first battle of Saratoga. A story of chaos, bloodshed, and death is projected onto the scene of pastoral tranquility. This contrast arises elsewhere on the tour road, so that one of its lessons is to see more in the landscape than is apparent on its face, to recognize and honor the sacrifices that have made possible our afternoon in the sunshine.

This lesson is perhaps most vivid at stop two. Press a button there labeled "history now" and you hear a voice claiming to be that of John Neilson, a historically documented person whose farmhouse at Bemis Heights was commandeered as field headquarters for General Enoch Poor. Neilson describes the "sorry sight" that greeted him when he returned from delivering his wife Lydia to a safe place south of the prospective battlefield: "The soldiers dug trenches and piled great walls of earth and logs all about my farm. They chopped my fences for firewood, cut hay from my mowin' ground and dug up my potatoes. They even trampled Lydia's little sauce garden—pumpkins, turnips and all." The tape station is so positioned that as you listen you stand before the actual farmhouse of John Neilson, carefully stripped of all nineteenth-century additions. The structure you see is, as far as historical research can determine, the exact one that existed in fall of 1777. But there are no trenches, no walls of earth and logs, no hay stubble, no trampled garden.

The house stands atop a gentle hill on a field of mown grass amid artfully placed trees and shrubs. It wears a coat of barn red paint that is probably more perfect than any it enjoyed during John Neilson's lifetime. You cannot enter the house, but you can look in and see Revolutionary-era military coats draped over the backs of chairs, and an old map spread open on the table. On peak-season weekends a park ranger in period costume stands outside the house to answer questions.

The farmhouse is neither what it was in 1777 nor what it became as the Neilson farm grew and flourished in the nineteenth century. Rather, it is an idealization, representing perhaps what John Neilson and Enoch Poor and the others were fighting for at Saratoga. And it serves as a screen upon which the audiotape script invites us to project an imagined picture of the Neilson farmhouse as it was in September and October of 1777, yielding an image that flickers back and forth between the reconstructed farmhouse actually before us and our mental picture of the disorder into which it was thrown by the necessities of warfare. The image of an idealized pastoral America alternates with the image of John and Lydia Nielson's sacrifice in pursuit of that ideal. It is like a cinematic montage that we can enjoy while pausing on a brisk bike ride or a quiet drive through the scenic countryside, depicting the Jeffersonian ideal of a United States made up of self-sufficient farmers living on land whose bounty and beauty were won by sacrifice, determination, and labor.

## Visualizing the History That Was Made Here

Each of the ten stops along the road has interpretive labels and one or more "history now" audiotapes. Some stops are marked by one or more of the stone monuments that were erected long before the tour road itself was developed, and there are a few monuments at sites along the route that are not marked as "official" stops. The monuments seem to have a curiously marginal status in the narrative of the tour road. Because most of the public thoroughfares along which they were originally placed were razed, a few of the monuments are now located well off the clearly marked paths of the tour road, almost as if they were dropped randomly in fields. With the single exception of the Arnold "boot monument," none of them is alluded to in any of the NPS signage, though all of them are well tended by the park maintenance staff.

As a consequence, more than one story is told along the tour road. Most obvious is a more-or-less coherent "official" story told by the labels and audiotapes that have been placed by the National Park Service at the ten marked stops. I call this story "more-or-less" coherent because the full narrative of the two battles that were fought at Saratoga is complicated and not easy to convey in signs and audiotapes designed for casual tourists and schoolchildren. One park official quipped to me that the average person probably leaves the park more confused than she was upon arrival. Part of the problem is the inherent difficulty of telling the story of two battles in a single circuit of a road whose one-way layout may lead the visitor to assume that the story will unfold chronologically. The assumption is in fact partly confirmed; the first stop overlooks the site of the initial skirmish that took place on September 19, and the last stop is the site to which the British withdrew after being defeated on October 7. But the intervening stops do not follow a straightforward chronology. Some are the sites of encampments and fortifications at which no discrete events are recorded, some focus on particular events that unfold for the tourist in no clearly discernable order. For the typical park visitor, the battles tend to become a jumble of disjointed moments— here's where Benedict Arnold made his charge, here's where Burgoyne had his headquarters, here's where Fraser was shot. It's of course quite likely that a jumble of disjointed moments is exactly what the battles were for the soldiers who experienced them, but that's probably not what FDR had in mind when he envisioned a park that would enable people "to visualize the history which was made here."

The metaphor of "visualizing" recurs often in documents in the park archive that record the development of its interpretive philosophy. Early planners believed that the park should provide visitors with an "overview" of the battles, a sense of their strategy and flow situated in a panoramic visual image of the landscape on which they unfolded. The Appleman report of 1939 argues at some length for a treatment of the site that would present "a simple clear picture" of the battles and eliminate "disconcerting detail" (4). Early on there was talk of erecting a high viewing tower that would allow people to look down upon the fields of battle (Slingerland letter to Lester Markel, 1926). A viewing tower already existed a few miles north of the battlefield, in the form of the 155-foot stone obelisk that was erected by the Saratoga Monument Association in 1883 at the site of Burgoyne's last encampment before his formal surrender. Like many similar structures of its era, it was designed in part to create an elevated platform from which people could enjoy a panoramic vista.

The plan for a viewing tower at the battlefield itself was either abandoned or forgotten. More limited panoramic views are afforded at the visitors' center itself and at several of the stops, but the interpretive materials do not take particular advantage of these places as viewpoints from which to develop a sense of the overall geography and flow of the battles. Maps and texts attempt to give visitors an understanding of what lies before them in the immediate field of vision—of where specific fortifications were located, or how the landscape might have looked somewhat different in 1777, for example—but little is done to help the visitor develop a larger mental map placing specific sites in relation to the others. Over time the interpretive emphasis seems to have shifted away from providing such a grand panoptic vision of the battles and toward providing a more intimate sense of how discrete events might have looked, sounded, and felt to the participants. The audiotapes are rich in sensory detail recorded from the vantage points of specific (though usually anonymous) characters. The result is an experience that is vivid in its particulars, but less clear than it might be in overall scope.

## The Tour Road as Palimpsest

Interjected into the already somewhat disjointed narrative told in the signs and audiotapes are the story fragments told by inscriptions on the stone monuments. Unlike the labels and audiotapes installed by the park service, these inscriptions were written not primarily to educate, but rather to memorialize and do homage. They consequently speak in an orotund voice quite unlike the "kindergarten" style imagined by FDR, and they assume knowledge that the average tourist probably does not have. One of my favorites is a five-and-a-half-foot-tall stone obelisk that stands along the road about halfway between stops one and two. Its inscription reads as follows: "Here Morgan, reluctant to destroy so noble a foe, was forced by patriotic necessity to defeat and slay the gentle and gallant Fraser. To commemorate the magnanimity of Morgan's heroic nature and his stern sense of duty to his country this tablet is here inscribed by Virginia Neville Taylor, great grand daughter of General Daniel Morgan."

Compare the orotund style and elevated sentiment of the Morgan inscription with the text of the "history now" audiotape at stop one. Recall that the position of the Morgan monument is such that the tourist will encounter it shortly after hearing this tape.

*Narrator:* History hovers over this scene like morning mist above the distant Hudson. Many historians believe the destiny of our newborn United States of America was decided here in the fall of 1777.
Relive those dramatic moments. In your mind, replace the modern road with twisting wagon ruts. Picture trees larger . . . the forest carpeted with thin undergrowth . . . the clearings dotted with tree stumps. It's a humid summer afternoon. A frontier farmer on horseback appears. Listen as he puts voice to his thoughts . . .
*Second voice:* Whoa! [Horse whinnies.]
How long since John and his son went to Canada? A month? Could be a year by the looks of his house. Corn's ripe for pickin'.
Wonder if John had a part in the fightin' at Ticonderoga? Cap'n Wright calls 'em traitors, John and his son and McBride and the other Tories. Reckon that's a mite harsh. Yet what must it be like to turn against your friends . . . even your own kin? But if the Redcoats aren't stopped, t'will be me hurryin' south plunderin' houses and t'will be John Freeman gazing at my deserted farm. Who'll be the cleverest fox then? Well, it's past time for talkin'. [Clucks to horse.] Time for doin'.
Gitup, Molly. (Saratoga National Historical Park)

The script seems marked by the conventions of radio drama. The narrator begins in plain but carefully ornamented syntax, with paired alliterations ("history hovers," "morning mist") and a nicely turned visual simile ("like morning mist above the distant Hudson") calculated to create a tone of high seriousness. He asks us first to reimagine the scenery, then to hear the thoughts of an ordinary farmer who pauses at the spot. The voice of the farmer is in a more vernacular style marked by fragmentary sentences, syntactic and phonetic elisions, and homely topical focus ("Corn's ripe for pickin'"). Like the inscription on the Morgan monument, the ruminating farmer considers the opposing side in the conflict ("John and his son and the other Tories"), but he moves on quickly from moral speculation to more pragmatic considerations. The voice on the tape concludes with a homely antithesis ("time for talkin' . . . Time for doin'") that gives expression to one of the classic topoi of commemorative oratory, the incommensurability of deeds and words. (Compare Lincoln, "The world will little note nor long remember what we say here, but it can never forget what they did here.")

The juxtaposition of this audiotape with the Morgan monument inscription in quick succession along the tour route is striking. From the musings of a hypothetical ordinary farmer, we move abruptly to an oracular moral pronouncement on the tragic death of one hero at the hands of another. The stylistic contrast is especially sharp in these two examples, but it is fairly consistent from beginning to end of the tour road. The monuments speak in tones of moral certainty and high seriousness, and they focus on notable acts and named persons. The labels and tape scripts speak in a vernacular style of more ordinary and often unnamed persons. At stop two we encounter a monument to the "noble son of Poland" Thadeus Koszyusco, at stop three we hear the taped voice of his nameless aide. The contrast between the two styles is heightened by the fact that the two take no notice of each other. With the single exception of stop seven where labels identify the "Arnold monument," the interpretive materials placed by the park service make no allusion to any of the stone monuments. It is as if the monuments were somehow invisible when the labels and tapes were installed and have since mysteriously reappeared.

The text inscribed on the landscape of the battlefield is like a palimpsest, a parchment manuscript on which writing that had been scraped off reappears as a shadowy image behind the new text that has been inscribed on the unsuccessfully reconditioned surface. Like the earlier text that a scribe had thought obliterated, the monument inscriptions "show through" the new writing that has been inscribed by the National Park Service. As a result, the concerns and the sensibility of those who placed the monuments stand in counterpoint with those of the National Park Service writers who sought to inscribe an official story of the battles. From the Saratoga Monument Association era, we can read an intense interest in heroes and heroic deeds, and a sophisticated literary and historical sensibility. A case in point is the boot monument, which manages to praise Benedict Arnold's heroism without mentioning his name. (A similarly sophisticated treatment of Arnold is evident in the Victory Monument at the site of Burgoyne's last camp, which includes life-size bronze statues of Daniel Morgan, Horatio Gates, and Philip Schuyler, and an empty niche with Arnold's name above it.) From the National Park Service era, we can read an interest in the experiences of ordinary farmers and soldiers and a sensibility formed less by literature, oratory, and history than by the media of radio, film, and television.

The palimpsest analogy applies similarly to the road system and the landscape itself. In planning the tour road, park administrators directed that the existing road system and all other postrevolutionary structures be "obliterated" so that the site could be restored to some approximation of its condition at the time of the battles. (The monuments were obviously not included in this directive, though I have not found an explicit exemption in any documents in the park archive.) Some early park planners even hoped to restore the flora at the site to the condition of the 1770s, a project that would have been made impossible by the extinction of some species and the firm establishment of some new ones. The roads were largely erased, but traces of them survive as horse trails and hiking paths. Buildings were razed, but I've happened upon foundations overgrown by brush. I've also managed to find a trace of old Route 32A along which my father once found a picnic spot. It's a disused and badly deteriorated $\Psi$ junction branching off from the segment of Route 32A that today establishes the southern boundary of the park. That $\Psi$ points like an arrow into the park grounds, along a route a few yards to the side of the present tour road and apparently directly over a line of wooden posts that have been driven by archeologists to mark the location of some American fortifications. As I recognized the apparent coincidence of old Route 32A with that line of American fortifications, I wondered how Route 32A might have come to follow that line of fortifications? Was it perhaps a road that existed at the time of the battles and was used by the colonial forces? How far back do the traces of the old public roads date?

The question brings into focus an inadequacy of my central metaphor: "writing" on the landscape. A landscape is not a blank surface, like a piece of paper or a computer disk. Its soil, climate, flora, fauna, and topography are specific and recalcitrant; they resist our efforts to reshape a place, so that the result of any effort to "write" on a landscape is necessarily an amalgam of the writer's efforts and the operation of chemical, biological, and climatological forces. And the resultant "text" will enforce its own somewhat different recalcitrance on the efforts of others to inscribe a new story at this place. A landscape thus has a history of its own in a way that no other kind of writing surface has.

Much of the history of the place at which the battles of Saratoga were fought remains unacknowledged in the story told by the interpretative materials placed by the park service along the tour road and at the visitors' center. These materials concentrate on specific historical *events* that occurred at the battlefield while ignoring the battlefield as a *place* with its own natural and cultural history. To cite another quite simple example, recall the phrase "Corn's ripe for pickin'" from the stop one audiotape quoted above. There's no corn to be found at the battlefield today, nor any explanation of why this is so. Stop five is the Barber Wheatfield, scene of the much celebrated shooting of British General Simon Fraser. There's no wheat, and no explanation of what happened to the wheat. One could argue that what needs most to be told at Saratoga is precisely the story of events that took place there in September and October of 1777, and that to complicate the story further with the natural and cultural history of the landscape where those events occurred would detract from it. And yet the traces inevitably show through, hinting at changed cultural sensibilities and economic realities.

## History Now (and Then)

I began studying how a historical tale is told at the Saratoga Battlefield as a "little" project that would produce a neat and possibly interesting paper. But the project turned out not to be so little, and the paper turned out not to be the tidy little QED I had expected to write. Answering one question often raised two or three more. Who were the people of the Saratoga Monument Association and what motivated them? Who composed their inscriptions and devised that wonderfully witty figure of the booted leg? What did the battlefield look like when it was a New York State Historical Park and what sorts of educational-ceremonial activities went on there? Who composed the labels and audiotape scripts that make up the official text now in place along the tour road? And how might the story of the battles change in future retellings? I expect to spend the next few years pursuing answers to these and other questions, and I expect that in the process of answering any one question I'm likely to discover two or three others at least as interesting.

What's made this project so very rich is the way it has made vivid and concrete for me something I had already known in an abstract way, namely that history is always written from a specific perspective. The godlike voice that speaks from monument inscriptions about Daniel Morgan, Simon Fraser, Benedict Arnold, and other great men relates a narrative of the Battles of Saratoga from the perspective of the post–Civil War era. The voices of the ordinary farmers and soldiers who speak from the audiotapes relate a narrative of the Battles of Saratoga as seen from the perspective of the Vietnam era. From the perspective of the post–9-11 world, the marker on the buttons we press to hear those voices—History Now—is inadvertently ironic, since the "now" in which the tapes were recorded has itself become history.

So if there is what Greg Clark calls an "American essence" to be discovered at the Saratoga Battlefield—or at Yellowstone or the Grand Canyon or any other of those "places that have been rendered by the culture symbolic of America"—it is an essence that cannot be articulated timelessly and finally. Any particular version of it will be specific to its own moment in time, and will have as much to tell us about that moment as it will about "America."

And what of rhetorical education at the Saratoga National Historical Park? Does it rise to the standard that Fred Antczak calls popularization? I believe my own experience of the park as I've studied it has indeed been "reconstituting" in Antczak's sense of that term. But I may not be a typical visitor to the park; my dogged readings and rereadings of the labels, tape scripts, and monument inscriptions are surely not typical. The most important things I've learned at the park I've learned not because of the efforts of those who composed the official text of the tour road, but in spite of them. The story told by the National Park Service in its labels and audiotapes, while told in a variety of voices of mostly ordinary people, comes across *in toto* as authoritative and timeless, not a story of the Battles of Saratoga, but The Story. It positions visitors to the park as passive recipients of the final word rather than as active inquirers. The presence along the tour road of monuments with a very different story of larger-than-life heroes presents an opportunity to call attention to the contingency of historical narratives, an opportunity the official text misses.

It may be that what I observe as a deficiency in the official text is itself simply one more mark of its contingency. It's of its time, just as the monuments are of their quite different time. A new master plan to govern interpretation at the park is in the works, and this will almost certainly mean new interpretive materials and a new text. Will a new tour road text teach a lesson in historiography and the contingency of civic identity by calling attention to the very different versions of the Battles of Saratoga that have been told in different historical moments? And what of the many parks, museums, historic houses, and other sites where historical stories are being told and retold for popular audiences? These are sites of rhetorical education, and the study of how they work to inform their visitors, and hence to form those visitors as citizens is a vast, inviting, largely unexplored, and deeply important field for rhetorical research.[5]

# Notes

1. See, in addition to Greg's essay in this volume, my essay "The Rhetoric of Picturesque Scenery" in Clark and Halloran, and our essay "It's a Nice Place to Visit But I Wouldn't Want to Live There" in Swearingen and Pruett.

2. For a historian's account of what has been called one of the fifteen most decisive battles in world history, see Richard Ketchum's *Saratoga: Turning Point of America's Revolutionary War*.

3. On FDR's interest in the general project of popularizing history and his role in getting the National Park Service involved with historical sites see also chapter 7 of Bodnar's *Remaking America*.

4. For a discussion of class issues at stake in the establishment of the park, see my "Text and Experience in a Historical Pageant."

5. For their generous assistance on this project, the author offers thanks to Superintendent Doug Lindsay and Rangers Dick Beresford, Joe Craig, and Linda White of the Saratoga National Historical Park; to RPI students Laura MacLemale and Lianne Webster; and to colleagues Tom Carroll, Greg Clark, and Tamar Gordon. Materials from the Saratoga National Historical Park Archives used with permission.

# 9
# Transcendence at Yellowstone
## Educating a Public in an Uninhabitable Place
### Gregory Clark

This essay describes an instance of rhetorical education in America that is cultural rather than curricular. It does so to suggest that in America successful formal instruction in theories and practices of public discourse may be founded upon a prior education in collective identity that is provided by experiences of the national culture. One important instance of that prior education occurs when individuals leave their homes and travel to places in America that have been rendered publicly symbolic of the national community. Beginning in the nineteenth century, a few places in the vast American landscape were set aside to provide those who would visit there a symbolic encounter with the whole nation, an encounter I am calling a "public experience." These are not places where Americans actually live. Indeed, they are far removed from the regional and home places with which individuals identify themselves. Most Americans first encountered public experience while still at home in representations in words and images that assign to certain distant sites a sort of American essence. So when they travel to see these places for themselves, thinking of themselves as tourists but acting as pilgrims, Americans find themselves meeting each other as strangers who have gathered there to experience together a shared sense of their national collectivity.

Yellowstone National Park is paradigmatic of those places, and it exists at least in part—like all of the U.S. national parks—for the purpose of providing individual Americans with a common experience of their national collectivity. This is the same sort of claim that S. Michael Halloran makes elsewhere in this volume: that shared experiences of American place, particularly as mediated by public institutions of the national culture (like the National Park Service), can enable the diverse individuals who live alienated from each other within this country's boundaries to understand themselves as part of a national community. That understanding is itself a lesson in public identity that is at the foundation of an individual's rhetorical education.

When Kenneth Burke introduced his pentadic method for explaining how rhetoric works, he emphasized the rhetorical power of context and circumstance—he called it "scene"—to shape and transform individual identity and action within it. "From the motivational point of view," he wrote, "there is implicit in the quality of a scene the quality of the action that is to take place within it" (*Grammar* 6–7). That, in Burke's nutshell, is the point I want to make about the sort of rhetorical education these publicly American places can provide. He was more specific about the rhetorical work done by such scenes in a later essay, "The Rhetorical Situation," where he wrote that both "the *words* one is using and the non-verbal circumstances in which one is using them" (263) prompt attitudes of "congregation" and "segregation" (269) that transform concepts of individual and collective identity.

This essay examines some of the prompts for that transformation of identity that Americans encountered in Yellowstone during its first century as a national park by describing ways that this American "scene" provided its visitors with experiences of, in Burke's favored term, "communion." Converging there as strangers, they find themselves inhabiting together temporarily a landscape they have learned to read as symbolic of their nation. This shared encounter in an uninhabitable place that has been made publicly symbolic of their collectivity is a rhetorically powerful public experience. It invites these fellow travelers to "transcend" their differences as they experience themselves as a community in this place that is an icon of their common homeland.

## Yellowstone Stories

I've always noticed license plates. When you are in your car, your license plate tells everyone where you come from. When traveling by car as a young child, I enjoyed leaving that localizing license plate in a parking lot and losing myself in a crowd of people from everywhere. I was from Utah, to me clearly a peripheral place in America. By the age of five I was well aware that America was in New York or Ohio or Washington, D.C., or California, but not Utah. I had only visited Idaho, another peripheral place. My grandparents had a farm there where, as their first grandchild, I would stay for weeks at a time. When the farm allowed it, we would take out the Buick and travel, and I would experience America. For me, America was only a morning's drive away, in Yellowstone National Park. As soon as we passed through the entrance gate, the cars I saw on the roads and in the parking lots were carrying colored plates from the full spectrum of states. Yellowstone, it seems to me, is where my rhetorical education began.

They probably took me there earlier, but the first trip to Yellowstone I remember was in 1955—the summer before I started school. I remember standing between them on the front seat reading aloud the names of the states from the plates that passed us on the pine-lined road. I remember lagging behind in a parking lot to stare at plates I had never seen—from places like Massachusetts and New Mexico and Florida and Texas. I remember blending into a crowd of people moving through clouds of sulfur steam along a trail that took us past mud pots and hot springs. The people marveled at them and I marveled at the feeling that just then I wasn't from Utah at all. Like the rest of the visitors to that place, I was from America.

To claim that my rhetorical education in America began in Yellowstone the summer before I started kindergarten requires some attention to definition. A rhetorical education includes many lessons, but prerequisite to them all is the instruction of individuals in a collective identity. Before people can do the practical rhetorical work of determining what they will believe and do together, they need to understand themselves as identified and interdependent with others. This sort of education in collective identity occurs both within and without the boundaries of formal schooling. Because inventing a national community has always been a deliberate and urgent project in the diverse and expansive United States, these prerequisite lessons pervade the public culture. School inculcates in individuals some conventionally civic attitudes and practices. But a broader education in collective identity informs almost every encounter with public life. My point is that the formal rhetorical education that enables participation in public discourse is enabled by almost constant informal instruction in a collective identity that occurs as individuals join crowds of their compatriots in the public experiences Americans are enculturated to seek. Such public experiences—like my trek through the parking lot and into the crowd to see the sights at Yellowstone—are not "civic" in their content or form. But they are civic in their function of prompting people to imagine themselves transcending the differences that divide them as they share a place that has been publicly designated their common ground.

John Sears notes in *Sacred Places* that the American landscapes that became tourist attractions in the nineteenth century were "points of mythic and national unity" where the diverse citizens of the new nation could gather (7). Symbolically, such places encompass the nation, at least in the imaginations of the people who visit them. As Benedict Anderson explains, because the actual collectivity of people that constitutes a nation is too expansive to encounter directly, citizens must develop a common language that enables them to *imagine* "their communion" (6–7). I am suggesting that this common "language" includes *experiences* that are shared. Public discourse provides people with the words that enable them to imagine that communion, and public experiences enable them to inhabit that imagined community, at least temporarily, as I did when I joined the crowd on the wooden walkways of a geyser basin. We had all left our homes to travel to this spectacular public place where none of us could live. Some of the most powerful symbolic images of the nation are such uninhabitable spectacles, places like Niagara or the Grand Canyon or Yellowstone, where the full spectrum of transient Americans gather to feel at home together.

It is because no one can live in these places that the visitors can imagine them symbolizing a collective home. Americans from Georgia or Minnesota have the same claim on Yellowstone as those who live a morning's drive away. That is even true across time: because no one lives there visitors can imagine themselves compatriots with others from a century before. Yellowstone and places like it offer visitors rhetorically powerful experiences of community that belie historical and practical facts. That is what the conclusion of an 1893 guidebook to the early national parks, *America's Wonderlands: A Pictorial and Descriptive History of Our Country's Scenic Marvels,* seems to promise.

> These [photographs] are fairly representative of the incomparable scenery that charmingly diversifies our native land, a land kissed by the lips of liberty, bounty, and beauty, and blessed with an amplitude of powers, under the exercise of which the largest freedoms, benefits, and sovereign rights are obtained for the whole people. (Buel 503)

This language enacts what Myra Jehlen has observed: that Americans imagine the American land—particularly when symbolized by its most spectacular places—as an "archetypal conjunction of personal identity and national identification" (2). Here real and persistent differences are denied as Americans gather out of time and territory in a place that is designated "fairly representative" of the nation that they should harmoniously compose. The experience overlays their individual identities with a collective one, the primary lesson in a rhetorical education.

My early trips to Yellowstone schooled me in a national identity, transcended the locality of my Utah home, and were shaped by published words and images of Yellowstone. What I experienced at Yellowstone that first trip was determined at least partially by a book that my grandmother would often read to me. Joyce Farnsworth's *Cubby in Wonderland* was first published in 1932, and my grandmother bought a copy then to read to my mother and her sisters. It was sufficiently popular—primarily among Yellowstone tourists, I suspect—to have gone through ten printings during the next six years, some of the hardest of the Great Depression. By the time *Cubby in Wonderland* was published, *wonderland* had long been a commonplace descriptor for Yellowstone. The term was connected to Yellowstone in the first detailed descriptions of the area that were published in the early 1870s as Lewis Carroll's new children's fantasy was being read throughout America. Soon the Northern Pacific Railroad—the first line to take tourists to Yellowstone—made "Wonderland" the title of its annual passenger guide, and by 1901 even John Muir, lover of Yosemite and the Sierra, would describe Yellowstone as a "Wonderland" where every year "thousands of tourists and travelers" can "wander about it enchanted" (39). In 1912, calendar maker Thomas D. Murphy published the first version of his gift book, *Three Wonderlands of the American West,* that described Yellowstone, Yosemite, and the Grand Canyon in florid language illustrated with black-and-white photographs and blurred color reproductions of Thomas Moran's famous paintings of those places. And in 1925, the Union Pacific Railroad made the allusion to Carroll's Wonderland explicit as it promoted its new Yellowstone service from the South in a brochure, titled *Geyserland,* where "the visitor walks through the looking-glass into a wonderland where incredible things happen" (5).

*Cubby in Wonderland* begins as mother and cub make their way down from their winter den in the Teton mountains to join the "two-legged tribe" in a summer pilgrimage to "Mother Nature's Wonderland" (134). Despite the fact they are bears, his mother tells him, they will all be tourists together there, for thanks to "Uncle Sam" (24), Yellowstone is "a very happy place for bears and people" (65). And after a few early misunderstandings, that description proves to be true as Cubby and his mother travel the park throughout the summer. Along the way they keep a respectful distance from the people but still witness with them all the famous marvels of the place. Bears and people together learn the lessons about natural history and about social relations that Yellowstone can teach them as they share the place for the summer. In the final chapter, awestruck with the rest of the crowd by the spectacle of Old Faithful, the bears forget themselves and join the two-legged tourists in a ranger-led tour through the Upper Geyser Basin: "Cubby and his mother and the people were very interested in all he had to tell them. When they came to a little bridge, the Ranger had the people counted as they walked across. There were just a hundred and ninety-seven people and a mother bear and her cub that morning" (133).

This is one of those "incredible things" that, according to the Union Pacific brochure, happens in "wonderland." And a wonderland is what I learned to imagine Yellowstone, and the nation it represented, to be. By the time my grandmother read that last chapter to me, I saw the park through Cubby's eyes, which may be why I experienced that stop at the geyser basin as I did. Before visiting Yellowstone, I had felt no more at home in the America I saw on television and in *Life* magazine than the little bear felt when he first walked into a valley that was dominated by that strange two-legged tribe. But by the end of a summer in Yellowstone, he and his mother could happily join the crowd for a tour, and the ranger could include them without comment in his count.

## Community, Conflict, and Public Identity

In 1955, Kenneth Burke wrote a new introduction for his 1937 book, *Attitudes Toward History* where he explained what he had meant both by *history*—"man's life in political communities"—and by *attitudes*—the "characteristic responses of people in their forming and reforming of congregations." He had first written the book to examine the circumstances of people who are embedded in what John Dewey had defined as a "public"—bound together by the "extensive and serious" consequences for all that can follow from the actions of one (Dewey 67). In 1937 Burke had offered this assessment: "getting along with people is one devil of a difficult task, [but] . . . in the last analysis, we should all want to get along with people (and do want to)." But in 1955, something more needed to be said. "In the twenty some years between the first edition of this book and its present reprinting," he wrote, "a momentous quantitative difference has entered the world." In 1937 Burke and his readers could assume that although "human stupidity could go to fantastic lengths of destructiveness, yet always mankind's hopes of recovery could be born anew." But now, with Auschwitz and Hiroshima in recent memory, clearly "a truly New Situation is with us" (v). So Burke reintroduced his book on "the forming and reforming of congregations" by declaring that "the invention of technical devices that would make the rapid obliteration of all human life an easily available possibility" has transformed what had been a set of recommendations for an ethical life into a prescription of essential "equipment for living"—or, more bluntly, for surviving.

That was also the year Burke published a proposal for a sort of educational reform that is "most urgent . . . in view of the new weapons that threaten not only our chances of living well but even our chances of living at all" ("Linguistic" 301). His "Linguistic Approach to Problems of Education" argued that the primary educational project in the United States should be the inculcation of the "attitudes"—the "characteristic responses"—that enable people who must live together in this "New Situation" to confine their conflicts to the rhetorical realm. Burke's *linguistic* approach to problems in education focuses critical attention on the power of language to create the realities that people collectively perceive, and the *problems in education* that Burke's approach addresses are those difficult ones that prevent people who must live together from identifying with each other as an interdependent community—as a public, in Dewey's sense of that term. What Burke proposed here is a rhetorical education of a very different sort from the conventional curriculum that he labels as "promissory." Rather than promising to provide students with skills to succeed individually in a competitive society, this education is "admonitory," teaching "attitudes" that admonish them to undermine the potential for violence that is inherent in their competition by attending critically to the collective consequences of individual discursive acts. Here it is in his summary terms:

In the educational situation, characteristically, the instructor and his class would be on good terms. They would preferably be under the sign of goodwill. And is not education ideally an effort to maintain such an attitude as thoroughly and extensively as possible without loss of one's own integrity? If, where we cannot "love" our neighbor's ways, we might at least "fearsomely *appreciate*" their form, and in methods that bring our own ways within the orbit of the "*fearsomely* appreciated," would we not then be at least headed in the right direction? (301)

This pedagogical statement has theological resonance. Burke would teach people to recognize and respect the power inherent in the rhetorical capacity of others in the same way that believers are taught to stand in fear of the power of God. To "fearsomely appreciate" that rhetorical capacity is a response somewhat analogous to the wary awe nineteenth-century Americans were taught to experience in places like Niagara Falls or Yosemite or Yellowstone. For Burke, a ready awareness of the power of each other's rhetoric is required if people are going to live constructively, rather than destructively, together.

Burke envisions communities in which people are educated in this ability to respond to discursive conflict with attitudes and acts of "transcendence." According to his "Dictionary of Pivotal Terms" that ends *Attitudes Toward History*, "transcendence" occurs when people identify themselves together with new "symbols of authority" and thereby "transcend" their differences: "When approached from a certain point of view, A and B are 'opposites.' We mean by 'transcendence' the adoption of another point of view from which they cease to be opposites" (336). He then offered the following example:

Primitive peoples recognize the process of transcendence in their initiation rites whereby, at different periods in the life of the individual, he is symbolically endowed with a new identity, as he enters some new corporate grouping within the tribe. The church tries to coach a similar process by its rites of communion. One discerns it behind even the crudest of hazing ceremonies that seek to impress, by picturesqueness, terror, or wound, the sense of a new identification (a new way of defining the individual's identity with relation to a corporate identity). (337)

What Burke is describing is an experience that enables diverse individuals to transcend their separateness as they strive to adopt as their own a collective identity. And the terms "Identity, Identification" stand at the conceptual as well as alphabetical center of his list of "Pivotal Terms." Burke notes in *Attitudes Toward History* that "all the issues with which we have been concerned"—all the concepts and problems surrounding that fundamental public problem of "forming and reforming of congregations"—"come to a head in the problem of identity." The problem is that identity is "*not* individual" (263); rather, "'identification' is hardly other than a name for the *function of sociality*" (266–67).

## Images of Yellowstone in the Rhetorical Education of a Public

In 1935, Burke tried to teach a group of Americans who were trying to redefine their national identity how to prompt individuals to transcend their separateness and identify with a collective. In a speech titled "Revolutionary Symbolism in America," Burke told the American Writers Conference that "cooperation" requires acceptance of a "unifying principle," one that individuals experience as a "subtle complex of emotions and attitudes." Particular "insignia" or icons that are presented publicly as "labels" for such unifying principles work as "myths" that enable "the carpenter and the mechanic, though differently occupied, [to] work together for common social ends" (267). In the public discourse, he continued, these myths are coded as images of collectivity with which individuals can, despite their differences, each identify. In the process, as Burke put it elsewhere, they make themselves over in the image of that imagery (*Philosophy of Literary Form* 281).

Places, as readily as words, can make these myths public, and they can do so with rhetorical power as they enable people to experience themselves inhabiting that symbolic imagery. Publicly symbolic places like Yellowstone have enabled the generations of Americans who have gathered there to imagine themselves a coherent community despite the unimaginable complexity of their actual collectivity. By the end of the nation's first full century, the rhetorical purpose of those symbolic places was institutionalized by their designation as national parks. The first ones, Yellowstone, Yosemite, and the Grand Canyon, were designated sites for public communion in places rendered legally uninhabitable and thus available to every citizen and have, ever since, remained prime destinations for American tourists. They may think of these trips as private vacations, but what they experience educates them as citizens. I began this essay by describing my first visit to Yellowstone as my first experience of my own national identity. Now I want to examine how some representations of Yellowstone have worked rhetorically in the nation's public discourse to enable Americans from across the continent and the century to imagine themselves as a coherent community.

In the early summer of 1871, *Scribner's Monthly* published in two parts an illustrated article that introduced Yellowstone to America. "The Wonders of the Yellowstone" was the first account sufficiently detailed and well distributed to bring this place into the national consciousness. Nathaniel P. Langford—eventually the first superintendent of the park and one of a group of prominent residents of the territory who had recently explored the area—submitted the article to the editors at *Scribner's*. They recognized the kind of interest it would provoke in their readers and commissioned the young landscape artist Thomas Moran to augment the text with engravings developed from Langford's rough sketches of Yellowstone scenes. The resulting article was widely read and prompted sufficient interest among people in business and government to fund the Hayden expedition, charged officially by the U.S. government to survey the Yellowstone region and assess its resources. A major contributor to that funding was the Northern Pacific Railroad, then constructing its transcontinental line across southern Montana, just north of Yellowstone, and it was the NPRR that arranged with Hayden himself for Moran to join the expedition. So late in 1871, Moran with his watercolor sketchbook, and William Henry Jackson with his wet-plate camera, began to record the scenery of Yellowstone as others developed the scientific data that would document its resources. Upon their return to the East, Moran proceeded quickly to paint in oil a monumental rendering of the Grand Canyon of the Yellowstone. The painting was immediately purchased by Congress and hung in the Capitol as the legislation that established the first national park moved with unprecedented speed to the president's desk.

Moran's career was founded upon that painting and its companion, *The Chasm of the Colorado*, that followed a year later. He continued to paint the spectacles of American landscape that would became national parks, and the American public began to encounter his images of these places everywhere—on travel posters and tourist brochures, train schedules and even luggage tags, as well as in art galleries, limited editions of chromolithographs, and illustrated books. As symbols of a vast American continent that is home to an incomprehensibly diverse people, these images portrayed uniquely American places that all of these people could imagine themselves inhabiting, at least temporarily, together. That he intended to contribute to this educational project is implicit in Moran's short essay, "American Art and American Scenery," that appears in a gift book titled *The Grand Canyon of Arizona*, published in 1906 by the "Passenger Department" of the Santa Fe Railroad. By this time, Moran's renderings of the Grand Canyon, like his renderings of Yellowstone, were almost universally familiar to Americans. The book, probably sold at Santa Fe stations and on the trains, introduced itself as a "book of words from many pens, about the Grand Canyon of the Colorado River in Arizona." The topic of Moran's essay was "nationalism in art." "That there is nationalism in art needs no proof," he wrote. "It is bred from a knowledge of and sympathy with . . . surroundings . . . and there is no phase of landscape in which we are not richer, more varied and interesting than any country in the world." Indeed, the triumph of American landscape art—as well as, we can probably assume, America itself—"only awaits the men of original thoughts and ideas to prove to their countrymen that we possess a land of beauty and grandeur with which no other can compare" (86–87). It is this common homeland that viewers of that art are prompted to value.

The essay expresses Moran's conviction that the American landscape and the national community it symbolizes are unique and probably superior in the world, a conviction he expressed by quoting another contributor to the volume, C. A. Higgins, listed as assistant general passenger agent of the Santa Fe Railroad, and likely the book's designer and editor. Higgins's description of the Grand Canyon as "an inferno swathed in soft, celestial fires," Moran wrote, expresses the "truth and perceptions of a poet" (87). Higgins evoked images of the otherworldly extremes of hell and heaven to describe the Grand Canyon, but descriptions of the Yellowstone region shifted very early from one to the other. Until about 1871 and the publication of the *Scribner's* articles, the Hayden expedition, and Moran's monumental painting of the Grand Canyon of the Yellowstone, the region was vaguely known to Americans by terms that coincided with its early description as "Colter's Hell." But with the scientific surveys and the aestheticized renderings of its landscape by people like Moran and Jackson, the public language of Yellowstone changed and by 1922 a guidebook for automobile tourists, subtitled *Wonders of the Yellowstone Dreamland,* could frankly proclaim the place "God's Country" (Chapple, 14). Moran's Yellowstone paintings and prints themselves certainly enabled this early rehabilitation of the popular conception of the place. As one art historian puts it, Moran's well-publicized images "transformed" Yellowstone "in the public's imagination from a land of hell on earth to a spectacular wonderland" (Kinsey 34).

Indeed, Yellowstone remained the primary American wonderland, a place where, as the Union Pacific Railroad's *Geyserland* insisted, "incredible things happen" (5). These "incredible things" are obviously the natural phenomena that are Yellowstone's famous attractions. From its beginnings, booklets and brochures describing Yellowstone have presented images of communing tourists that belie the differences that divide the American people. These, too, are "incredible things." The cover of the Northern Pacific Railroad's 1903 guidebook, *Wonderland,* presents a familiar Yellowstone vista with an Indian in loincloth and feathers in the foreground, beckoning to readers, with peace pipe in hand, to join him in enjoying the place (Wheeler). The cover of another NPRR promotional booklet, this one published in 1917 and titled *The Land of the Geysers,* has a panoramic view of Old Faithful and its massive log lodge. Again in the foreground, standing together as common witnesses to the icon of an eruption, are an affluent woman tourist, an Indian in traditional dress, and a buckskin-clad trapper with musket in hand. For Joe Mitchell Chapple, whose 1922 auto-touring guide to the park was subtitled *Wonders of the Yellowstone Dreamland,* Yellowstone is simply "the camping ground of Uncle Sam" where "everybody feels at home" (13). Chapple strongly encouraged his readers to culminate their visits at the Grand Canyon of the Yellowstone, and to gather there at a place above Artist's Point where "there is room for all" (61) to view the scene together in "silent reverence" (63).

My point is that the rhetorical power of such places follows as much from this public recognition that they are "the camping ground of Uncle Sam" where "everybody feels at home," as it does from the spectacles to be viewed there. The legislation that established Yellowstone as a national park in 1872 distinguished it from all other American places by proclaiming it a place "reserved and withdrawn from settlement, occupancy, or sale under the laws of the United States, and dedicated and set apart as a public park or pleasure ground for the benefit and enjoyment of the people" (quoted in Murphy 57–58). Two decades later, President Theodore Roosevelt laid the cornerstone for the first formal entrance to the park with this reaffirmation of that status: nowhere else "is there to be found such a tract of veritable wonderland made accessible to all visitors." He then dedicated this place to the project of educating a nation: Yellowstone, like "the Grand Canyon of the Colorado, and Yosemite," is destined to be visited by "a steadily increasing number of our people" who seek there a "liberal education" (quoted in Chapple 98–99). This education comes as the nation's citizens gather there to experience together "the incomparable scenery" that is a public symbol of "our native land" (Buel 503).

## Touring Yellowstone: Leaving Home for Homeland

When encountered along with compatriot strangers, this dedicated scenery affords a concrete experience of community that is nonetheless ephemeral. Having left their separate homes to gather where none of them can live, they experience being at home together temporarily in a place that is constituted of symbols where they can imagine themselves "transcending" their differences. This is in the tradition of nineteenth-century experiences of the natural sublime: as they gather to witness together the awesome power of nature, people take temporary refuge from the violence that lies latent in their own differences. It is in that way these places are "sacred," in a secular and civic sense. Perhaps Yellowstone in vacation season is the same sort of place a church is on a Sabbath day—a place where people can retreat from their conflicts and competitions to experience a communion that temporarily transcends it all. The scenic icons of the American Wonderland offer Americans that sort of experience of transcendence.

For a century, Americans were taught to experience Yellowstone in precisely that way. W. W. Wylie's "Complete Hand, or Guide Book for Tourists," titled *Yellowstone National Park, or the Great American Wonderland* (1882), is an example of that instruction. Published when "plain roads are now open to all points of interest" and to attract to the park tourists who "do not feel able to hire guides" (3), Wylie's guide prescribes a particular itinerary. "For the following reasons," he wrote, "the natural and most satisfactory way to visit the Park is to enter at Mammoth Hot Springs, and go around by the Geyser Basins, over to Lake, and down by Falls and Canyon . . . " (9).

The reasons are these: By this route all the objects of interest are seen in order of a climax, the less interesting after leaving Mammoth Springs first, and the more wonderful toward the last. In this way the tourist is always deeply interested and fully appreciates what he sees; while if he enters at the upper end of the park, he sees the most wonderful first. These objects of lesser importance have very little interest to him afterward, and are only seen with something of a disappointed feeling (9–10).

This is more than mere tour. It is an aesthetic experience that has narrative form and rhetorical function. Nearly every description of the park through its first fifty years follows that same counterclockwise circle through scenes of intensifying wonder, culminating at the Grand Canyon of the Yellowstone River. Wylie's description of this climactic place is typical: "This is the part of the Park that tongue or pen can give no adequate account of" (59). By almost every description, ending a tour of the park with a visit to this place is a transformative experience. Indeed, forty years after Wylie, Joe Mitchell Chapple concluded his guidebook for automobile tourists with a description of the Grand Canyon of the Yellowstone that begins with this single-sentence paragraph: "Here is Yellowstone transcendent!" (63).

Kenneth Burke defined "transcendence" in *Attitudes Toward History* as "the adoption of another point of view from which [opposites] cease to be opposites" (336), and later as the consequence of a successful dialectical exchange through which individual motives are transformed into motives that are shared with the others with whom the individual is engaged (*Grammar* 422). My point is that a firsthand encounter with a place that has been given the symbolic meaning of a public experience—the sort of experience people share when they leave their homes to witness together the spectacle of the Grand Canyon of the Yellowstone—prompts a transformation in one's sense of identity. Such places wield rhetorical power through the experiences they offer that enable people to imagine themselves—despite the distances and differences that actually divide them at home—as a national community. The members of that national community then perpetuate the power of that image among themselves with photographs, postcards, and souvenirs, as well as written and oral descriptions that they take with them out of the park and back to their separate homes.

This is a long way around to a point that can be stated quite briefly. When individual Americans gather in an uninhabitable landscape that has been rendered publicly symbolic of their nation, they can experience themselves as a national community. Images of this experience prepare them, and prompt them later, to recognize and remember this collective identity they felt there. Places in the national landscape that symbolize a common homeland but are, in fact, no one's home, can school people in a common identity. Embedded in this point are two observations about rhetorical education in America. First, rhetorical education—understood as an education in the collective identity of citizenship that enables rhetorical participation—seems to be pervasive in Americans' cultural experience. Second, public discourse in that culture may be sustained on the foundation of that sense of collective identity that follows, for individuals, from what I am calling here "public experiences." When individuals share experiences that have been rendered symbolic of their community, those experiences themselves—whether of language or of landscape—wield considerable rhetorical power.

# IV
# Rhetorical Education:
# Back to the Future

## 10

# (Re) Turning to Aristotle

## Metaphor and the
## Rhetorical Education of Students

*Sherry Booth and Susan Frisbie*

Over the last decade, a number of scholars, notably Robert Scholes in *The Rise and Fall of English,* have issued calls to return rhetoric to the center of English education. To do so may save English from the fate of the dodo—and of classics departments—and also make rhetoric the core around which to unify the various facets of English education, from composition to literature to creative writing. We concur that rhetoric and a rhetorical education are central, not just to traditional English departments, but to students who will, over the course of their lives, participate in the academic world, in business and government, and in public, civil discourse. Rhetoric offers a bridge between worlds private and public, academic and civil—and we argue that the role of metaphor is a central place to begin. Metaphor's power to create knowledge is crucial to our students, as consumers and producers of texts. By spelling out metaphors, investigating the narratives buried within them, and examining the assumptions that framed their creation, we can lead our students to a richer understanding of how metaphor, like language more generally, can shape, reshape, and even create a reality.

Lauded as the "most beautiful of *tropes*" (Quintilian) and excoriated as a "perfect cheat" (Locke 3:105), metaphor over the centuries has been praised and pilloried, sometimes by the same individual. Aristotle, for example, believed command of metaphor "the greatest thing by far" but distrusted its use in argument (*Rhetoric and Poetics* 5–7). In the Middle Ages, metaphor was linked to the allegorical rather than to individual expression; in the Renaissance, writers from Shakespeare to Donne reveled in the copiousness of language and used metaphor in ways later considered extravagant. Dr. Samuel Johnson, for example, criticized the use of metaphor by the metaphysical poets: "The most heterogeneous ideas are yoked by violence together," but in spite of his criticism also evinces grudging respect for them, because even though "the reader commonly thinks his improvement dearly bought, . . . [the poets'] learning instructs, and their subtilty [sic] surprises" (1:14). The Romantic poets tended to be less ambivalent, seeing "metaphor as inseparable from language" (Hawkes 90). Shelley's view melds the aesthetic, linguistic, and cognitive: ". . . language is vitally metaphorical; that is, it marks the before unapprehended relations of things, and perpetuates their apprehension, until words which represent them, become through time signs for portions or classes of thoughts instead of pictures of integral thoughts . . . " ("Defense of Poetry" 791).

Poets, novelists, rhetoricians, linguists, educators, and philosophers who have attempted to define metaphor and its role in human communication tend to polarize into two positions that can be roughly labeled as the classical and the romantic (Hawkes 90). Andrew Ortony uses "non-constructivism" and "constructivism" to describe these opposing views. Nonconstructivists hold the classical view of "metaphor as deviant and parasitic upon normal usage" whereas constructivists take the romantic view of metaphor "as an essential characteristic of the creative use of language" (2). Most twentieth-century theorists bear the romantic/constructivist standard, positing metaphor not as an appendage, easily removed from speech and writing, but as a natural and organic aspect of language, which itself is metaphorical: it stands for the essence and nuance of presumed physical and intangible realities with which it shares no formal ground.

While critics who have thought diligently about metaphor may agree, many of us—teachers and students—hold no such informed opinion, because it is a topic that we may not have systematically considered. If we rely on most handbooks, old or new, we find metaphor defined as a figure of speech, a thing, static. James Seitz notes that the "prevailing definition of metaphor remains almost identical" across composition handbooks (38), focused on its similarity to, and formal difference from, simile. In composition we are left with a simplistic view that urges teachers to help students avoid mixed or strained metaphors but does not address the role of metaphor in conveying and receiving—in constructing—meaning. Fortunately, composition handbooks are not the latest word. In discussions of literature and creative writing, we find a richer treatment of metaphor. The name most commonly associated with the literary analysis of metaphor is I. A. Richards, who was the first to attempt to analyze and name the "two ideas" in metaphor. His analysis offered the now familiar terms *tenor* and *vehicle,* but his great contribution was his assertion that metaphor is natural and "omnipresent" in the language of all speakers (91). Next, Kenneth Burke suggested that we consider metaphor as "perspectival incongruity." Looking back at this analysis of metaphor in the literary context, Paul Ricoeur argues that Richards "made the breakthrough" (84) in analyzing the ways words in metaphor interact in "the living utterance" (79). In one sense, this tradition introduced by Richards has continued in literary considerations of metaphor, such as those found in handbooks of literary terms. However in the last fifteen years, with the shift to postmodern schools of literary theory, the emphasis on metaphor in literary criticism has declined, replaced by attention to feminist, new historicist, postcolonial, and other theoretical approaches.

Unlike the situation in literature, attention to language has remained central to creative writing, both theory and pedagogy. Evidence of this appears in creative writing textbooks, such as the widely adopted *Writing Fiction: A Guide to Narrative Craft* (6th ed.) by Janet Burroway. Her treatment of metaphor is undergirded by theory, seen in her assertion that "Comparison is not a frivolity. It is, on the contrary, the primary business of the brain. [ . . . ] metaphors acknowledge [ . . . ] that comparison is the basis of all learning and all reasoning" (328). Such assertions, however, are not discussed in depth but are followed by examples and analysis of particular metaphors from fiction, not surprising given that this is a creative writing textbook, aimed ultimately at helping students generate metaphor themselves. Thus, despite the greater discussion in creative writing, the deepest, most useful and illuminating work on metaphor comes from other disciplines, where the links between metaphor and cognition appear to be firmly established.

Linguist Max Black, for example, argues for the cognitive function of metaphor because a "special, emergent 'new thing' is created when a novel metaphor is understood—something new that is attributable to the metaphor rather than to its novelty" (Ortony 10). Andrew Goatly believes that "metaphor and the mental processes it entails . . . are basic to language and cognition" (1), and George Lakoff and Mark Johnson articulate, from linguistic evidence, metaphor not as "a device of the poetic imagination and rhetorical flourish" but "pervasive in everyday life, not just in language but in thought and action" (3). Eva Feder Kittay stresses metaphor's cognitive function. A complete theory of metaphor will, she suggests, "advance our understanding of cognitive and creative processes" (9). Investigation into metaphor, then, provides certain kinds of insight into the way the mind works.

## A Process Definition of Metaphor

Given the limitations of the traditional handbook definitions of metaphor, more useful are definitions developed by linguists and philosophers of language. We turn again to Richards, who began such analysis, writing that "In the simplest formulation, when we use a metaphor we have two thoughts of different things active together and supported by a single word or phrase, whose meaning is a resultant of their interaction" (93) (echoes of Dr. Johnson's "two ideas for one"). Note that Richards is describing action—"we use metaphor"—not defining a static thing. Like language itself, like rhetoric and the rhetorical situation, metaphor is a process, an action, a combining. We argue that metaphor is not an artifact (nor art, nor fact). It is a process of creation and association that involves developing or recognizing a fundamental but not necessarily obvious link between two elements, one or both of which may be explicitly present in the text of the metaphor. (In the metaphor "Investment is the fuel that runs the engine of the American economy," both elements are present. The following example provides one element, in context: "There's a cancer on the Presidency.")

## How Metaphor Works

Major scholars on metaphor, regardless of discipline, basically agree on what metaphor does to the mind of the perceiver, though they use different terminology. The first important feature is incongruity, the key to metaphor. Metaphor cannot simply be paraphrased—it is not reducible—because of the "incongruity between the domains of the topic [tenor] and the vehicle" (Kittay 37). Metaphors create "incongruity" (Burke, "Four" 423), "surprise" (Sticht 485), or "cognitive anomaly" (Petrie 444) when a reader or hearer recognizes, at some level of awareness, that an assertion (metaphor) that is literally untrue is being presented as a speech act that in fact conveys meaning. The resulting attempt to "make sense" of metaphor forces the reader to "accommodate his/her cognitive structure to account for the anomaly" thus created (Petrie 444). A "successful" metaphor thus paradoxically orients the reader through apparent disorientation. A complex locus of social, experiential, and linguistic and syntactic elements makes this apparent paradox viable. The metaphor must be expressed in such a way that it shares with its literal analog enough specific and translucent features to allow the connection to register, but not so many that the connection is obvious, easily and epigrammatically reducible. Most of us are so facile in dealing with metaphor that we are oblivious to the fine lines on either side, one crossing into the literal, the other into the inscrutable.

Scholars also concur on the process of this accommodation, though they again use different terminology. It is described as "perspectival incongruity" (Burke, "Four" 423), or as a process that involves "mapping," "regrouping," "reordering," and "restructuring" features in two domains (Schön 278), or as "triangulation" from more familiar to less familiar or even unfamiliar experience (Petrie 450). Accommodating the metaphor is an "iterative process of successive approximations" from a more to a less familiar domain (Ortony 16). When the process works effectively, the perceiver comes to new knowledge. Significantly, all the scholars mentioned use verbs like "examine," "inquire," "attend to," and "construe" to describe how metaphor must be engaged in order for cognitive shifts to register consciously.

## Generative Metaphors

Donald Schön argues that some metaphors—not all, but those he calls "generative"—both reveal and further shape our view, or in his words, "frame" the issue. For Schön, narrative is a central organizing principle: to make sense of the myriad images and information we receive daily, we create a narrative of events to explain what is happening or what has happened. It is here, in this narrative description, that metaphor plays a crucial role, helping us create a "story" we can make sense of and identify with. We are all familiar with the experience of telling a story from different perspectives, adding or deleting—or altering—details depending on our observations, feelings, thoughts. This selection process is driven by the metaphor maker's worldview, which comes out of the nexus of assumptions, life experiences, moral and religious beliefs, political affiliations, and so on that shape us. This is an ideological as well as cognitive aspect of metaphor. Ideologically, metaphorizing differs from categorizing because when we create metaphors, we categorize ad hoc on the basis of particular interests (Kittay 22). While metaphors often seem superficially clear and pleasing, at the same time they are complex and messy, their inner workings invisible to the unreflecting—and often unsuspecting—reader. We need to help our students understand these aspects of metaphor, thereby making them better readers and more audience-aware writers.

Consider, for example, how Schön applies his investigation into metaphoric frames to social policy and urban planning. Although introducing metaphor into such controversies is not always troublesome, Schön examines how in certain situations, some metaphors in effect enclose or frame a narrative that is far more than merely descriptive. If metaphor were merely decorative, as the classical view has it, then it would pose no problem because a decoration can be removed, detached. But as Schön's examples demonstrate, metaphor is not just decorative; "generative" metaphors contain what appear to be natural conclusions to the narrative being told about the problem, and thus the "solutions" are naturalized (262–68).

Using an urban housing example, one common "generative" metaphor posits slums as "cancer." Clearly, if the complex issue of urban housing is seen in terms of a deadly disease, then the housing must be cured, cut out, eradicated. But, as Schön notes, another group might frame the issue very differently, employing a very different metaphor and thus foregrounding a different set of variables and a different end, or solution, to the narrative. For example, what one person or group might see as urban cancer, others might perceive as an island in a swelling sea of gentrified neighborhoods, an island that has arisen gradually to meet various human needs, such as low-cost housing, familiar landscapes and structures, and sustained and sustaining relationships among the inhabitants. If framed this way, Schön would argue, the solution would hardly be to cut out or eliminate the very housing that the residents depend on, because their "island" is a safe haven amid the threatening sea of higher rents and social and human dislocation. Metaphor is obviously deeply implicated in many such frame conflicts. If Nixon had accepted John Dean's metaphor of "a cancer on the Presidency," he might have acted to avoid his own systematic political demise. When Operation Desert Shield, an apt metaphor for a militarily defensive exercise, changed to an offensive endeavor, it became Operation Desert Storm: an unstoppable regional force of nature (imagine instead, for example, Operation American Saber).

## Metaphor, Local Sites, and Social Contexts

Increasing our understanding of metaphor, and passing our insights along to our students, is more difficult than it might appear, particularly if we look to composition textbooks (as we did) for guidance. Textbooks reflect and shape practice. It is troubling to see in them a representation of metaphor so contrary to the view of those most aware of metaphor's cognitive force, its potential to shape a writer's prose or a reader's views. Scholars on metaphor can do for us as teachers precisely what these scholars say metaphors themselves do—provide a new way of perceiving how central metaphor is in language and, by extension, in a rhetorical education.

Our own classroom experiences illustrate metaphor's cognitive function. Some years ago we were part of a collaborative project to enhance coherence across first-year composition classes at our university. To that end, we chose a common text, Mike Rose's *Lives on the Boundary,* which engaged us in part because it addressed a topic we felt had been neglected at our small, private university: how factors such as race, class, and gender affect access to higher education in America. Rose's book provided not only an interesting personal narrative but also extensive analysis and interpretation. It is important to consider the political and social context surrounding our project: the 1994 national election, since identified as the opening salvo of the Republican Revolution (a bellicose metaphor discussed later). The contentious debates over welfare reform, the role of government, affirmative action in business and education, immigration, and women's issues created an unsettled climate in the United States (consider, incidentally, the metaphorical implications of "climate"—as contrasted to, for example, "season" or "weather"). The competing ideologies behind these debates naturally found their way into the university classroom and were reflected in students' responses to Rose's book. In this historical moment we examined how ambient cultural metaphors might affect our students' perception of, and reaction to, issues and the texts that communicate them. We looked in particular at how students in our classes internalized, applied, and adapted metaphor from a common text, and at novel metaphors in their responses to the text.

Schön's "frame conflict" theory (269) describes exactly what we experienced that year. Outside our classrooms, two competing narratives— conservative and liberal—were framed by generative metaphors, each telling the story of the current condition of the United States, the causes of that condition, and, by implication, the solution(s). The metaphors framing the Right's narrative included war, corruption, and decay. Target loci included the government and especially institutions serving the poor, such as public education. We've all become familiar with the phrases "culture wars" and "Republican Revolution," which clearly frame the debate over social issues as so desperately dangerous that the entire nation is in peril. So pervasive and imminent is the threat, in fact, that all that's left is to arm ourselves and prepare to fire in defense—or "lock and load" in Pat Buchanan's famous phrase, beginning a second American Revolution.

Behind the call to armed conflict are equally pervasive metaphors of contamination and decay. George Will, urging election of Republican candidates, complained of the "curdled 103rd Congress" and recommended electing neophytes because "currently the talent pool from which elected officials are drawn is small and brackish" (92). William Bennett uses the frame of illness: "The disease of Congress runs deeper than any process of reform can cure. . . . Rot is beginning to set in" (231). Newt Gingrich uses this rot metaphor to conclude his *Contract with America:* "To renew or to decay, that is the choice each of us makes, one at a time, day by day. To renew or decay." Expressed metaphorically, the problem—rot has spread throughout various governmental systems such as education—contains the solution. Rot must be cut out, amputated, all of it, as far as it has spread. And if the rot has taken over the entire organism, then the situation calls for extreme measures.

Attitudes like Will's and Gingrich's are contested by many in the educational establishment, whose generative metaphors might be the same, but framed differently. Rot—of course. But for this more liberal group, it is the status quo that causes decay. Rose's *Lives on the Boundary,* a personal and academic critique of the status quo, highlights the metaphors pervasive in the profession—metaphors of boundary and territory, illness and wellness, and conversation and invitation. Rose too uses metaphors of contest and struggle (if not war, then sports), but almost always to describe the harm done not to the nation, the group as a whole, but to individuals, to students, to children.

Sometimes the harm comes from the profession itself, which uses medical terminology to "diagnose" and "treat" the child. Rose writes of the medieval goddess of grammar, Grammatica, pictured with pincers and scalpel—a reminder to teachers who must inspect students' work for error and "cut it out with the coldest tool" (2). He criticizes "the atomistic, medical model of [the] language" (210) used in schools: metaphors of testing, diagnosing, clinical settings and reports, assessments and final evaluations. "The supreme irony . . . is that the very means we use to determine [student] needs—and the various remedial procedures that derive from them—can wreak profound harm on our children," especially the poor (127).

Rose uses metaphors of friendship and romance to indicate how teachers can connect with students, speaking of "relationships," "invitation," and "intellectual embrace." The book describes powerfully how various students are affected by the presence or absence of the sorts of rich conversations—with books, with ideas, with teachers—that Rose benefited from. Rose couches the story of teaching in metaphors of conversing, of learning a specialized language of the academy, of learning how to read, write, and think as part of a larger discussion. From this conversation comes the chance for him and the students he writes about to cross boundaries, to enter new realms. Rose uses other travel or space metaphors too, especially for the transcending or liberating experience of students: his mentor Jack McFarland gave him a "Baedeker to a vocabulary of ideas" (36); his Loyola professors gave him "cognitive maps" by which to navigate new domains of knowledge.

We had hoped that Rose's metaphor-rich text would help students appreciate the problems he addresses. But we found that metaphors can be extremely problematic. We had recognized from the start that many of the students at our privileged university were not familiar with Rose's perspective, the notion that access to a good education is often seriously enhanced or hampered by factors of race and class (and, we would add, gender). The predictable (at least in retrospect) happened: many students experienced not cognitive growth but cognitive dissonance, caused, as we came to see, by the clash of differing conceptual schemes revealed by analysis of metaphors. Our students' experiences suggest that metaphors may complicate, not clarify, the already complex processes of reading, thinking, and writing clearly, let alone coming to new knowledge.

Our intent was not to polemicize but to help students see issues more clearly, consider them more fully, and articulate their own views more lucidly. The metaphors students identified with, and used, reflected their own perceptions and opinions. And their discomfort with views they did not share, and in most cases had never considered, was reflected in their discomfort with the metaphors expressing those alien views. Metaphor reminds us of how difficult acquiring new knowledge can be. Thoughtful teachers have long known that the place to begin is with the familiar: "If we insist, as current conventional wisdom would have it, that learning must always start with what the student presently knows, then we are faced with the problem of how the student can come to know something radically new" (Petrie 440). When students are taught how to examine how metaphor functions, metaphor itself becomes the means to knowledge: "Metaphor is one of the central ways of leaping the epistemological chasm between old knowledge and radically new knowledge" (440). Metaphor acts like a wormhole, moving readers to a new understanding that could only be achieved much more laboriously and deliberately through conventional linear explication.

What we had hoped would happen—and what philosophers of language say can happen—did not, because we had not paid sufficient attention to the link between metaphor and rhetoric. For our students to be able to work with metaphor, they must understand how metaphor works. And grasping metaphor as a reader/consumer or writer/producer requires a greater understanding of the elements and assumptions at play in any rhetorical situation: purpose, audience, author, material, and medium.

To help students do this kind of analysis, we need to help them hone their analytical and empathetic abilities by asking critical questions, which are in fact rhetorical questions: What does the material tell us about what the speaker has assumed the audience already knows? How does the tone of the speech support the speaker's purpose? How might the same tone strike a different audience? How might a pamphlet with the same text achieve a different purpose than a live speech? Such analysis can be difficult because the elements may not be easy to pin down, because the text provides insufficient clues, or because students lack certain critical extratextual information. For example, a complete analysis of the variable of audience in relation to the Declaration of Independence requires an understanding of the historical context on both sides of the Atlantic.

Creating and analyzing metaphors involve exactly the same variables, with at least some elements, by definition, not explicit in the text. The presumption of common experience and perspective that underlies all successful rhetoric is particularly important, and fragile, in metaphor. To understand, for example, how George Bush's metaphor of "a thousand points of light" works, one must presume an audience sympathetic to Bush's political agenda (note that Bush's political opponents claimed, rather disingenuously, not to understand his metaphor); one must discern the difference between a thousand points of light and a single, central source of illumination; one must know that Bush supported charity but opposed large-scale government welfare programs; one must understand that Bush was speaking in that context; one must have positive associations with light—and, with all that, perhaps one can process the metaphor.

This process of addressing metaphor may be more extensive than is required in some "standard" instances of rhetorical analysis and may include a higher proportion of wild cards, but it is not substantively different. One can, in fact, argue that metaphor exists not apart from conventional rhetoric but as part of a matrix in which some variables of audience and tone are more tightly controlled and more clearly delineated and other variables of material and purpose have to be inferred.

Not surprisingly, students did not take (no doubt because we had not yet learned to help provide) such a systematic approach. A review of student responses to Rose's work and its collateral issues—from papers to questionnaires to a timed-writing assignment—showed our students in various stages of learning and/or confusion, reflecting varying degrees of cognitive dissonance and cognitive growth. For some, especially students of color, there was little dissonance between Rose's story and the metaphors he employed. His metaphors—and the "truths" they contained—meshed with their own stories and metaphors. These students often, seemingly unconsciously, generated metaphors reminiscent of Rose's, metaphors of boundaries, of illness, of conversation. One young woman wrote a paper in which she attempted to explain to her more privileged classmates how she often felt. When she, a Chicana, walked into her engineering classes, she said she was "a bum in Bloomingdale's" (R-4).[1] Nor were most of these students troubled when it came to the final timed-writing assignment; they simply adopted Rose's metaphors, using them to explain their own position in response to the question (which asked them which of two editorials on access to education they found more "effective"). Rose's metaphors became a kind of linguistic shorthand, especially valuable under timed-writing conditions, but their rhetorical control of their essays suggested that the shorthand was just that—an abbreviation of a position, a perspective, they understood deeply.

Similarly, students whose experiences more closely matched that of privileged conservatives also had little difficulty with metaphors, either in addressing Rose's or in proffering their own. For these students, Rose and his metaphors were easy to analyze, attack, and refute. We had never, of course, insisted on a political agenda for our project, so these students freely appropriated the war and disease metaphors, a choice that reflected a political position as well as a rhetorical strategem. But we ourselves had not yet fully realized how metaphor and frame almost always grew out of ideology, so we were underprepared to show students the ideological grounds and the embedded frames and stories in Rose's metaphors and in the ones they chose. One student, for example, argued that everyone would feel better if the United States had a *filtration* system for education, one that channeled students into either academic or vocational programs from an early age, a metaphor with interesting associations of science, purification, and health.

For a fortunate few, metaphor performed its cognitive function, leading them to new knowledge about the lives of others. At first we did not recognize what had happened in some of these cases and thought that such students were applying Mike Rose's metaphors to their own far different lives, claiming for themselves a status as "sufferer" that by any external valuation they would certainly not warrant. For instance, one honors program standout wrote about her own life beyond a boundary, burdened with a label: a GATE (gifted and talented education) student! At first we wanted to protest, to insist that the comparison between her and Mike Rose was silly, revealing that under her privileged label she hadn't really been exposed to, and so had not grasped the perils of, the marginalization Rose addresses. But in fact, this student *was* using Rose's metaphors to help her negotiate the gap between her life of middle-class security and educational advantage and the reality of those other lives and stories Rose tells.

Some students were not as successful in arriving at new knowledge and experienced considerable cognitive dissonance. The timed writing—quite predictably—was the occasion for verbal meltdown, resulting in not just mixed, but jumbled, metaphors, such as the following from a student who wanted to side with the article favoring reduced admissions to colleges, based on rigorous testing, but also wanted to endorse the traditional American view of education as the key to success and opportunity: "While this system may be reducing the luster of the 'American Dream,' it is ensuring a greater level of success and reducing the disillusionment of not achieving the dream" (U-18). Another student misquotes Rose and combines Rose's metaphor of students rising to the level a teacher sets for them with the student's own metaphor, thus fracturing Rose's metaphor and meaning in revealing ways: "Mike Rose says that 'students float to the margins' set for them. If we close down schools, where are all those floaters to go?" "Raise the margin," the student continues, "and the number of educated people will also rise" (J-10). Two other students wrote the following sentences, revealing their confusion: "Henry's [author of the conservative article] views caused tidal waves of restraint" (K-15); and "I have a huge container of mixed feelings and true emotions churning inside me regarding education" (S-6).

What we have learned about metaphor, not least from analyzing our own students' manipulation of, and by, metaphor, has shaped our views about the role of metaphor in rhetorical education. But how precisely to teach metaphor remains the problem, for a number of related reasons. First, metaphor seems natural, if not invisible, because of the profusion of dead metaphors that have become literal: terms like "branch banks," "greenhouse effect," "spin-offs," "organizational deadwood," and "underground economy" no longer raise more than an image of the thing described.

But what about metaphors that are fresh, or generative, that have the power to function cognitively? James Seitz argues that teachers of English fail to mobilize metaphor "not because [they] lack . . . interest in change but because it is far from certain just what sort of change such a perspective on metaphor should bring to the teaching of English. . . . Paradoxically, what may prove most instructive about metaphor is the extent which it refuses instruction" (49–50). Seitz then moves to Aristotle's claim that metaphor alone cannot be taught, a statement that seems to end the discussion. But, with apologies to Aristotle, we *can* make metaphor part of rhetorical education. For what rhetoric offers students is the knowledge of how to "read" a metaphor and thus to understand better how language operates. The metaphors we use to teach should come from various locations: literature, the belletristic essay, the technical report, the speeches of politicians and public figures, the anthologized essay. A variety of texts will demonstrate compellingly how pervasive—and persuasive—metaphor is. It is easier to teach students first to recognize and analyze metaphor in texts than to create their own, and the more analytical experience they get, the greater their potential to create metaphor in their own writing.

## A Rhetorical Education and the Role of Metaphor in the Twenty-first Century

Every age constructs a rhetoric that both maintains and attempts to promulgate the values of that culture at its particular historical moment. We need to ask ourselves what our cultural values are and what rhetoric best expresses and promotes those values. For the Greeks and Romans, the ideal of good citizens participating in the discourses of political, judicial, and ceremonial acts was paramount, and the education given to (appropriate male) members of the group was intended to create, to shape, an involved citizenry. This approach prevailed at least until the Renaissance, when another set of values emerged that largely reduced rhetoric to the study of style, of schemes and tropes. The point here is simple—different ages value different things, and thinkers, writers, artists, and the broader population choose to invest time and energy into those topics that seem most important at that historical moment. A rhetorical education at the dawn of the twenty-first century reflects— or should reflect—the major preoccupations, media, and modes of our time.

The "central preoccupation of our time," writes Michael Holquist in his introduction to Bakhtin, "[is] language" (xvii). Holquist, of course, is not the only one who sees language at the heart of human life. In their insightful introduction to twentieth-century rhetoric in *The Rhetorical Tradition: Readings from Classical Times to the Present,* Patricia Bizzell and Bruce Herzberg write that "the themes of language and meaning, ethics and ideology, and argument and knowledge recur and overlap at each stage in the formulation of rhetorical theories during the twentieth century" (899). Thinkers as diverse as Richards, Burke, Derrida, and Foucault are each, in fact, grappling with basic questions about language, the answers to which have had profound effects on our understanding of how language works, and profound effects on how we choose to teach writing in college classrooms. We hope we have sketched the outlines of what, in part, a rhetorical education might look like at the end of one century and the beginning of another, and what role metaphor can play in this education.

Bizzell and Herzberg provide a definition of rhetoric that reissues the call to return rhetoric to its central place in education.

> Rhetoric still means the practice of effective speaking and effective writing; rhetoric still means teaching the strategies for effective discourse; but rhetoric, drawing on centuries of theoretical analysis of the relation between discourse and psychology, between discourse and social order, between discourse and knowledge, is also a field of inquiry, a complex and sensitive theory of language that seeks to describe its operation in human affairs. (919)

Not surprisingly, the above definition also applies to metaphor. Metaphor, as a means to provide a new perspective or to persuade, links language and psychology and spans the spectrum of human endeavor and inquiry. Schön's analysis of metaphor's role makes clear how social issues can be framed as both problem and solution. Heather Brodie Graves and Roger Graves's current investigation of metaphor in technical communication demonstrates the above definition of rhetoric in action—as a "sensitive theory of language that seeks to describe its operation in human affairs"—in that their analysis reveals disturbing metaphors with insidious effects on the way humans are figured into technology. For example, "infant mortality" as a metaphor to describe the failure of a newly delivered technological device blurs the line between human and machine in troubling ways (389). These brief examples remind us of how important it is for readers and writers to analyze texts—and the texts' metaphors—rhetorically to determine: Who is speaking? Who is addressed? What assumptions about the world frame the writer's language choices? What end or whose interests are being served? The need for such questions extends far beyond college writing classrooms into the daily lives of students who are and will be citizens, workers, and leaders.

To rhetoricians, ancient or modern, rhetoric is a means to both synthesis and analysis, a series of moves for readers and writers who need, as Scholes argues, an understanding of both a "usable cultural past" and the "cultural present" (104). Metaphor, as a constant component of rhetoric through the ages, has a role to play in English studies as our students negotiate the contemporary world. Students, all citizens, in fact, require many different kinds of literacies—print, electronic, television, film, and advertising—to function effectively in civil and academic spheres, and metaphor pervades all of these. The study of metaphor is inseparable from the study of language, and language as a means to communicate, to persuade, to explicate—in short, to play a role in human affairs—is rhetoric. By studying metaphor, learning how it functions in deeply cognitive ways, and in turn by teaching metaphor to students, we can be part of a revived practical and useful rhetorical education for students as civil members of a society increasingly rife with incivility. Sustained and careful attention to metaphoric language at various levels can enable students to be critical readers and writers of texts of all kinds: personal, political, and academic.

## Notes

1. All student papers used in this project were assigned a number and letter identifier to ensure students' anonymity.

# 11

# Cyberliteracy

## Toward a New Rhetorical Consciousness

*Laura J. Gurak*

By "literacy" I mean . . . not only the ability to read and write but
an activity of the mind . . . capable of recognizing and engaging
substantive issues along with the ways that minds, sensibilities,
and emotions are constructed by and within communities whose
members communicate through specific technologies. In other
words, literacy has to do with consciousness: how we know what
we know and a recognition of the historical, ideological and technological forces that inevitably operate in all human beings.

Kathleen Welch, *Electric Rhetoric* 67

There's no turning back. Once a novelty, the Internet is now
transforming how Americans live, think, talk, and love; how we
get to school, make money, see the doctor, and elect presidents.
This isn't just about the future—it's about the here and now.

*Newsweek* special report on e-Life 39

Until recently, this quote from *Newsweek* may have been impossible
to comprehend. Yet today, many of us live in a constantly mediated
state between our physical lives and our virtual ones (voice-mail boxes,
e-mail, and chat sites). We do all of this without thinking very much
about it, despite the fact that this way of living is radically different from
what most of humankind has experienced until now. And we do it, almost
always, without much critical observation of our behavior. We're almost
too busy moving along the superhighway, the metaphor that brought us
to this place, to stop and wonder how much we like it, how it affects our

social spaces, or whether the current Internet offers the best model for the long-term good of society.

I must admit that, in many ways, I like our new world, where the global blends with the local, the physical with the virtual, the human with the machine. But, on the other hand, I am not always happy with all the prospects of our wired lives: more and more of the Internet is being commercialized; people seem far more edgy after a long day online; personal privacy is completely up for grabs in cyberspace; students write based on the coded templates and forms created by Microsoft. Yet what we teach, for the most part, is how to *use* the technology, not how to critique it, participate in it, and take control of it. We don't need any more manuals on how to create a Web site. What we need instead is a new literacy, a critical literacy for this new medium, one that should be at the heart of rhetorical education in the twenty-first century. Unless we become familiar with the rhetorical features of digital communication, we will be led into cyberspace with only a limited understanding of both the power of and the problems with this technology. To become cyberliterate, we need to understand the new rhetorics of digital space so we become more sophisticated about critiquing, challenging, and anticipating these technologies.

By thus inviting readers to view the Internet with a critical eye, this essay offers background and key concepts for rhetorical education and cyberliteracy. It asks us to be active participants in cyberspace and suggests that, to be truly literate online, we must understand the technology historically and contextually. Cyberliteracy involves, as Welch suggests, a *conscious* interaction with the new technologies: one that embraces and enjoys the technology but at the same time is critical, looking beyond the pretty Web images or speedier data connections that dominate our image of cyberspace.

## Literacy as Consciousness

What is cyberliteracy? The term *literacy* is a highly contested one; a brief overview of this discussion will help illustrate how I am using the concept in my notion of cyberliteracy. In addition, an overview of literacy leads to the logical conclusion that, in the digital age, this concept must be reconfigured if it is to be a useful heuristic and critical tool for the sorts of discourse that will take place in the future.

Kathleen Tyner provides a succinct overview of the history of literacy scholarship. She notes that, in general, the term *literacy* is often equated with the ability to read and write. Before World War II, literacy scholars wrote about "literacy as a tool for transforming higher psychological processes" (25). This perspective—that being skilled in print literacy over oral culture was somehow transformative and brought people to a "higher level" of cognitive ability—valued certain abilities over others, and scholars were making vast judgments about the superiority of cultures. Western cultures, living in the post-Gutenberg world of print, were, according to this pre–World War II work, superior to many traditional, indigenous cultures, cultures that communicated their history and cultural knowledge via oral communication (stories, poetry, song, and so on).

As anthropology and other studies of human society became more culturally sensitive, this older view of literacy was contested, and what became evident is that what counts as literacy in one culture may not in another. Tyner characterizes current scholarship on literacy as research that values "literacy as discourse" (28). All forms of discourse are a form of literacy, depending on the context, culture, and situation. Electronic discourse is no exception.

And yet, popular understandings of the term *literacy* often harken back to an earlier period of time, valuing reading and print over any other form of communication. This view of literacy is what might be labeled as "performative": that is, the ability to do something is what counts. We hear about literacy in this way almost every day when we watch the television news or read the paper and learn that people need to become more "computer literate" or "technology literate," which, translated, usually means that these people need to learn how to use a computer and keyboard. (See figure 1.) Indeed, this view of literacy is so common that it makes difficult the task of enacting cyberliteracy, which relies on the ability to understand, criticize, and make judgments about a technology's interactions with and effects on culture. In addition to literacy as performance, most people understand literacy to mean "print," and thus we have come to favor the book over the screen. As Welch, Tyner, and others have argued, print dominance has profound implications for higher education because, while students spend hours watching television and playing on the computer, their schoolwork still focuses on printed books.

## Cyberliteracy and Secondary Orality

Walter Ong's work is a useful place to augment this print-limited view of literacy and help open up the discussion to include cyberdiscourse.

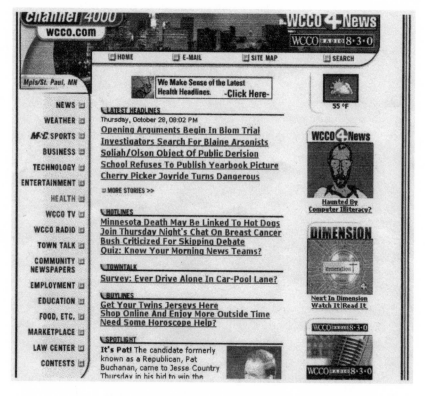

1. This television station Web site features a Halloween pun link, asking if anyone is "haunted by computer illiteracy." Clicking on this link sends you to a story about how to become more "literate" in the performative sense: that is, how you can become better at using computers and the Internet. This definition of computer literacy is probably the most common, and it does not suggest anything like a critical cyberliteracy.

Ong, whose notion of secondary orality is often used to help describe the kinds of language appearing on cyberforums (e-mail, Usenet news, the Web), has also been criticized for some of his thoughts that appear to make biased claims suggesting the inevitability of print and the superiority of those who live in the Gutenberg world. Ong has taken his share of criticism, and he has since modified his position.[1] Such views about the superiority of print over oral literacies can be viewed as racist and culturally biased because they favor the white, European, post-Gutenberg world of print over numerous other oral traditions. Yet Ong's specific concept of "secondary orality" is helpful in relation to cyberliteracy and can be invoked in a way that does not bias one view over another. Others, too, have also found this concept useful in relation to computer-mediated communication, and the reasons become obvious with a simple analysis of almost any e-mail message or Usenet news posting (figure 2).

According to Ong, secondary orality suggests new forms of communication, ones that combine features of print culture with those of oral culture. Like print, electronic text is typed. It is fixed in a medium, for however long, and, like a printed book, can be distributed widely.[2] Yet like oral communication, electronic text, particularly e-mail messages and online chats, sounds more liked typed conversations than formal printed texts. Spelling and capitalization are often ignored, for example. Ong identifies nine features of oral discourse; Welch (184–86) and others have used these features to analyze electronic text. For example, Ong notes that an oral style is "additive rather than subordinative" (37). Ong's characteristics of oral discourse—that it be abbreviated, redundant, conservative, agonistically toned, empathetic, participatory, homeostatic, situational, and that it close the human lifeworld—are useful in seeing how the "written" texts of electronic discussions and e-mail resemble both writing and speech (again, see figures 1 and 2).

For the purposes of this essay, it is the overall concept of secondary orality rather than a point-by-point analysis that is most useful, because the concept helps us see that cyberliteracy is not purely a print literacy, nor is it purely an oral literacy. It is an electronic literacy that combines features of both print and the spoken word, and it does so in ways that change how we read, speak, think, and interact with others. By understanding that online texts are not exactly written and not exactly spoken, we begin to understand that cyberliteracy requires critical thinking skills, because online rhetoric is not quite like anything we have yet encountered. Written messages are usually created slowly and with more reflection, affording time for thought and revision as the document is chugging away at the printer. Electronic discourse, on the other hand, seems to encourage us to reply quickly, often in a more oral style. Traditional rules about writing, editing, and revising a document do not make much sense in this environment. So it is not adequate to simply assume a performative literacy stance and think that if we teach people to use computers, they will become "literate." Cyberliteracy, again noting Welch's epigram to this essay, is about consciousness. It is about taking a critical perspective on a technology that is radically transforming the world and about understanding how this technology changes certain ac-

2. A typical e-mail message contains features of writing and speech, illustrating Ong's notion of secondary orality and, more broadly, the idea that cyberliteracy requires reading and listening skills not usually accounted for in print. Notice that although the message is printed, normally a more formal form (like a letter), the replier is informal, signing her name "l-a" and using short phrases. The format is also "aggregative" in that each locution builds on the previous one.

cepted distinctions (such as writing versus speaking) and conventions (such as punctuation and spelling).

## A Brief Narrative of Western Literacy Technologies (One Version)

To be cyberliterate is to understand the relationship between our communication technologies and ourselves, our communities, and our cultures. It may be hard to see the effects of the Internet on our daily lives, in large part because we are living in the midst of these changes. Yet technologies play a part in how we view the world. A quick review of communication technologies in Western history reminds us of the relationship between communication technologies, rhetoric, and worldviews.

In the Western story of literacy and technology, we often begin by looking at the stone counting devices used by ancient people to keep track of commerce, such as the sale of domesticated animals or grain (Faigley). These technologies created what Kaufer and Carley call a "technological situation . . . a set of available [communication] technologies and their distribution across individuals in the society" (99). Along with word of mouth and memory, farmers and tradespeople could rely on these inscribed pieces of clay to remind them about who owed them a sheep or some wheat or barley. This technology increased the "reach" (Kaufer and Carley) of this communication, because individuals did not need to be near each other to have a record of their transaction. A similar discussion takes place around the papyrus scroll; Aristotle's manuscripts were the length that they were in part because they needed to fit the size of a standard scroll. Social conditions changed, as Plato's oft-quoted Phaedrus dialogue tells us, when people began to record oral discourse onto these paper scrolls.

And when the Catholic church controlled manuscripts, another set of social conditions was created: knowledge was in the hands of the priests and monks who maintained and copied these documents. As moveable type and the improved Gutenberg printing press caught on, everyday people could own a bible or a novel. Books, pamphlets, and who could print and own them became subject to many political battles but, in the end, the book—particularly the paperback—became what some would say is a very profound communication technology.[3] It is small and lightweight. It does not require batteries. You can read it and pass it along to someone else. Indeed, from stone etchings to paperback novels, the shapes we have given the technologies of reading and writing have in turn become the shapes of how we live with each other.

Next in this narrative come electronic technologies, which speeded up the transmission of information, increased reach and multiplicity (the number of people who receive the information; see Kaufer and Carley, 103), and began to move information from hard, tangible ink on the page to soft, electrified characters and sounds sent over wires. The impact of the telegraph and train, telephone, radio, and television has been studied widely by media critics, social historians, and historians and critics of technology. Each technology, based on the choices made when it was designed and developed, has changed the rhetorical context in which we live.

People born in the midst of a new technology, before it becomes ubiquitous, are often keenly aware of these social and cultural changes. Many of us in the forty-something age group learned to write first with paper and pencil, then with a typewriter. We then adapted our writing styles to word processing, then to the Web, but most of us still tend to rely on paper. People in their twenties and younger have been born into a world surrounded by screens and buttons and are more comfortable with writing, editing, and navigating completely within digital space because they were born into it. Before they can speak, infants watch people channel surf, press buttons on microwave ovens, and surf the Web. This generation does not create a document with the end goal of printing it (a feature of early word processing); what they produce on the screen often *is* the final product (a Web page, for example). Our technologies condition our comfort, and the more ubiquitous a technology is, the more natural it seems.

But the relationship between our communication technologies and our lives is not only a cognitive one. It is a political one as well. For example, we reach for old paradigms—laws, business ideas, political institutions—to create our new technological spaces. We often do this because it is easier to imagine a technology in terms of what we already understand. But also, the desire to create new technologies in relation to older ones operates so that certain power centers stay in control. On the Internet, this phenomenon is readily apparent. Even though the Internet inspires new models for business (grassroots, bottom-up sites where people are in control, such as eBay and other auctions), these sites are now being bought on the traditional stock market, with CEOs, profit margins, large mergers (like AOL and Time Warner), and so on. Another example is copyright, which by all thinking should be opening up in light of the ability to share via the Internet. But instead, copyright is getting even more restrictive: recent U.S. legislation just extended the term of copyright, and most proposed legislation favors copyright holders and not the public.

Cyberliteracy, then, takes into account many features. It recognizes that, on the Internet, communication is a blend of oral and written (as well as visual). Communication via cyberspace has broad reach like television but it is interactive like a conversation. In addition, the technology, like many before it, shapes our social spaces, replacing the slower methods of handwriting and typing with the speed and frenzy of digitized text. These features must be understood by anyone who teaches or performs research in rhetoric. But wait, there's more . . .

## Literacy as a Value System

One other facet of literacy must be considered when invoking a definition of cyberliteracy. In some cases, the term *literacy* not only means performance and reading/writing versus oral/spoken, it also ascribes exactly what one should read and write. E. D. Hirsch's *Cultural Literacy* is the paradigm case. Hirsch's canon of what counts as knowledge has been widely criticized for reasons similar to criticisms of the valuing of print over orality. Canons are always problematic, because what they include will always privilege some people's stories, plays, art, and ideas over others. Welch's definition of literacy at the end of the millennium reminds us that, as with all attempts to define what counts as literacy, cyberliteracy is also not value neutral. Drawing on her own analysis and the work of literacy theorist Brian Street, she argues that literacy in an age of electric rhetoric

> constitutes intersubjective activity in encoding and decoding screen and alphabetic texts within specific cultural practices and recognizes the inevitable deployment of power and the control that larger entities have over these media. . . . While literacy now and historically is conditioned by communication technology, it is not determined by it; changes in consciousness bring about social constructions in which some writing and speaking activities are privileged and others are devalued. (136)

Because the most common definitions of electronic or computer literacy concentrate on the performative aspects, they often ignore this important lesson. Approaches to literacy that value certain forms of knowledge over others are, as mentioned previously, biased toward a white, Western, rational model of thinking and communicating. When settlers of European descent forced Native American people to give up their language and stories and adopt the language and stories of the

Western world, they were taking an overtly racist stance in how they defined what counts. Likewise, we must be careful that definitions of computer literacy do not favor some groups over others. Online communication, which resounds with the marks of both speech and writing, is rich with possibilities for restoring an oralness to our inherently Western print world, and it is rich with possibilities for what kinds of information are considered valid.

But these possibilities will not become probabilities unless people who are traditionally underrepresented in the computer culture (African Americans, Native Americans, women) are encouraged and welcomed into the world of computing. Even though Internet use is increasing, not everyone has access. According to a recent Commerce Department study, while more than 40 percent of households in the United States owned computers, 25 percent had Internet access. But, the report notes, "the bright picture is clouded by data that show significant disparities continue between certain demographic groups and regions and, in many cases, the gap between these groups has grown over time" (U.S. Commerce Dept.). And even though we assume it, not everyone has access to the basic infrastructure. In a different study, the National Telecommunications Information Administration (NTIA) reported that high percentages of the Native American population do not even have phone service (R. Anderson 1999).

Finally with regard to access, it is important to return for a moment to the most basic concept of literacy: the ability to read and write. Even if people have computers, if they cannot understand printed text, they will not be able to access this new, exciting online technology. We forget that there are still people in the United States who cannot read: a recent study showed that 21 to 23 percent of those studied were unable to fill out an employment application, follow written instructions, or read a newspaper (Literacy Volunteers of America).

This "access" question is important. For cyberliteracy, it means making sure that cyberspaces of the future represent the range of human cultures and are not dominated by corporations, media conglomerates, and the predominantly white male world of engineering and computing. Cyberspace should be accessible to all: via hardware and phone access and via online spaces that are open to a range of cultural perspectives. Individuals and groups representing a range of cultures, viewpoints, and ideas should stake out a claim in cyberspace before it is too late.

## Challenging Technological Determinism

For most citizens, it is hard to imagine that the course of any technological development might have been different. That is because we are raised on a model of technological development based on the theory of evolution. Historian and critic David F. Noble best describes this mythos in his case study of factory automation, where he argued that

> It is a staple of current thinking about technological change that such a "successful" technology, having become dominant, must have evolved in some "necessary" way. Implicit in the modern ideology of technological progress is the belief that the process of technological development is analogous to that of natural selection. It is thus assumed that all technological alternatives are always considered, that they are disinterestedly evaluated on their technical merits, and that they are then judged according to the cold calculus of accumulation. Any successful technology, therefore—one which becomes the dominant and ultimately the only solution to a given problem—must, by definition, be the best, for it alone has survived the rigors of engineering experimentation and the trials of the competitive marketplace. And, as the best, it has become the latest, and necessary, step along the unilinear path of progress. (144)

Noble easily could have been describing the Internet, which is constantly being hyped in overtly Darwinian terms. Media reports, Internet sites, and everyday discussion suggest that somehow, the Internet is what it is because it followed some natural path of selection. Examples abound; in an article for the *New York Times* discussing Microsoft's next corporate strategy, we read that "Microsoft Corporation conceded today that the company now [faces] an even greater challenge in the next phase of the Internet's *evolution,* as the role of traditional desktop software recedes and the power center of computing shifts from the operating system to the World Wide Web" (Lohr C-1; emphasis added). This short sentence is rife with unspoken but key premises. Invoking "evolution" suggests that there is only one predefined path for how the Internet will develop. The desktop will recede and the Web will become the center of operations. While this model is certainly possible and has some redeeming qualities (software will always be updated, for example), it is not the only possibility. Unlike what this sentence suggests, the Web is not a biological entity that will somehow evolve on its own.[4] In fact, the very Microsoft at the center of this sentence is one of the key players in how personal computing and the Internet will develop. If Microsoft, with all of its power and control, decides that the operating system should still be the "power center" of computing, it is hard to imagine that this would not happen. In this sentence, however, Microsoft is set up as a neutral observer, watching from afar the "evolution" of this thing called the Internet and speculating on how the company can keep up with the forces of natural selection.

Technological Darwinism suggests that the power of the consumer is equivalent to the forces of natural selection, and that, if a product is faulty, it will drop off the evolutionary tree simply because people do not purchase it. But major forces—Internet companies, the telecommunications and cable industry, entertainment and media conglomerates, government officials (who make laws based mostly on what they learn from lobbyists)—are making clear and overt choices about what the Internet will be and do.

Other visions of the Internet do not come into focus not because they fail the test of economic evolution but because they are not supported by the major powers that be. For example, in the early days, just before the great hubbub of Web shopping mania and overpriced IPOs, many people were speculating about the role the Internet could play in democratic discourse, education, and public information. But with legislators favoring a laissez-faire policy toward the Internet and at the same time reducing any remaining NSF funding, the Internet is quickly turning into a space that is predominantly commercial. Alternate possibilities seem less and less likely unless we invoke an activist cyberliteracy, becoming energized cybercitizens who challenge determinism in our research, in what we teach, and in the technologies we favor.

## Beyond Media Hype

Most of the trade books having to do with literacy and the Internet are, in the end, no more than how-to manuals: how to log in, surf the Web, find information, use e-mail, and chat with friends. Even publications that do touch on issues of a more critical sort would have us believe that one is cyberliterate once one knows how to use the tools. Paul Gilster, in a recent book with the promising title *Digital Literacy,* appears to break this mold and discuss issues of online credibility (how to know if a Web site is credible or not). But in the end, he suggests that digital literacy is literacy of the performance sort, that it "involves acquiring the necessary survival skills, the core competencies [described in his book] to take advantage of this environment" (28). Even if and when Internet software changes, you will still be "literate" if you can use the Internet to "find, verify, and incorporate [Internet] content into [your] work" (230).

As I have argued thus far, cyberliteracy is not simply a matter of learning how to keep up with the technology or how to do a Web search. Cyberliteracy means learning to be aware and awake: to be a critical user and consumer of these new technologies, to be conscious of how these technologies change our rhetorical spaces and habits. Cultures are composed of their rhetorics, and online technologies are at the center of our current culture. Just consider how various communication technologies have changed our notions of space and relationships. Oral cultures relied on storytellers; it was necessary to be physically present to hear the story, and entire communities often gathered to hear the latest news. Radio culture began by entire families sharing one radio and listening to one program together. But in many homes today, every kid has a radio, a TV, a phone, and even an Internet connection. This individualist ethos inspires a completely different sense of family and community. Clearly, the tendencies built into computers, cell phones, personal digital assistants, and the like change.

Cyberliteracy means being awake and conscious of these implications. And, it requires a sense of activism, voicing an opinion about what this technology should become and being an active, not passive, user of these technologies. To become conscious of technology should be to become curious about the forces behind it. A wonderful slogan by the group Computer Professionals for Social Responsibility (www.cpsr.org) asks "Technology is driving the Future. Who is Steering?" Yet we are not conditioned to ask this sort of question. Note, for example, the word *user,* a standard computer term that describes the person on the keyboard/mouse/joystick end of the machine. The term echoes throughout the software field: user-interface design, user-friendly documentation, user manuals, and so on. Yet the only other area to refer to people as "users" is the area of drug addiction, where the term *user* implies someone who is controlled by the substance. To be cyberliterate, you need to be more than a user. You need to become an active participant in the discussion, critiquing, challenging, and anticipating how these technologies are designed, implemented, and used. Almost anyone can learn to code in HTML and surf the Web, but hardly anyone becomes conscious of the social and cultural implications of these new technologies.

Media coverage does not always help in this regard. Most media stories are designed to ask questions that feed mainstream ideas of what counts and what does not. In the *New York Times* article quoted earlier, the focus is on the "browser wars." Yet while the competition between Netscape and Microsoft Explorer is interesting, it could easily be argued that the real wars on the Internet are not browser wars. They are the battles between public space and private space, between public information and information that is controlled and dispensed at a pay-per-view fee. We hear very little discussion about how the Internet has gone from a research space to a commercial space (.com is now the most popular domain name). Yet this shift is significant in terms of the content that gets most widely promoted online. Cyberliteracy requires us to ask whether we like this shift and if not, how we can retain public e-spaces.

## Seeking a Balance in Cyberspace

Part of being cyberliterate also requires us to be realistic. While a totally commercial Internet would not be a good thing, commercial forces in relation to the Internet are not all bad. Competition leads to new ideas and often makes products cheaper and more available to consumers. Prices on computer hardware have dropped dramatically in the last three years. Newer and better Web sites and search engines are available. And new business models, inspired by the Internet's people-driven, bottom-up style, are competing in the marketplace and changing how we do business. Yet the obvious concern comes when these are the only forces, when we take a medium with such potential and leave its development entirely within a laissez-faire model. Especially in today's climate, this model ignores issues of social good, public space, and citizen access. A blend of the two would be preferable and, given the current trend toward anything governmental, it will be up to the citizenry—an informed, cyberliterate group—to take action and create new e-spaces that balance out the commercialization of the Internet.

Commenting on the development of the Internet, Freeman Dyson argues that this balance is "out of control and tilting sharply." He believes it is "our task as humans to keep the balance in equilibrium" (118).

The networks are driving us into a world of cut-throat competition that many of us find destructive. [They] impose cultural and economic constraints that we feel powerless to resist [and] mostly serve the rich and are inaccessible to the poor and uneducated, thereby increasing the barriers and inequalities between rich and poor. . . . But we have the power as individuals to make our needs and desires heard. As creators of the machines and protocols by which the networks live, we have the power to understand them and to influence their functioning. We have the responsibility for making the networks serve the interests of social justice and human freedom. (118)

Cyberliteracy requires us to look beyond the commercial side and see that, ultimately, this is a technology of rhetorical exchange, not just one of selling. It is a technology of reading, writing, and speaking, and it brings with it changes in all things affected by human communication, changes in everything from grammar and style to conceptions of community, expectations about speed, differing senses of gender and identity, and new ways to do politics.

Mine is not the only view in this regard (though it may be the only one to characterize it as literacy). Several groups, including Computer Professionals for Social Responsibility and People for Internet Responsibility (www.pfir.org), share the idea that cyberspace should be more than online shopping malls. PFIR notes that

with the rapid commercialization of the Internet and its World Wide Web, there are increasing concerns that decisions regarding these resources are being irresponsibly skewed through the influence of powerful, vested interests (in commercial, political, and other categories) whose goals are not necessarily always aligned with the concerns of individuals and the people at large. . . . The Internet can be a fantastic tool to encourage the flow of ideas, information, and education, but it can also be used to track users' behaviors and invade individuals' privacy in manners that George Orwell never imagined in his 1984 world. (PFIR)

Rhetoric, and rhetorical education, offers an important way to balance this trend.

## Conceptions of Cyberliteracy in Rhetorical Education

The future of cyberliteracy needs to be critical, observant, and activist. Yet, how to begin? As teachers and scholars, how can we illustrate this blend of oral, written, and visual communication as a new rhetorical form, and how can we show that these technologies are not neutral? The key is to stay rooted in the specific. Case examples, ones that highlight the unique features of online discourse and expose the underpinnings of the technology and its uses, are excellent tools, for, as with most criticism, they raise the specific case as a point of discussion, departure, and active reaction.

It is no longer enough (was it ever?) to speak of "*the* rhetoric of technology," because each case is different, and each case offers unique insights into the nexus between machine, language, and culture. Case studies allow us to examine key issues of the technology and its rhetorical context so students and researchers have specific critical terms through which to understand and critique it. Take, for example, issues of gender and computing. In my study of the online protest over a government-proposed encryption standard (the Clipper Chip), I noted that one of the only women to participate in the discussion was flamed, called the "Wicked Witch of the East," and generally treated with less respect than any of the other (male) participants, even though this particular woman is a well-known mathematician and encryption expert. The oral-written nature of e-mail contributed to this treatment, as did the historical lack of access to the computer culture by women and the resulting hostile nature of many Usenet newsgroups (Gurak, *Persuasion*). More recently, in a new study, I examine the visual images available for kids on the Internet, including two computers advertised widely during the holiday season of 1999: the Barbie computer just for girls (in pink), and the HotWheels computer just for boys (in blue)[5] (Gurak, *Cyberliteracy*). In both cases, I am able to offer a grounded instance that illustrates specific gender-biased features of online discourse (see figure 3). These features become the basis for questioning the standard, media-imposed view that the Internet is a neutral place where anyone can be anything they like. The criticism becomes part of the action of cyberliteracy.

Another relevant case would be any of the recent upsets over personal privacy and the Internet. These cases illustrate that while online discourse is painted as a place where users can remain anonymous, technologies like Web cookies, the Pentium III chip, or RealJukeBox software

3. Popular computer advertisements showing gender-biased features of online discourse.

are secretly collecting personal information. A comparative analysis of the rhetoric surrounding these technologies is immensely informative. While the corporations who create these programs would have you believe that they are only doing so to make your life better (by allowing you, for example, to connect more quickly or shop with more expediency) or that your private information is all over the place anyway (so, what's the problem), discussion by privacy advocates reveals that privacy-grabbing technologies are intrusive and at odds with the standards of other countries: the recently passed European Data Directive does not allow personal information to be collected without explicit permission from the individual. In addition, survey after survey of regular citizens reveals that many are uncomfortable with the growing databases of personal information so readily created and, often, accessed via the Internet. The exigencies caused when these three points of view come together make for a wonderful site of rhetorical analysis.

After these individual critiques reveal the problems, the activist side of cyberliteracy should encourage us to use rhetoric as a tool for action: to send letters to our elected representatives asking them to vote for privacy protection laws, to make sure our local schools are giving girls equal access at computers, to complain to companies that sell products that surreptitiously invade our personal privacy. In addition, if enough individual case studies begin to point out the same issues, we can strive for a (not the)—temporal to be sure—"rhetoric of the Internet": a rubric of key terms and issues for cyberliteracy in the early part of this new century.

Many other issues arise that can be used as the basis for technological/ rhetorical critique. These include the rhetoric of anger and flaming, the popularity of hoax messages on the Internet, the persuasive messages of e-commerce, and the fate of physicality in a virtual age. Cyberliteracy demands that we maintain a critical eye on the social, political, and economic premises that drive Internet technology, because if we— rhetoricians and critics—do not, hardly anyone else will.

Thus, I invite you—the scholar, the citizen, the student, the teacher, the parent, the advocate, the rhetorician—to create cyberliteracy by rejecting technological determinism and embracing an active, critical stance toward Internet technologies. Only then will we see these technologies go beyond the obvious and toward new experiences that are inclusive, educational, accessible, and exciting.[6]

# Notes

1. See Welch 55–68 for a concise summary of the "Ong debate."

2. This feature is called "reach" by Kaufer and Carley.

3. Thank you to John Logie for reminding me of this when I asked him why he thought that the number-one e-commerce site, Amazon.com, ironically happens to sell hard copy books.

4. Of course, even biological organisms don't always evolve apart from human intervention. Humans have been selectively breeding plants and animals for thousands of years, and recent work in genetic engineering suggests that perhaps the old ideas of natural selection may be on their way out.

5. Thank you to Josephine Lee for first bringing these to my attention.

6. Portions of this essay are previously published by Yale University Press in the book *Cyberliteracy: Navigating the Internet with Awareness* (2001) and are used with permission.

# Afterword: Lessons from *Rhetorical Education in America*

## Wendy B. Sharer and Margaret M. Lyday

"Rhetorics," James Berlin has written, "provide a set of rules about the dispositions of discourse at a particular moment. They codify who can and cannot speak . . . ; what can and cannot be said . . . ; who can and cannot listen and act . . . ; and the very nature of the language to be used." Rhetorical education helps students understand and apply these many rules, but, Berlin suggests, a thorough study of rhetorics also interrogates the "junctures of discourse and power" in which the rules are grounded ("Revisionary" 116–17). To accomplish all of these goals, rhetorical education necessarily involves teachers and students in an incredibly complex set of pedagogical endeavors, including

- studying and practicing language conventions in a variety of educational, professional, and public contexts;
- developing a critical awareness of hierarchies that structure communication within these various contexts; and
- recognizing the discursive presence of cultural, economic, and political interests within these various contexts.

The essays collected here form a starting point from which to navigate the complex territory of rhetorical education. Several themes—lessons, if you will—emerge from these diverse contributions and suggest possibilities for curricular development and classroom practice. As new generations of teachers and students traverse the terrain of *Rhetorical Education in America,* these lessons may help light the way.

# Lesson One: The history of rhetorical education in America has implications for current classroom practice.

Many of the essays suggest that teachers of rhetoric can learn from the struggles of their predecessors and can strengthen contemporary rhetorical pedagogy by revisiting educational practices that have been ignored or overshadowed in the history of rhetorical education. William Denman opens the collection by exploring what he sees as an ignored, but critically important, goal of past rhetorical curricula in America—the development of citizen-orators. According to Denman, "[t]he disappearance of the concept of 'citizen-orator' from American education has deprived our students, and the citizens they become, of a central ability to function effectively in democratic life" (3). After providing readers with a history of the concept of the "citizen-orator" from classical times through the present, Denman concludes that teachers of communication courses—in both speech and composition—must resuscitate the once-valued connections between rhetoric and democratic empowerment. Past constructions of the citizen-orator, Denman asserts, quoting James Murphy, are not simply "antiquarian hogwash"; rather, they are ideas worth exploring in the twenty-first century (16).

Rhetorical educators can also learn from the past by reconsidering pedagogies used by historically marginalized groups. The "various contexts in which African Americans' rhetorical education and performance took place during the nineteenth century," Shirley Wilson Logan explains, "suggest ways in which we can prepare our students to enact a rhetoric of social change" (39). Early black rhetorical activists learned to write and speak persuasively in order to influence the conditions and the people that oppressed them. Their work thus illustrates a path contemporary rhetorical education might follow as it moves away from the study of "language use for self-improvement" to a focus on language use for sociopolitical action (45).

Susan Kates's study of James Watt Raine also contributes to this lesson. Raine's instructional approaches to dialects, Kates argues, might help current teachers develop a responsible and effective pedagogy for linguistically marginalized groups: "By returning to the past—by recovering it—we can discover that our contemporary debates over the issue have an important history, one that we need to attend to if we wish to address this pedagogical dilemma more effectively" (77).

Other contributors to this volume propose that contemporary teachers might benefit from considering historical moments in which rhetorical education served oppressive or contradictory purposes. Nan Johnson's essay, for example, reminds readers of the need to question rhetorical pedagogies that are touted as liberatory or democratic. As Johnson explains, the parlor rhetoric movement's promise to expand literacy veiled the movement's intentions of reinforcing gender roles. Similarly, Jill Swiencicki's detailed study of *The Columbian Orator* demonstrates how the historical study of pedagogical texts can help current educators locate contradictory discourses within their pedagogical materials. Swiencicki analyzes *The Columbian Orator*'s "contents, arrangement, and instructional preface"—in both its nineteenth- and twentieth-century editions—"less as a coherent example of neoclassical civic rhetoric . . . and more as a conflicted statement about eloquence, social power, and public culture" (58). All texts in the field of rhetorical education, Johnson and Swiencicki prompt us to recall, contain such conflicted statements and, for this reason, need to be continually interrogated if we desire a pedagogy that does not perpetuate oppressive constructs of language.

## Lesson Two: We can learn from the past, but we cannot simply "go back."

While many of the essays presented here suggest that we can learn from the past of rhetorical education, they also offer a caution: we cannot uncritically transfer materials or methods from the past into the present. The goal of surveying rhetorical education is not to "resurrect" past pedagogy that necessarily embodies specific prejudices, but, as Swiencicki suggests, to "realiz[e] what [that pedagogy] enables and associat[e] these features with forward-thinking pedagogies from our own millennial moment" (73). Although much from the past perhaps should be reconsidered as part of today's curriculum, we cannot, Logan reminds us, "return to some sentimentalized good old days of oratory before computers and television and mass media, when children read" (38).

Instead, contemporary material, cultural, and theoretical contexts must inform today's rhetorical curriculum. While Sherry Booth and Susan Frisbie encourage readers to consider metaphor—"a constant component of rhetoric through the ages"—in contemporary pedagogy, they are careful to note that our understandings of metaphor must be expanded and complicated if they are to be of use for teaching critical reading and writing skills to today's students. Metaphor, they assert, can be an extremely effective teaching tool if teachers help students understand how it "functions in deeply cognitive ways." To accomplish this goal, however, our understandings of metaphor must draw not only on past understandings of metaphor from ancient rhetoric, literary history, and creative writing, but also from current work in linguistics and psychology. A more complex understanding of the psychology of metaphor, derived from both historical understandings of metaphor and the work of contemporary scholars of language and culture, can "enable students to be critical readers and writers of texts of all kinds: personal, political, and academic" (178).

Furthermore, instructional practices that may have pervaded rhetorical education in the past must be adapted to a rhetorical curriculum that provides exposure to many different kinds of texts. Our students, Booth and Frisbie point out, "require many different kinds of literacies—print, electronic, television, film, and advertising—to function effectively in civil and academic spheres" (177–78). The expanding world of electronic communication in particular requires new pedagogical approaches. Teachers of rhetoric today must be prepared to instruct students in "cyberliteracy"—the ability to read and write critically in digital environments. As Laura Gurak warns, "unless we become familiar with the rhetorical features of digital communication, we will be led into cyberspace with only a limited understanding of both the power of and the problems with this technology" (180). "To become cyberliterate," Gurak explains, "we [and our students] need to understand the new rhetorics of digital space so we become more sophisticated about critiquing, challenging, and anticipating these technologies" (180). Simply learning the technology—the shortcuts and quirks of various software—is not enough. Students, if they are to exercise rhetorical choice, must be able to critique the limits and possibilities of software design.

## Lesson Three: The experience of identities—national, racial, regional, ethnic, professional, and gendered, to name but a few—is intricately entwined with rhetorical education.

Just as they must accommodate new media and new writing technologies, current curricular models of rhetorical education cannot simply imple-

202 / Wendy Sharer and Margaret Lyday

ment classical ideals of citizenship because those ideals are premised upon a public sphere that is limited to upper-class men. As Miller suggests, "civic philosophies of rhetoric will need to be redefined to move beyond the classical ideal of the individual citizen speaking for the common good" and to incorporate lessons learned from recent work in feminism and cultural studies (31).

Incorporating these lessons reveals that rhetorical education in America has often served to privilege certain identities while significantly restricting others. Nan Johnson suggests in this volume that nineteenth-century women learned to behave and to understand themselves in specific ways as they read parlor rhetorics that "reinscribed relatively separate and distinctly unequal rhetorical spheres for the sexes" (107). Rhetorical education served a similarly suppressive function in American colleges of the late nineteenth and early twentieth century. The teaching of English at that time, Miller explains, "was institutionalized to teach Anglo-Saxon culture" (24). Rich Lane suggests that the teaching of restrictive cultural norms continues today as a result of the unrhetorical stance of many English-education programs. Even though "many teacher preparation courses attempt to use texts that challenge the nationalist, literature-based content of teaching English at the secondary level," Lane explains, most of those programs "fall short of offering the strategies and philosophies needed to prepare teachers to implement more-rhetorical approaches." As a result, "a literature-based strategy continues to reinforce national and local standards movements" (88).

Rhetorical education need not, however, serve conservative purposes. While the parlor rhetoric movement and the emergence of English as a discipline in the late nineteenth century served to normalize and limit the experience of identity, students at Berea College most likely learned a much more empowering lesson about identity through the rhetorical scholarship and pedagogy of James Watt Raine. As mainstream institutions of higher education strove to standardize language and create a homogenous "educated culture" by stigmatizing any evidence of regionalism, Raine created a pedagogy that "argues that the roots of Appalachian English are in Elizabethan English; . . . traces many Appalachian words to Chaucer and Shakespeare and celebrates the ingenuity of many of the expressions used by the people of Kentucky" (77–78). Rhetorical education in the twenty-first century might serve as a location to recognize and critique oppressive language practices such as those elaborated by

Johnson, Miller, and Lane, while also acknowledging and promoting the subversive language curriculum of teachers such as Raine.

The connections between rhetorical education and the experience of identity are not just curricular. As Gregory Clark and Michael Halloran suggest, a sense of national identity is also constructed through rhetorical education outside of the classroom. Both writers explain that we are taught how to identify with one another and with a particular construction of America through public landscapes and tourist destinations such as Yosemite National Park and the tour road at Saratoga Battlefield. Learning national identity through such public attractions, Clark suggests, provides an important foundation for schooled rhetorical education: "Before people can do the practical rhetorical work of determining what they will believe and do together, they need to understand themselves as identified and interdependent with others" (147).

Our ability to recognize and use certain persuasive strategies, in other words, depends upon our identification with others and with certain elements of American culture. Clark suggests the images of scenic national parks that are circulated nationwide through photographs and artwork come to serve "as symbols of a vast American continent that is home to an incomprehensibly diverse people," while also bringing these diverse populations together by "portray[ing] uniquely American places that all of these people could imagine themselves inhabiting, at least temporarily, together" (155). The tour road at Saratoga Battlefield, Halloran explains, serves a similar purpose, creating a shared history of national heroes for visitors: "The story told by the tour road inculcates shared ideals that can become the stuff of ethos and enthymemes, the common ground that allows us to argue our differences in public discourse" (130). The tour road leads visitors through a shared experience and thus contributes to their ability to understand and communicate with one another.

## Lesson Four: How we construct rhetorical education will influence the structure of our public institutions and our students' abilities to participate therein.

Another prominent theme present in many of these essays asks the reader to consider how we might connect rhetorical education with public participation. Indeed, this idea motivates many of the calls for us to reconsider the past of rhetorical education in America—to consider revitalizing the "citizen-orator" and to reexamine the "rhetoric for social change" studied and practiced by black activists of the nineteenth century. A reinvigorated rhetorical curriculum, this theme suggests, might lead to a reinvigorated civic arena. Denman promotes rhetorical education in public speaking and writing in a way that "link[s] those skills to a wider goal: the betterment of civic life" (16). Along similar lines, Miller urges teachers of rhetoric within English departments to challenge the predominant literary studies model of pedagogy and instead push for a literacy studies model. By focusing on literacy rather than literature, Miller argues, rhetorical education in English departments can help students see themselves as active rhetorical agents rather than as passive recipients of other people's texts. Unlike the previously dominant literary model of pedagogy, "literacy involves not just interpretation but action," Miller explains, "and our research, teaching, and service work on literacy need to attend to how citizens can act equitably on behalf of social justice" (35).

Because rhetorical education has tremendous implications for students' abilities to participate in public conversations, several contributors to this volume also suggest that rhetorical education in the university is best situated with one foot in the community. Service learning projects, which ask students to write for and/or about their local communities, make rhetorical education a joint endeavor between instructors and members of the local community. Service learning projects not only expand responsibility for rhetorical education—no longer is it solely the duty of the individual writing teacher—but such projects also expand the benefits of rhetorical education by encouraging and training students for civic participation. Other community-classroom collaborations, such as the Scholar/Practitioner Project described by Logan, are expanding the opportunities and impacts of rhetorical education by linking students, scholars, and community members in the formulation and promotion of public policy.

## Pondering the Future of Rhetorical Education in America

These certainly are not all of the lessons from *Rhetorical Education in America,* yet they all have important implications for how we approach the study and teaching of rhetoric in the twenty-first century. Keeping these lessons in mind, we can begin to approach some of the critical questions that face teachers, scholars, and students of rhetoric today. We conclude with a brief elaboration of some of these questions and we invite you to ponder them, debate them, and expand on them as you join in the conversations started by the contributors to this book.

Question One: What role(s) should rhetorical education play in the formation of national and international identities?

Understanding how national identity is constructed through various discourses is a critical goal for rhetorical education in the post–September 11th world. Working from the insights gleaned through studies such as those by Gregory Clark and S. Michael Halloran in this collection, we might think about how to construct curricula that interrogate and expand the geographical boundaries of rhetorical education in America. How are inhabitants of and visitors to this country taught to understand the construct of America? Through what images and narratives of shared experience do Americans learn to identify themselves and to exclude others? What are the global implications of this rhetorical education in national identity?

Certainly, students should know the rhetorical traditions of their own cultural heritage, but the global scope of twenty-first-century life also requires that students have some historical and cross-cultural perspective. They should understand why different cultures—or the same culture in different times—rank values differently and why people in those cultures define who they are in different ways. Such historical and cross-cultural understanding might enable students to critically examine the arguments behind events of global import, such as wars, treaties, elections, and terrorist acts. Students need to learn firsthand how to analyze and participate in the rhetorical activities of local, national, and international discourse communities. In short, future teachers of rhetorical education in America need to consider how to incorporate global contexts into their curricula.

Question Two: How should we assess the quality of our curricula?

Given the expanding diversity of student populations and the growing pressure on higher education to prove its worth, those of us who teach rhetoric face increasingly complex questions about the "outcomes" of our educational programs. Many educators and administrators believe that we should look at the "products" of our labor—the students. But how do we measure true learning and advancement in writing ability, especially the ability of those immersed in cultures that depend on another dialect or language? If we ignore these variables, we risk excluding critical and growing populations from higher education.

Furthermore, what kind of improvements do we wish to see as a result of our efforts in rhetorical education? Many of us who study and teach rhetoric would argue that fewer surface errors do not necessarily indicate a great improvement in rhetorical ability. Instead, we prefer to measure rhetorical ability in terms of careful consideration of alternative viewpoints, keen awareness of audience, and intricate yet clear articulation of ideas. Many people beyond the field of rhetoric, however, continue to equate excellence in writing and speaking with the absence of error. How do we change these views? And, if we can change them, how do we then assess the work our students produce? On what measures should we judge student work? What background should evaluators have to judge the quality of these measures? Answering these questions becomes even more complex and significant if we assume that rhetorical education in America needs to incorporate international perspectives. How would we measure the success of attempts to incorporate such perspectives? Who would be qualified to assess the international aspects and impacts of rhetorical education in America?

Question Three: How should teachers of rhetorical education respond to the increasing presence and power of technology?

Computer technology is part of twenty-first-century life and, hence, needs to be considered in curricula for rhetorical education. An increasing number of colleges and universities require students to have personal computers. Ninety-five percent of the elementary and secondary schools in America are now linked to the Internet. A quick review of federal and state grant opportunities will show that, while there is little money for new faculty and smaller classes, grants to create and improve technological infrastructure abound. It is safe to say that technology will continue to have a powerful presence in what we do as teachers and scholars.

As Laura Gurak suggests in this collection, the presence of technology creates new educational needs. Yet these educational needs go beyond simply teaching students how to use a computer when drafting a paper. Because the distribution of technology remains problematic, leaving certain Americans and certain nations at a significant disadvantage educationally, politically, and economically, teachers, scholars, and students of rhetoric should explore the material and economic factors of technological access.

"Computers continue to be distributed differentially along the related axes of race and socioeconomic status," Cynthia Selfe cautions, and this distribution "contributes to ongoing patterns of racism and to the continuation of poverty" within national and international contexts (420). Given this continued and dangerous pattern of technological distribution, teachers of rhetorical education need to consider many tough questions as they determine where and how to use technology in their work. Who has access to computers in their writing? How much access do different groups of people have (at home, at school, at work, etc.)? Who has access to the internet? What locations and populations lack the telephone, cable, and/or computer equipment necessary to participate in cyberspace? How do different levels of computer access affect performance and rewards in school and/or on the job? How do computer and software manufacturers determine the design of their products? How do these designs impact communication and the teaching of rhetorical skills?

The magnitude of the questions facing teachers, scholars, and students of rhetoric seems overwhelming, yet we do not have time to be overwhelmed. As we learned in the 1960s and 70s when we were slow to develop practical degrees for business and many of the larger companies— Ford, General Electric, Westinghouse—began to develop their own "degrees," time is often critical in curriculum development. Furthermore, the volatile international climate of today immediately requires critical thinkers and careful rhetors. The very possibility of international negotiation and global democracy depends upon them and the education through which they develop the rhetorical skills to communicate in international arenas. As John Dewey argued more than seventy-five years ago (if we may learn from the past), "democracy . . . will have its consummation when free social inquiry is indissolubly wedded to the art of full and moving communication" (112). How do we cultivate "free social inquiry" and "full and moving communication" in the twenty-first century? This question lies at the heart of rhetorical education in America.

# References

Adams, David Wallace. *Education for Extinction: American Indians and the Boarding School Experience, 1875–1928*. Lawrence: U of Kansas P, 1997.

*The American Orator*. Chicago: Kuhlman, 1901.

Anderson, Benedict. *Imagined Communities; Reflections on the Origin and Spread of Nationalism*. London: Verso, 1993.

Anderson, Rachel. "Native Americans and the Digital Divide." Communications Policy and Practice (Benton Foundation). 16 November 1999. <http://www.benton.org/DigitalBeat/db101499.html>.

Antczak, Frederick. *Thought and Character: The Rhetoric of Democratic Education*. Ames: Iowa State UP, 1985.

Appleman, Roy Edgar. "Recommendations on Development of Policy and Work Program, Saratoga National Historical Park, Aug. 15, 1939." Saratoga NHP archives, Administrative Reports File. CRBIB 001112, SARA.053.

Aristotle. *On Rhetoric: A Theory of Civic Discourse*. Trans. George A. Kennedy. New York: Oxford UP, 1991.

———. *The Rhetoric and the Poetics of Aristotle*. *Rhetoric* translated by W. Rhys Roberts; *Poetics* translated by Ingram Bywater. New York: Modern Library, 1954.

Bailyn, Bernard. *Education in the Forming of American Society*. New York: Norton, 1960.

Batteau, Allen. *The Invention of Appalachia*. Tucson: U of Arizona P, 1990.

Beale, Walter H. "Richard M. Weaver: Philosophical Rhetoric, Cultural Criticism, and the First Rhetorical Awakening." *College English* 52.6 (Oct. 1990): 626–40.

Belenky, Mary Field, Blythe M. Clinchy, Nancy R. Goldberger, and Jill M. Tarule. *Women's Ways of Knowing: The Development of Self, Voice and Mind*. New York: Basic Books, 1986.

Bennett, William. *The Devaluing of America: The Fight for Our Culture and Our Children*. New York: Touchstone P, 1994.

Berlin, James. "Revisionary Histories of Rhetoric: Politics, Power, and Plurality." *Writing Histories of Rhetoric*. Ed. Victor Vitanza. Carbondale: Southern Illinois UP, 1994. 112–27.

——. "Rhetoric and Ideology in the Writing Class." *College English* 50 (1988): 477–93.

——. *Rhetoric and Reality: Writing Instruction in American Colleges, 1900–1985*. Carbondale: Southern Illinois UP, 1987.

——. *Rhetorics, Poetics, and Cultures: Refiguring College English Studies*. Albany: SUNY P, 1996.

——. *Writing Instruction in Nineteenth-Century American Colleges*. Carbondale: Southern Illinois UP, 1984.

Berlin, James, and Michael J. Vivion, eds. *Cultural Studies in the English Classroom*. Portsmouth, NH: Heineman-Boynton/Cook, 1992.

Berube, Michael. *The Employment of English: Theory, Jobs, and the Future of Literary Studies*. New York: New York UP, 1998.

Berube, Michael, and Cary Nelson, eds. *Higher Education Under Fire: Politics, Economics, and the Crisis of the Humanities*. New York: Routledge, 1995.

Billings, Dwight. Foreword. *The Land of the Saddle-bags: A Study of the Mountain People of Appalachia* by James Watt Raine. 1924. Lexington: UP of Kentucky, 1997.

Bingham, Caleb. *The Columbian Orator: Containing a Variety of Original and Selected Pieces; Together with Rules; Calculated to Improve Youth and Others in the Ornamental and Useful Art of Eloquence*. Philadelphia: J. B. Lippincott, 1803. Ed. David Blight. New York: New York UP, 1998.

Bizzell, Patricia. "Beyond Antifoundationalism to Rhetorical Authority: Problems Defining Cultural Literacy." *Rhetoric in an Antifoundational World: Language, Culture and Pedagogy*. Ed. Michael Bernard-Donals and Richard R. Glejzer. New Haven: Yale UP, 1998. 371–88.

Bizzell, Patricia, and Bruce Herzberg, eds. *The Rhetorical Tradition: Readings from Classical Times to the Present*. Boston: Bedford Books, 1990.

Black, Max. "More About Metaphor." Ortony 19–43.

Blackwell, Alice Stone. *Lucy Stone: Pioneer of Woman's Rights*. Boston: Little, 1930.

Blair, Hugh. *Lectures on Rhetoric and Belles Lettres*. New York: Carvill, 1829.

Bledstein, Burton J. *The Culture of Professionalism: The Middle Class and the Development of Higher Education in America*. New York: W. W. Norton, 1976.

Blight, David W. "Introduction: The Peculiar Dialogue Between Caleb Bingham and Frederick Douglass." *The Colombian Orator*. New York: New York UP, 1998. xiii–xxix.

Bloom, Allan. *The Closing of the American Mind: How Higher Education Has Failed Democracy and Impoverished the Souls of Today's Students*. New York: Simon & Schuster, 1987.

Bloom, Lynn Z., Donald A. Daiker, and Edward M. White, eds. *Composition in the 21st Century: Crisis and Change*. Carbondale: Southern Illinois UP, 1995.

Bodnar, John. *Remaking America: Public Memory, Commemoration, and Patriotism in the Twentieth Century.* Princeton: Princeton UP, 1992.

Bourdieu, Pierre. *Distinction: A Social Critique of the Judgment of Taste.* Trans. Richard Nice. Cambridge, MA: Harvard UP, 1984.

Brereton, John C. *The Origins of Composition Studies in the American College, 1875–1925.* Pittsburgh: U of Pittsburgh P, 1996.

Brody, Miriam. *Manly Writing: Gender, Rhetoric, and the Rise of Composition.* Carbondale: Southern Illinois UP, 1993.

Brown, Charles Walter. *American Star Speaker and Elocutionist.* Chicago: M. A. Donohue and Co., 1902.

Brown, Richard D. *Knowledge Is Power: The Diffusion of Information in Early America, 1700–1865.* New York: Oxford UP, 1989.

Brueggemann, Brenda Jo. *Lend Me Your Ear: Rhetorical Constructions of Deafness.* Washington, DC: Gallaudet UP, 1999.

Brydon, Steven R., and Michael D. Scott. *Between One and Many: The Art and Science of Public Speaking.* 2nd ed. New York: Mayfield, 1997.

Buel, J. W. *America's Wonderlands: A Pictorial and Descriptive History of Our Country's Scenic Marvels.* Denver: World Publishing Company, 1893.

Buell, Lawrence. *New England Literary Culture: From Revolution through Renaissance.* Cambridge: Cambridge UP, 1986.

Bullock, Richard, John Trimbur, and Charles Schuster, eds. *The Politics of Writing Instruction: Postsecondary.* Portsmouth, NH: Heinemann-Boynton/Cook, 1991.

Burke, Jim, and Mary Frances Claggett. *The English Teacher's Companion.* New York: Boynton/Cook, 1999.

Burke, Kenneth. *Attitudes Toward History.* 3rd ed. Berkeley: U of California P, 1984.

———. "Four Master Tropes." *The Kenyon Review* 3 (1941): 421–38.

———. *A Grammar of Motives.* Berkeley: U of California P, 1969.

———. "Linguistic Approach to Problems of Education." *Modern Philosophies and Education.* Ed. Nelson B. Henry. *National Society for the Study of Education Yearbook* 54, Part 1. Chicago: U of Chicago P, 1955. 259–303.

———. *Philosophy of Literary Form.* 3rd ed. Berkeley: U of California P, 1974.

———. "Revolutionary Symbolism in America. Speech by Kenneth Burke to American Writers' Congress, April 26, 1935." *The Legacy of Kenneth Burke.* Ed. Herbert W. Simons and Trevor Melia. Madison: U of Wisconsin P, 1989. 267–73.

———. "The Rhetorical Situation." *Communication: Ethical and Moral Issues.* Ed. Lee Thayer. London: Gordon and Breach Science Publishers, 1973. 263–75.

Burroway, Janet. *Writing Fiction: A Guide to Narrative Craft.* New York: HarperCollins, 1996.

Campbell, George. *The Philosophy of Rhetoric.* London: William Tegg, 1850.

Campbell, John C. *The Southern Highlander and His Homeland.* 1921. Lexington: UP of Kentucky, 1969.

Campbell, Karlyn Kohrs, ed. *Man Cannot Speak for Her*. Vol. 1–2. Westport, CT: Greenwood, 1989.

Casteen, John T. "Letter to the University Community on Equal Opportunity in Admissions." 30 September 1999. U of Virginia. 15 October 1999. <http://www.virginia.edu/president/spch_admission99.html>.

Chapple, Joe Mitchell. *A' Top O' The World: Wonders of the Yellowstone Dreamland*. Boston: Chapple Publishing Co., 1922.

Chesnutt, Charles W. *Essays and Speeches*. Ed. Joseph McElrath, Robert Leitz, and Jesse Crisler. Stanford: Stanford UP, 1999.

———. *The Journals of Charles W. Chesnutt*. Durham: Duke UP, 1993.

Clark, Gregory, and S. Michael Halloran, eds. *Oratorical Culture in Nineteenth-Century America: Transformations in the Theory and Practice of Rhetoric*. Carbondale: Southern Illinois UP, 1993.

Cmiel, Kenneth. *Democratic Eloquence: The Fight over Popular Speech in Nineteenth-Century America*. Berkeley: U of California P, 1990.

Cohen, Herman. *The History of Speech Communication: The Emergence of a Discipline, 1914–1945*. Annandale, VA: Speech Communication Association, 1994.

Connors, Robert. *Composition-Rhetoric*. Pittsburgh: U of Pittsburgh P, 1997.

Connors, Robert, and Edward P. J. Corbett. *Classical Rhetoric for the Modern Student*. New York: Oxford UP, 1998.

Conway, Kathryn M. "Woman Suffrage and the History of Rhetoric at the Seven Sisters Colleges, 1865–1919." *Reclaiming Rhetorica*. Ed. Andrea Lunsford. Pittsburgh: U of Pittsburgh P, 1995. 203–26.

Coppin, Fanny Jackson. *Reminiscences of School Life, and Hints on Teaching*. 1913. New York: G. K. Hall, 1997.

Coulter, Xenia. "The Hidden Transformation of Women through Mothering." *All about Mentoring* 22 (Fall 2001): 46–49.

Crowley, Sharon. *Composition in the University: Historical and Polemical Essays*. Pittsburgh: U of Pittsburgh P, 1998.

———. *The Methodical Memory: Invention in Current-Traditional Rhetoric*. Carbondale: Southern Illinois UP, 1990.

———. "A Personal Essay on Freshman English." *Pre/Text* 12 (1991): 155–76.

———. "A Plea for the Revival of Sophistry." *Rhetoric Review* 7 (1989): 318–34.

Crowley, Sharon, and Debra Hawhee. *Ancient Rhetorics for Contemporary Students*. New York: Allyn & Bacon, 1999.

Cushman, Ellen. "The Public Intellectual, Service Learning, and Activist Research." *College English* 61 (1999): 328–36.

Derrida, Jacques. *Archive Fever: A Freudian Impression*. Trans. Eric Prenowitz. Chicago: U of Chicago P, 1996.

Dewey, John. *The Public and Its Problems*. Athens, OH: Ohio UP, 1985.

Dickson, Chidsey. "Now Is the Time for All Good Rhetors." WPA-L@ASU.EDU posted 2 Feb. 2003.

Dillard, J. L. *Toward a Social History of American English*. New York: Mouton, 1985.

Donawerth, Jane. "Textbooks for New Audiences: Women's Revisions of Rhetorical Theory at the Turn of the Century." *Listening to Their Voices: The Rhetorical Activities of Historical Women*. Ed. Molly Meijer Wertheimer. Columbia: U of South Carolina P, 1997. 337–58.

Douglass, Frederick. "My Bondage and My Freedom." *Autobiographies: Narrative of the Life of Frederick Douglass, An American Slave; My Bondage and My Freedom; Life and Times of Frederick Douglass*. New York: Library of America, 1994.

———. "Narrative of the Life of Frederick Douglass." 1845. *The Oxford Frederick Douglass Reader*. Ed. William L. Andrews. New York: Oxford UP, 1996. 21–97.

Dyson, Freeman J. *The Sun, the Genome, and the Internet: Tools of Scientific Revolutions*. Oxford: Oxford UP, 1999.

Eagleton, Terry. *The Ideology of the Aesthetic*. Oxford: Blackwell, 1990.

Earley, Tony. "The Quare Gene." *The New Yorker* 21 September 1998: 80–85.

Eberly, Rosa. *Citizen Critics: Literary Public Spheres*. Urbana: U of Illinois P, 2000.

Emmel, Barbara, Paula Resch, and Deborah Tenney, eds. *Argument Revisited; Argument Redefined: Negotiating Meaning in the Composition Classroom*. Thousand Oaks, CA: Sage Publications, 1996.

Erickson, Joseph A., and Jeffrey B. Anderson. *Learning with the Community*. Washington, DC: American Association for Higher Learning, 1997.

Ervin, Elizabeth. "Encouraging Civic Participation among First-Year Writing Students; or, Why Composition Class Should Be More Like a Bowling Team." *Rhetoric Review* 15.2 (Spring 1997): 382–99.

Fahnestock, Jeanne, and Marie Secor. "Classical Rhetoric: The Art of Argumentation." *Argument Revisited; Argument Redefined: Negotiating Meaning in the Composition Classroom*. Ed. Barabara Emmel et al. Thousand Oaks, CA: Sage Publications, 1996. 97–123.

Faigley, Lester. "Material Literacy and Visual Design." *Rhetorical Bodies*. Ed. Jack Selzer and Sharon Crowley. Madison: U of Wisconsin P, 1999. 171–201.

Farnsworth, Frances Joyce. *Cubby in Wonderland*. New York: Abington, 1932.

Fisher-Fishkin, Shelley, and Carla Peterson. "'We Hold These Truths to Be Self-Evident': The Rhetoric of Frederick Douglass's Journalism." *Frederick Douglass: New Literary and Historical Essays*. Ed. Eric Sundquist. New York: Cambridge UP, 1990. 189–204.

Flower, Linda. "Partners in Inquiry: A Logic for Community Outreach." *Writing the Community: Concepts and Models for Service-Learning in Composition*. Ed. Linda Adler-Kassner, et al. Washington, DC: American Assoc. for Higher Education, 1997. 95–118.

Franklin, Phyllis, David Laurence, and Elizabeth B. Welles. *Preparing a Nation's Teachers: Models for English and Foreign Language Programs*. New York: MLA, 1999.

Frink, Henry Allyn. *The New Century Speaker*. Vol. 1. 1898. New York: Books for Libraries, 1971.

Foucault, Michel. *Discipline and Punish: The Birth of the Prison*. New York: Vintage, 1979.

——. *Power/Knowledge: Selected Interviews and Other Writings*. Ed. Colin Gordon. New York: Pantheon Books, 1980.

Fox, John. *The Kentuckians*. New York: Harper and Brothers, 1897.

Franklin, Phyllis. "Postscript: Imagining America: Artists and Scholars in Public Life." *MLA Newsletter* 31.3 (1999): 6.

Freire, Paulo. *Pedagogy of the Oppressed*. New York: Continuum, 1970.

——. *Teachers as Cultural Workers: Letters to Those Who Dare Teach*. Boulder, CO: Westview, 1998.

Gadotti, Moacir. *Pedagogy of Praxis*. New York: SUNY P, 1996.

Ganter, Granville. "The Active Virtue of *The Colombian Orator*." *New England Quarterly* 70 (1997): 463–76.

Genung, John Franklin. *Handbook of Rhetorical Analysis*. Boston: Ginn, 1888.

——. *The Practical Elements of Rhetoric*. Boston: Ginn, 1886.

——. *The Working Principles of Rhetoric*. Boston: Ginn, 1900.

Gere, Anne Ruggles. *Intimate Practices: Literacy and Cultural Work in U.S. Women's Clubs, 1880–1920*. Urbana: U of Illinois P, 1997.

*Geyserland: Yellowstone National Park*. Omaha, NE: Union Pacific System, 1925.

Gilster, Paul. *Digital Literacy*. New York: Wiley & Sons, 1998.

Gilyard, Keith. *Let's Flip the Script: An African American Discourse of Language, Literature, and Learning*. Detroit: Wayne State UP, 1996.

Gingrich, Newt, and Dick Armey. *Contract with America: The Bold Plan by Rep. Newt Gingrich, Rep. Dick Armey, and the House Republicans to Change the Nation*. New York: Times Books, 1994.

Giroux, Henry. "Beyond the Ivory Tower." Berube and Nelson 238–58.

——, ed. *Education and Cultural Studies: Toward a Performative Practice*. New York: Routledge, 1997.

——. *Pedagogy and the Politics of Hope*. Boulder, CO: Westview, 1997.

——. *Schooling and the Struggle for Public Life: Critical Pedagogy in the Modern Age*. Minneapolis: U of Minnesota P, 1988.

——. *Teachers as Intellectuals: Toward a Critical Pedagogy of Learning*. Boston: Bergin & Garvey, 1988.

Goatly, Andrew. *The Language of Metaphors*. London: Routledge, 1997.

Graff, Gerald. *Professing Literature: An Institutional History*. Chicago: U of Chicago P, 1987.

Graff, Gerald, and Michael Warner, eds. *The Origins of Literary Studies in America: A Documentary Anthology*. New York: Routledge, 1989.

Graff, Harvey. *The Labyrinths of Literacy*. London: Falmer-Taylor, 1987.

——. *The Legacies of Literacy: Continuities in Western Culture and Society*. Bloomington: Indiana UP, 1988.

Gramsci, Antonio. *The Prison Notebooks: Selections*. Trans. Quintin Hoare. New York: International Publishers, 1971.

Graves, Heather Brodie, and Roger Graves. "Masters, Slaves, and Infant Mortality: Language Challenges for Technical Editing." *Technical Communication Quarterly* 7 (Fall 1988): 389–414.

Greer, Jane. "'No Smiling Madonna': Marian Wharton and the Struggle to Construct a Critical Pedagogy for the Working Class, 1914–1917." *College Compostion and Communication* 51 (1999): 248–71.

Griggs, Sutton. *Imperium in Imperio.* Cincinnati: Sutton L. Griggs Publishing, 1899.

Gurak, Laura J. *Cyberliteracy: Navigating the Internet with Awareness.* New Haven: Yale UP, 2001.

——. *Persuasion and Privacy in Cyberspace: The Online Protests over Lotus Market-Place and the Clipper Chip.* New Haven: Yale UP, 1997.

Habermas, Jurgen. *The Structural Transformation of the Public Sphere: An Inquiry into a Category of Bourgeois Society.* Cambridge, MA.: MIT UP, 1989.

Halloran, S. Michael. "From Rhetoric to Composition: The Teaching of Writing in America to 1900." *A Short History of Writing Instruction: From Ancient Greece to Twentieth-Century America.* Ed. James J. Murphy. Davis, CA: Hermagoras Press, 1990. 151–82.

——. "Rhetoric in the American College Curriculum: The Decline of Public Discourse." *PRE/TEXT* 3.3 (Fall 1982): 245–69.

——. "Text and Experience in a Historical Pageant: Toward a Rhetoric of Spectacle." *Rhetoric Society Quarterly* 31 (Winter 2001): 5–7.

Harper, Frances. "Duty to Dependent Races." *With Pen and Voice: A Critical Anthology of African-American Women.* Ed. Shirley Wilson Logan. Carbondale: Southern Illinois UP, 1995. 36–42.

——. *Iola Leroy or Shadows Uplifted.* Boston: Beacon, 1987.

Harris, Joseph. "Negotiating the Contact Zone." *Journal of Basic Writing* 14.1 (1995): 27–42.

——. *A Teaching Subject: Composition since 1966.* Saddle River, NJ: Prentice-Hall, 1997.

Hart, Roderick P. "Why Communication? Why Education? Toward a Politics of Teaching." *Communication Education* 42 (April 1993): 97–105.

Hawisher, Gail E., and Cynthia Selfe. *Passions, Pedagogies and Twenty-First Century Technologies.* Urbana, IL: NCTE, 1999.

Hawkes, Terence. *Metaphor.* The Critical Idiom Series 25. London: Methuen, 1972.

Hayes, Ira, ed. *Great Beginnings.* Urbana, IL: NCTE, 1998.

Hedge, Levi. *Elements of Logick, or a Summary of the General Principles and Different Modes of Reasoning.* Boston: Hilliard, Gray, Little, and Wilkins, 1831.

Heidegger, Martin. "The Origin of the Work of Art." *Martin Heidegger: Basic Writings.* Ed. David F. Krell. San Francisco: Harper Collins, 1977. 139–213.

——. "The Question Concerning Technology." *Martin Heidegger: Basic Writings.* Ed. David F. Krell. San Francisco: Harper Collins, 1977. 307–43.

Herzberg, Bruce. "Service Learning and Public Discourse." *JAC* 20.2 (2000): 391–404.

Hewett, Beth L. "Samuel P. Newman's *A Practical System of Rhetoric:* The Evolution of a Method." *Advances in the History of Rhetoric: Disputed and Neglected Texts in the History of Rhetoric* 1 (1997): 51–68.

Hill, Adams Sherman. *Beginnings of Rhetoric and Composition*. New York: American, 1902.

———. *The Foundations of Rhetoric*. New York: American, 1892.

———. *The Principles of Rhetoric and Their Applications*. New York: Harper and Row, 1878.

Hochmuth, Marie, and Richard Murphy. "Rhetorical and Elocutionary Training in Nineteenth-Century Colleges." *A History of Speech Education in America: Background Studies*. Ed. Karl R. Wallace. New York: Appleton-Century-Crofts, 1954. 153–77.

Hollis, Karyn. "Liberating Voices: Autobiographical Writing at the Bryn Mawr Summer School for Women Workers, 1921–1938." *College Composition and Communication* 45 (February 1994): 31–60.

Holquist, Michael, ed. *The Dialogic Imagination: Four Essays by M. M. Bakhtin*. Trans. Caryl Emerson and Michael Holquist. Austin: U of Texas P, 1981.

Hook, J. N., and W. H. Evans. *The Teaching of High School English, 5th Ed*. New York: John Wiley, 1982.

hooks, bell. *Teaching to Transgress*. New York: Routledge, 1994.

Hopkins, Pauline. *Contending Forces: A Romance Illustrative of Negro Life North and South*. 1900. New York: Oxford UP, 1988.

Horwitz, Tony. *Confederates in the Attic: Dispatches from the Unfinished Civil War*. New York: Vintage-Random House, 1999.

Howell, W. S. *Eighteenth-Century British Logic and Rhetoric*. Princeton: Princeton UP, 1971.

Hoyle, Francis P. *The Complete Speaker and Reciter*. New York: George A. Parker, 1905.

———. *The World's Speaker, Reciter, and Entertainer*. Philadelphia: World's Bible, 1905.

"Impact of Welfare Reform on Low-Income Citizens Examined." *Outlook: The University of Maryland Faculty and Staff Weekly Newspaper* 28 September. 1999: 1.

*The International Speaker and Popular Elocutionist*. Chicago: International Publishing Company, 1895.

Jablonski, Carol J. "A Reflection on Curricular Reform: A Challenge and a Role for Rhetorical Studies." *Southern Communication Journal* 63.4 (1998): 337–45.

Jarratt, Susan. "Feminism and Composition: The Case for Conflict." *Contending with Words*. Ed. Patricia Harkin and John Schilb. New York: MLA, 1991. 105–23.

———. *Rereading the Sophists: Classical Rhetoric Refigured*. Carbondale: Southern Illinois UP, 1991.

———. "Rhetorical Power: What Really Happens in Politicized Classrooms." *ADE Bulletin* 102 (Fall 1992): 34–39.

———. "Sapphic Pedagogy: Exploring Women's Difference in History and in the Classroom." *Learning from the Histories of Rhetoric. Essays in Honor of Winifred Bryan Horner*. Ed. Theresa Enos. Carbondale: Southern Illinois UP, 1993. 75–90.

Jehlen, Myra. *American Incarnation: The Individual, the Nation, and the Continent.* Cambridge: Harvard UP, 1986.

Johnson, Nan. *Nineteenth-Century Rhetoric in North America.* Carbondale: Southern Illinois UP, 1991.

———. "The Popularization of Nineteenth-Century Rhetoric: Elocution and the Private Learner." Clark and Halloran 139–57.

Johnson, Samuel. *Dictionary of the English Language.* 2 vols. London, 1755.

Kaestle, Karl. *Pillars of the Republic.* New York: Hill-Farrar, 1983.

Kammen, Michael. *In the Past Lane: Historical Perspectives on American Culture.* New York: Oxford UP, 1997.

Kates, Susan. "The Embodied Rhetoric of Hallie Quinn Brown." *College English* 59.1 (1997): 59–71.

Kaufer, David S., and Kathleen M. Carley. *Communication at a Distance: The Influence of Print on Sociocultural Organization and Change.* Hillsdale: Erlbaum, 1993.

Kephart, Horace. *Our Southern Highlanders: A Narrative of Adventure in the Southern Appalachians and a Study of Life among the Mountaineers.* 1913. Knoxville: U of Tennessee P, 1976.

Ketchum, Richard M. *Saratoga: Turning Point of America's Revolutionary War.* New York: Henry Holt, 1997.

Kinsey, Joni L. "Thomas Moran's Surveys of Yellowstone and the Grand Canyon: The Coalition of Art, Business, and Government." *Splendors of the American West: Thomas Moran's Art of the Grand Canyon and Yellowstone.* Ed. Anne R. Morand, et. al. Birmingham: Birmingham Museum of Art and U of Washington P, 1990. 29–41.

Kirkham, Samuel. *English Grammar in Familiar Lectures.* New York: Robert B. Collins, 1829.

Kittay, Eva Feder. *Metaphor.* Clarendon Library of Logic & Philosophy. Oxford: Oxford UP, 1989.

Lakoff, George, and Mark Johnson. *Metaphors We Live By.* Chicago: U of Chicago P, 1980.

*Land of the Geysers.* St. Paul: Northern Pacific Railroad, 1917.

Langford, Nathaniel P. "The Wonders of the Yellowstone." *Scribner's Monthly* May 1871: 1–17 and June 1871: 113–28.

Lehuu, Isabelle. "Sentimental Figures: Reading *Godey's Lady's Book* in Antebellum America." *The Culture of Sentiment: Race, Gender, and Sentimentality in Nineteenth-Century America.* Ed. Shirley Samuels. New York: Oxford UP, 1992. 73–91.

Lindemann, Erika C. *A Rhetoric for Writing Teachers.* New York: Oxford UP, 1995.

Lisman, C. David. *Toward a Civil Society: Civic Literacy and Service Learning.* Westport, CT: Bergin and Garvey, 1998.

Literacy Volunteers of America. "About LVA and Literacy." 16 November 1999. <http://www.literacyvolunteers.org/about/index.htm>.

Locke, John. *Essay Concerning Human Understanding (1690).* Ed. J. W. Yolton. London: Dent, 1961.

Logan, Shirley Wilson. "Frederick Douglass and *The Colombian Orator.*" Presentation delivered at the Rhetoric Society of America's thirtieth biennial conference. Pittsburgh, PA, 1998.

Lohr, Steve. "Microsoft Starts the Recruiting for Its Next War." *New York Times* 9 September 1999: C1; C10.

Lucas, Stephen E. *The Art of Public Speaking.* 5th ed. Boston: McGraw Hill, 1995.

Lumm, Emma Griffith. *The Home School Speaker and Elocutionist.* New York: Boland, 1899.

———. *New American Speaker.* Chicago: C. W. Stanton Company, 1898.

———. *The Twentieth Century Speaker.* New York: Boland, 1899.

Lyons, Scott Richard. "Rhetorical Sovereignty: What Do American Indians Want from Writing?" *CCC* 51.3 (2000): 447–68.

Mailloux, Steven. "Misreading as a Historical Act: Cultural Rhetoric, Bible Politics and Fuller's 1845 Review of Douglass's Narrative." *Readers in History: Nineteenth-Century American Literature and the Contexts of Responses.* Ed. James L. Machor. Baltimore: Johns Hopkins UP, 1993. 3–31.

———. "Reading Typos, Reading Archives." *College English* 61.5 (May 1999): 584–90.

———. *Reception Histories: Rhetoric, Pragmatism, and American Cultural Politics.* Ithaca: Cornell UP, 1998.

McAfee, Ward M. *Religion, Race, and Reconstruction: The Public School in the Politics of the 1870s.* Albany: SUNY P, 1998.

McAllister, Catherine, and Evelyn Ting. "Analysis of Discussion Items by Males and Females in Online College Courses." Saratoga Springs: Empire State College, 2000: 1–25. <http://www.esc.edu>.

McCracken, H. Thomas, and Richard L. Larson with Judith Entes. *Teaching College English and English Education: Reflective Stories.* Urbana, IL: NCTE, 1998.

McCrorey, Henry Lawrence. "A Brief History of Johnson C. Smith University." *The Quarterly Review of Higher Education among Negroes* 1 (July 1933): 29–36.

McCroskey, James, ed. *An Introduction to Rhetorical Communication.* 7th ed. New York: Allyn & Bacon, 1997.

McFeely, William S. *Frederick Douglass.* New York: Norton, 1991.

Mencken, H. L. *The American Language: An Inquiry into the Development of English in the United States.* New York: Alfred A. Knopf, 1936.

Miller, Carolyn R. "Genre as Social Action." *Quarterly Journal of Speech* 70 (1984): 151–67.

Miller, J. Hillis. Foreword. *Publishing in Rhetoric and Composition.* Ed. Gary A. Olson and Todd W. Taylor. Albany: SUNY P, 1997. xi–xv.

Miller, Richard. *As If Learning Mattered: Reforming Higher Education.* Ithaca: Cornell UP, 1998.

Miller, Susan. *Assuming the Positions.* Pittsburgh: U of Pittsburgh P, 1998.

———. *Rescuing the Subject*. Carbondale: Southern Illinois UP, 1989.

———. *Textual Carnivals: The Politics of Composition*. Carbondale: Southern Illinois UP, 1991.

Miller, Thomas P. *The Formation of College English: Rhetoric and Belles Lettres in the British Cultural Provinces*. Pittsburgh: U of Pittsburgh P, 1997.

———. "Teaching the Histories of Rhetoric as a Social Praxis." *Rhetoric Review* 12 (Fall 1993): 70–82.

Miller, Thomas P., and Melody Bowdon. "A Rhetorical Stance on the Archives of Civic Action." *College English* 61.5 (May 1999): 591–98.

Moran, Thomas. "American Art and American Scenery." *The Grand Canyon of Arizona*. Passenger Department of the Santa Fe Railroad, 1906. 85–87.

Morreale, Sherwyn P., Michael S. Hanna, Roy M. Berko, and James W. Gibson. *The Basic Communication Course at U.S. Colleges and Universities: VI*. Annandale, VA: National Communication Association, 1998.

Morrison, Toni. *Playing in the Dark: Whiteness and the Literary Imagination*. Cambridge, MA: Harvard UP, 1992.

Muir, John. *Our National Parks*. Boston: Houghton Mifflin, 1901.

Murphy, Thomas D. *Three Wonderlands of the American West*. Boston: The Page Company, 1912.

National Park Service. "Master Plan: Saratoga National Historical Park, New York." U.S. Department of the Interior, National Park Service, 1969.

National Park Service. Saratoga National Historical Park Web site. <http://www.nps.gov/sara/>.

*National Service-Learning Clearinghouse*. University of Minnesota. 10 October 1999. <http://www.nicsl.coled.umn.edu/who/status/htm>.

Newman, Samuel P. *A Practical System of Rhetoric*. New York: Dayton and Newman, 1842.

*Newsweek*. Special report on e-Life. 20 September 1999.

Noble, David F. *Forces of Production: A Social History of Industrial Automation*. New York: Oxford UP, 1986.

North, Stephen P. *The Making of Knowledge in Composition: Portrait of an Emerging Field*. New York: Boynton/Cook, 1987.

Northrop, Henry Davenport. *The Ideal Speaker and Entertainer*. New York: Geo. W. Bertron, 1910.

O'Connor, Lillian. *Pioneer Women Orators: Rhetoric in the Antebellum Reform Movement*. New York: Columbia UP, 1954.

Ong, Walter J. *Orality and Literacy: The Technologizing of the Word*. London: Routledge, 1988.

Ortony, Andrew. "Metaphor: A Multidimensional Problem." Ortony 1–18.

———, ed. *Metaphor and Thought*. Cambridge: Cambridge UP, 1979.

Osborn, Michael, and Suzanne Osborn. *Public Speaking*. 2nd ed. New York: Houghton Mifflin, 1996.

Osborne, Peter. *A Critical Sense: Interviews with Intellectuals*. New York: Routledge, 1996.

Peck, Elizabeth. *Berea's First 125 Years, 1855–1980*. Lexington: UP of Kentucky, 1982.

People for Internet Responsibility (PFIR). "Why was PFIR formed?" 24 November 1999. <http://www.pfir.org/>.

Perelman, Chaim, and L. Olbrechts-Tyteca. *The New Rhetoric: A Treatise on Argumentation*. Trans. John Wilkinson and Purcell Weaver. Notre Dame: U of Notre Dame P, 1969.

Perkins, Linda Marie. "Quaker Beneficence and Black Control: The Institute for Colored Youth, 1852–1903." *New Perspectives on Black Educational History*. Ed. Vincent P. Franklin and James D. Anderson. Boston: G. K. Hall, 1978.

Persi, Nina C., and William N. Denman. *Civic Responsibility as a Justification for the Teaching of Public Speaking: An Analysis of Basic Course Textbooks*. Huntington, WV: The John Deaver Drinko Academy, Marshall University, 1997.

Peterson, Carla. *Doers of the Word: African American Women Speakers and Writers in the North, 1830–1880*. New Brunswick, NJ: Rutgers UP, 1998.

Petrie, Hugh G. "Metaphor and Learning." Ortony 438–61.

Phillips, Christopher. *Freedom's Port: The African-American Community of Baltimore, 1790–1860*. Urbana: U of Illinois P, 1997.

Phillips, Michael M. "Documented Legislative History of Saratoga National Historical Park." January 16, 1973; edited and updated March 1988. File, "The Roosevelts and the Park." Saratoga NHP archives.

Pinneo, T. S. *The Herman's Reader for Female Schools*. New York: Clark, 1847.

Porter, Dorothy B. "The Organized Educational Activities of Negro Literary Societies, 1828–1846." *The Journal of Negro Education* 5 (October 1936): 555–76.

Porter, Ebenezer. *Analysis of the Principles of Delivery*. Andover, MA: Newman, 1827.

Potter, David. *Debating in the Colonial Chartered Colleges: An Historical Survey, 1642–1900*. New York: Teachers College, 1944.

Powell, Malea. "Rhetorics of Survivance: How American Indians *Use* Writing." *CCC* 53.3 (Feb. 2002): 396–434.

Quackenbos, G. P. *Advanced Course of Composition and Rhetoric*. New York: Appleton, 1879.

Quintilian. *Institutio Oratoria*. Trans. H. E. Butler. 4 vols. London: Loeb Classical Library, 1920–22.

Raine, James Watt. *The Land of the Saddle-bags: A Study of the Mountain People of Appalachia*. Lexington: UP of Kentucky, 1997.

Rich, Adrienne. "Notes toward a Politics of Location." In *Blood, Bread and Poetry: Selected Prose 1975–1985*. New York: Norton, 1986. 210–31.

Richards, I. A. *The Philosophy of Rhetoric*. London: Oxford UP, 1965.

Ricoeur, Paul. *Freud and Philosophy; An Essay on Interpretation*. New Haven: Yale UP, 1970.

Rodman, George, and Ronald B. Adler. *The New Public Speaker*. New York: Harcourt Brace, 1997.

Roosevelt, Franklin Delano. Memorandum to Hon. Ebert K. Burlew, December 6, 1939. File, "The Roosevelts and the Park." Saratoga NHP archives.

———. "Remarks of Governor Roosevelt on Occasion of Visit to the Saratoga Battlefield, October 17, 1929." File, "The Roosevelts and the Park." Saratoga NHP archives.

Rose, Mike. *Lives on the Boundary: The Struggles and Achievements of America's Underprepared*. New York: Free Press, 1989.

———. "Rigid Rules, Inflexible Plans and Stifling Language." *CCC* 31.4 (1980): 389–401.

Royer, Daniel. "The Process of Literacy as Involvement in the Narratives of Frederick Douglass." *African-American Review* 28 (Spring 1995): 363–74.

Royster, Jacqueline Jones. *Traces of a Stream: Literacy and Social Change among African American Women*. Pittsburgh: U of Pittsburgh P, 2000.

Royster, Jacqueline Jones, and Jean C. Williams. "History in the Spaces Left: African American Presence and Narrative of Composition Studies." *CCC* 50 (June 1999): 563–84.

Rudolph, Frederick. *The American College and University: A History*. New York: Random House, 1962.

Russell, David R. *Writing in the Academic Disciplines, 1870–1990: A Curricular History*. Carbondale: Southern Illinois UP, 1991.

Salvatori, Mariolina Rizzi, ed. *Pedagogy: Disturbing History 1819–1929*. Pittsburgh: U of Pittsburgh P, 1996.

Sanchez, Rene. "Gates to Give $1 Billion for Minority Scholarships." *Washington Post* 17 September 1999: A1.

Saratoga National Historical Park. Audiostation Scripts. June 1975. Saratoga NHP archives, Administrative Reports file.

Schilb, Jonathan. "Difference, Displacements, Disruptions: Revisionary Histories of Rhetoric." *PRE/TEXT* 8 (1987): 29–44.

Scholes, Robert. *The Rise and Fall of English*. New Haven and London: Yale UP, 1998.

Schön, Donald A. "Generative Metaphor: A Perspective on Problem-Setting in Social Policy." Ortony 254–83.

Sears, John. *Sacred Places: American Tourist Attractions in the Nineteenth Century*. New York: Oxford UP, 1989.

Secor, Marie, and Davida Charney, eds. *Constructing Rhetorical Education*. Carbondale: Southern Illinois UP, 1991.

Seitz, James E. *Motives for Metaphor: Literacy, Curriculum Reform, and the Teaching of English*. Pittsburgh: U of Pittsburgh P, 1999.

Selfe, Cynthia. *Technology and Literacy in the Twenty-First Century: The Importance of Paying Attention*. Carbondale: Southern Illinois UP, 1999.

Shelley, Percy Bysshe. "A Defence of Poetry." *The Norton Anthology of English Literature*. 7th ed. Ed. M. H. Abrams. New York: Norton, 2000. 789–802.

Sheridan, Thomas. *British Education: Or the Source of the Disorders of Great Britain;*

*Being an Essay towards Proving, that the Immortality, Ignorance and False Taste, which so Generally prevail, are the Natural and Necessary Consequences of the Present Defective Systems of Education*. 1756. Menston: Scolar Press, 1971.

Shor, Ira. *Empowering Education: Critical Teaching for Social Change*. Chicago: U of Chicago P, 1992.

Showalter, Elaine. "Presidential Address 1998: Regeneration." *MLA* 114 (1999): 318–28.

Sisco, Lisa. "Writing in the Spaces Left: Literacy as a Process of Becoming in the Narratives of Frederick Douglass." *American Transcendental Quarterly* 9 (September 1995): 195–227.

Siskin, Clifford. *The Work of Writing: Literature and Social Change in Britain, 1700–1830*. Baltimore: Johns Hopkins UP, 1998.

Slingerland, George O. Letter to Lester Markel, Sunday Editor, *New York Times*. August 12, 1926. George Slingerland papers, box 1, folder 8. Saratoga NHP archives.

Smagorinsky, Peter. *Standards in Practice Grades 9–12*. Urbana, IL: NCTE, 1996.

Smagorinsky, Peter, and Melissa E. Whiting. *How English Teachers Get Taught: Methods of Teaching the Methods Class*. Urbana, IL: NCTE, 1995.

Smith, Emily Ann, and Elizabeth Peck. *Berea's First 125 Years: 1855–1980*. Lexington: U of Kentucky P, 1982.

Smitherman, Geneva. "CCCC's Role in the Struggle for Language Rights." *College Composition and Communication* 50.3 (1999): 349–76.

Spellmeyer, Kurt. *Common Ground: Dialogue, Understanding, and the Teaching of Composition*. Englewood Cliffs, NJ: Prentice Hall, 1993.

Spillers, Hortense J. "Mama's Baby, Papa's Maybe: An American Grammar Book." *Diacritics* (Summer 1987): 65–81.

Sprague, Rev. Delos E. *Descriptive Guide of the Battlefield of Saratoga*. Ballston Spa, NY: Battlefield Publishing, Inc., 1930.

Sproule, J. Michael. *Speechmaking: Rhetorical Competency in a Postmodern World*. 2nd ed. Madison, WI: Brown and Benchmark, 1997.

Sticht, Thomas G. "Educational Uses of Metaphor." Ortony 474–85.

Stone, William L. *Visits to the Saratoga Battle-Grounds, 1780–1880*. 1895. Port Washington, NY: Kennikat Press, 1970.

Stratton, Josephine W., and Jeannette M. Stratton, eds. *The New Select Speaker*. New York: D. Z. Howell, 1902.

Street, Brian V. *Literacy in Theory and Practice*. Cambridge: Cambridge UP, 1984.

Swearingen, C. Jan, and David Pruett, eds. *Rhetoric, the Polis, and the Global Village: Selected Papers from the 1998 Thirtieth Anniversary Rhetoric Society of America Conference*. Mahwah, NJ: Lawrence Erlbaum, 1999.

Tchudi, Stephen, and Paul J. Morris III. *The New Literacy: Moving Beyond the 3Rs*. Portland, ME: Calendar Islands Publishing, 1996.

*Texas Center for Service Learning Home Page*. October 1997. Texas Commission on Volunteerism and Community Service. 10 October 1999. <http://www.txserve.org/servlrn/general/aboutsl.html>.

Tompkins, Jane P., ed. *Reader Response Criticism: From Formalism to Post-Structuralism.* Baltimore: Johns Hopkins UP, 1980.

Tonkovich, Nicole. "Rhetorical Power in the Victorian Parlor: *Godey's Lady's Book* and the Gendering of Nineteenth-Century Rhetoric." *Oratorical Culture in Nineteenth-Century America: Transformations in the Theory and Practice of Rhetoric.* Ed. Gregory Clark and S. Michael Halloran. Carbondale: Southern Illinois UP, 1993. 158–83.

Trimbur, John. "Essayist Literacy and the Rhetoric of Deproduction." *Rhetoric Review* 9 (1990): 72–86.

Tyner, Kathleen. *Literacy in a Digital World: Teaching and Learning in the Age of Information.* Mahwah, NJ: Lawrence Erlbaum, 1998.

Union Pacific System. *Geyserland: Yellowstone National Park.* Omaha, NE: Union Pacific, 1925.

United States Commerce Department. July 8, 1999. "New Commerce Report Shows Dramatic Growth in Number of Americans Connected to Internet." 15 January 2000. <http://204.193.246.62/public.nsf/docs/070799-new-report-falling-through-the-net-digital-divide>.

Villanueva, Victor. *Bootstraps: From an American Academic of Color.* Urbana, IL: NCTE, 1993.

———, ed. *Cross-Talk in Comp Theory.* Urbana, IL: NCTE, 1997.

Walworth, Ellen Hardin. *Battles of Saratoga 1777; The Saratoga Monument Association 1856–1891.* Albany: Joel Munsell's Sons, Publishers, 1891.

Warner, Michael. *The Letters of the Republic: Publication and the Public Sphere in Eighteenth-Century America.* Cambridge: Harvard UP, 1990.

Watson, Martha, ed. *Lives of Their Own: Rhetorical Dimensions in Autobiographies of Women Activists.* Columbia: U of South Carolina P, 1998.

Watters, Ann, and Marjorie Ford. *A Guide for Change: Resources for Implementing Community-Service Writing.* New York: McGraw-Hill, 1995.

———. *Writing for Change: A Community Reader.* New York: McGraw-Hill, 1995.

Welch, Kathleen E. *Electric Rhetoric: Classical Rhetoric, Oralism, and a New Literacy.* Cambridge: MIT P, 1999.

Wells, Ida B. *Crusade for Justice.* Chicago: U of Chicago P, 1972.

Wells, Susan. "Rogue Cops and Health Care: What Do We Want from Public Writing?" *CCC* 47.3 (October 1996): 325–41.

Whately, Richard. *Elements of Rhetoric.* Carbondale: Southern Illinois UP, 1963.

Wheeler, Olin D. *Wonderland.* St. Paul: Northern Pacific Railroad, 1903.

Whiting, Samuel. *Elegant Lessons of the Young Lady's Preceptor.* New Haven: S. Converse, 1824.

Wilken, Curtis B. "*The Columbian Orator* and Frederick Douglass's Development as a Citizen-Orator." Unpublished Masters Thesis, 1994.

Will, George. "The Curdled Congress." *Newsweek* 17 October. 1994: 92.

Wilshin, F. F. "Evaluation of Proposed Administration—Museum and Utility Building Sites." October 10, 1940. NYS Civilian Conservation Corps, National Park Service Records, 1933–1969, box 2, folder 2. Saratoga NHP archives.

———. "Narrative Report." November 2, 1940. NYS Civilian Conservation Corps, National Park Service Records, 1933–1969, box 2, folder 3. Saratoga NHP archives.

Wilson, Edward O. *Consilience: The Unity of Knowledge*. New York: Alfred A. Knopf, 1998.

Winegarten, Ruthe. *Black Texas Women: A Sourcebook*. Austin: U of Texas P, 1996.

Winterowd, Ross W. *The English Department: A Personal and Institutional History*. Carbondale: Southern Illinois UP, 1998.

Witherspoon, John. *Selected Writings*. Ed. Thomas P. Miller. Carbondale: Southern Illinois UP, 1990.

Woodruff, Bertram L. "Curriculum Adjustments for the Improvement of English in Negro Colleges." *The Quarterly Review of Higher Education Among Negroes* 1 (July 1933): 1–6.

Wylie, W. W. *The Yellowstone National Park, or the Great American Wonderland*. Kansas City, MO: Ramsey, Millett, and Hudson, 1882.

Zaluda, Scott. "Lost Voices of the Harlem Renaissance: Writing Assigned at Howard University, 1919–1931." *CCC* 50.2 (December 1998): 232–57.

Zarefsky, David. *Public Speaking: Strategies for Success*. 1st ed. New York: Allyn and Bacon, 1996.

Zavarzadeh, Mas'ud, and Donald Morton. "A Very Good Idea Indeed: The (Post)Modern Labor Force and Curricular Reform." Berlin and Vivion 66–86.

Ziolkowski, Thad. "Antitheses: The Dialectic of Violence and Literacy in Frederick Douglass's *Narrative*." *Critical Essays on Frederick Douglass*. Ed. William Andrews. Boston: G. K. Hall, 1991.

# Contributors

**Sherry Booth** teaches women's studies and writing classes at Santa Clara University. Her research interests in rhetoric include *ethos* as well as nineteenth-century Scottish rhetoric. She is currently working with the novels of Margaret Atwood.

**Gregory Clark** is professor of English at Brigham Young University. This essay is part of a larger project exploring the sort of rhetorical experiences that are prompted by encounters with landscapes.

**William N. Denman** is a professor of communication studies at Marshall University. His chapter was produced while serving as a fellow of the John Deaver Drinko Academy for American Political Institutions and Civic Culture at Marshall.

**Susan Frisbie** teaches writing and literature courses at Santa Clara University. Her research interests include composition and rhetorical theory, the intersection of reading and writing, assessment of student writing, and nineteenth-century British literature, particularly Jane Austen.

**Cheryl Glenn** is an associate professor of English and women's studies. Former president of the Coalition of Women Scholars in the History of Rhetoric and Composition, she is the author of *Rhetoric Retold: Regendering the Tradition from Antiquity through the Renaissance,* which won the best book/honorable mention from the Society for the Study of Early Modern Women, and *Making Sense: A New Rhetorical Reader.* She coauthored *The New St. Martin's Guide to Teaching Writing.* Her rhetorical research has earned her three awards from the National Endowment for the Humanities and the Richard Braddock Award from the Conference on College Composition and Communication.

**Laura J. Gurak** is a professor in and the director of the Internet Studies Center in the rhetoric department at the University of Minnesota, where she is also a faculty fellow in the law school. Her specialties include rhetoric of technology, intellectual property, and Internet studies. She is the author of *Cyberliteracy: Navigating the Internet with Awareness* (Yale UP, 2001) and *Persuasion and Privacy in Cyberspace: The Online Protests over Lotus MarketPlace and the Clipper Chip* (Yale UP, 1997). Gurak has also authored two textbooks and two edited collections and has published numerous book chapters and articles. She is an occasional commentator on *Future Tense: A Journal of the Digital Age* from Minnesota Public Radio.

**S. Michael Halloran** is a professor of rhetoric and communication at Rensselaer Polytechnic Institute, where he received his Ph.D. in 1973. He is coeditor (with Gregory Clark) of *Oratorical Culture in Nineteenth-Century America: Transformations in the Theory and Practice of Rhetoric* (Southern Illinois UP, 1993) and has published articles in *College English, Rhetoric Review, Rhetoric Society Quarterly, Quarterly Journal of Speech,* and other journals, and in a number of essay collections. At Rensselaer he has served as director of graduate studies in the Department of Language, Literature, and Communication; as chair of that department; and as associate dean of the School of Humanities and Social Sciences.

**Nan Johnson** is a professor of English at the Ohio State University. Her research interests include the history and theory of rhetoric and composition. She is the author of *Gender and Rhetorical Space in American Life, 1866–1910* (Southern Illinois UP, 2002), *Nineteenth-Century Rhetoric in North America* (Southern Illinois UP, 1991), and numerous reviews and articles published in *Rhetoric Review, College English, English Quarterly, ADE Bulletin,* among others.

**Susan Kates** is an associate professor of English and women's studies at the University of Oklahoma where she teaches in the composition, rhetoric, and literacy program. She is the author of *Activist Rhetorics and American Higher Education, 1885–1937* (Southern Illinois UP, 2000). Her essays have appeared in *College English* and *College Composition and Communication*.

**Rich Lane** teaches courses in composition and rhetoric and teacher education at Clarion University of Pennsylvania. He has directed English-education programs at the University of Utah and Murray State University and was the recipient of the Lowell Bennion Public Service Professorship in 2000–2002 for his work in forming the Family Literacy Center in Salt Lake City, Utah. He has published articles on composition and popular culture, approaches to teaching popular culture in secondary language-arts curricula, and the novels of Margaret Atwood. He lives with Pamela and his son, Maxfield, in Clarion, Pennsylvania.

**Shirley Wilson Logan** is an associate professor in the Department of English at the University of Maryland. Past director of the department's Professional Writing Program, she teaches courses in composition pedagogy, rhetorical theory, and nineteenth-century black women's rhetorical practices. She is currently researching sources of black rhetorical education in nineteenth-century America. Publications include *With Pen and Voice: An Anthology of Nineteenth-Century African-American Women* (Southern Illinois UP, 1995), *We Are Coming: The Persuasive Discourse of Nineteenth-Century Black Women* (Southern Illinois UP, 1999), and essays in various collections, most recently, " 'What Are We Worth': Anna Julia Cooper Defines Black Women's Work at the Dawn of the Twentieth Century" in *Sister Circle: Black Women and Work* (Rutgers UP, 2002).

**Margaret M. Lyday** is an associate professor at Penn State University, where she teaches courses in rhetorical theory, writing, and editing, and where she cochaired the conference at which many of these essays were first aired. She has served as associate dean of liberal arts, and as founding director of the Lehigh Valley Writing Project and of the Graduate School Communication Enhancement Program. At present she directs the composition program.

**Thomas Miller** is an associate professor of English and the director of composition at the University of Arizona. His book, *The Formation of College English: Rhetoric and Belles Lettres in the British Cultural Provinces* (U of Pittsburgh P, 1997), is the first part of a two-volume study of the introduction of the modern culture into higher education and was named the cowinner of the Mina Shaughnessy Award from MLA.

**Wendy B. Sharer** is an assistant professor of English at East Carolina University where she also serves as the associate director of composition. Her work on the rhetorical practices of early-twentieth-century women's organizations has appeared in *Rhetoric Society Quarterly, Rhetoric Review,* and received the 2002 James Berlin Memorial Outstanding Dissertation Award from the Conference on College Composition and Communication.

**Jill Swiencicki** is an assistant professor of English at California State University, Chico, where she teaches courses in rhetoric, writing, and women's studies. She is currently at work on a book-length project titled "Eloquent Identities: Rhetoric, the Public Sphere, and Social Difference in Antebellum America."

# Index

76, 82, 83–86; media, 98; mediating feature of, 84; medical model of, 171; and metaphor, 178; politics of, 76, 77; regional, 76, 82; shaping of views of reality, 13, 151; as a type of gene, 85. *See also* Appalachian language; Ebonics
language-arts curricula, xiv, 93–94
language-in-education controversies, xiii
Larson, Richard L.: *Teaching College English and English Education*, 89
Lawson, Charles, 67
lectures, 25
Leff, Michael: "In Search of Ariadne's Thread," 12
letter-writing handbooks, 107, 113
liberalism, 39
Lincoln, Abraham, 66, 112, 134
linguistically marginalized groups, 199
"linguistic turn," 87
literacy: ascribing what should be read, 187; as consciousness, 180–81; as discourse, 181; history, 180–81; as multiple ways people communicate, 100; as performance, 181; popular understandings of as print, 181, 182; as a social praxis imbedded in history, 18; and teaching of rhetoric, xvi; as a value system, 187–88
literacy crisis: associated with the evolution of print culture, 19; at the end of the nineteenth century, 18, 25
"literacy myth," 38
literacy studies model, 27, 204
literacy technologies, 184–87, 191
literary anthologies, 98
literary classics, 18
literary-research paradigm, xii
literary scholarship, divorced from the teaching of reading and writing, 26
literary societies, 22, 45
literature, demarcation from the work of reading and writing, 24
literature-based strategy, 88
literature surveys, 29
local discourse, 50

"loci of contradictions," 39
Logan, Shirley Wilson, xi, xii, 66, 127n2, 199, 204
Lucas, Stephen E.: *The Art of Public Speaking*, 17n3
Lumm, Emma Griffith: "Alike to Those We Love, and Those We Hate," 120, 122–23; *The Home School Speaker and Elocutionist*, 113, 120, 122–23, 125, 126; "Let It Be Patriotism First—Then Love," 126; *The New American Speaker*, 113–14, 120, 122–23
lyceum circuit, 45, 46, 130
Lyday, Margaret, xvin1
Lyons, Scott Richard, ix

Macaulay, Thomas, 112
Mailloux, Steven, 30, 44, 64, 73n1
Malcolm X, 50
manufacturing, emergence of, 5
manuscripts, controlled by priests and monks, 185
Markel, Lester, 137
Mather, Cotton, 21
Mattingly, Carol, 127n2
McCarthy era, 10
McCracken, H. Thomas: *Teaching College English and English Education*, 89
McCroskey, James: *An Introduction to Rhetorical Communications*, 17n3
McFarland, Jack, 171
mechanical correctness, 10
media language, 98
media texts, analysis of, 92
Mencken, H. L.: *The American Language*, 80
metaphor: cognitive function, 169; in composition handbooks, 164; in contemporary pedagogy, 200–201; definition of, 177; of friendship and romance, 171; generative, 167–68; how it works, 166–67; ideological aspect, 167–68; incongruity, 166–67; literary analysis of, 165; means to knowledge, 163, 172; process definition of, 166; and rhetorical

Saratoga Battlefield Association, Inc., 132
Saratoga Battlefield Tour Road: as an educational text, 130, 134–38; as palimpsest, 138–42; shared ideals, 203
Saratoga Monument Association, 132, 137, 140, 142
Saratoga National Historical Park, xiv, 129–44, 132, 143
"scene," 146
Schilb, John, 57
Scholar/Practitioner Project, 51, 204
Scholes, Robert: *The Rise and Fall of English*, xvin4, 18, 30, 163, 177
Schön, Donald: frame conflict theory, 169; on generative metaphor, 167–68
Schuyler, Philip, 140
Schuylerville, 132
Schwalter, Elaine, 20
Scott, Michael D.: *Between One and Many: The Art and Science of Public Speaking*, 17n3
*Scribner's Monthly*, 154
Sears, John: *Sacred Places*, 148
secondary curriculum: literature as primary class content, 90, 92; state of, 88–89
secondary orality, forms of communication that combine features of print culture with those of oral culture, 183
secondary teachers: call for preparation of students for civic action, 96; education of, 87; primarily literary training, 94; as "rhetorical authority," 96
Secor, Marie: "Classical Rhetoric: the Art of Argumentation" (and Jeanne Fahnestock), 15–16
segregation, 39–40
Seitz, James, 164, 175
Selfe, Cynthia, xvin4, 207
service learning: pedagogies, 98; and rhetorical education, vii, 32, 50, 204; rhetorical training, 50; in

teacher education and the secondary curriculum, 101–2
"service units," 34
Seven Sisters colleges, viii
Sharer, Wendy, xvin1
Sharp Street African Academy, 41
Shelley, Percy Bysshe, 164
Sheridan, Thomas: *British Education: Or the Source of the Disorders of Great Britain; Being an Essay towards Proving, that the Immortality, Ignorance and False Taste, which so Generally prevail, are the Natural and Necessary Consequences of the Present Defective Systems of Education*, 26–27
"She Would Be a Mason," 116–17
Showalter, Elaine, 31
Siskin, Clifford, 23
Slingerland, George O., 137
Smagorinsky, Peter: *How English Teachers Get Taught: Methods of Teaching the Methods Class* (and Whiting), 89, 91–93
Smiley, Tavis, 50
Smith, Adam, 20
Smith, Emily Ann: *Berea's First 125 Years: 1855–1980*, 86n1
Smitherman, Geneva: "CCCC's Role in the Struggle for Language Rights," 83; Ebonics work, 76
social role of rhetorical art, loss of, 10
Society of Friends, schools for free blacks in the North, 41
Sophists: critiques of, vii, 30; study of discursive practices, 96; teaching methods, 95–96; truth as a relative type of knowledge produced by process of argument through language, 95
"Speakers": allocation of rhetorical categories along gender lines, 125; depiction of women as the embodiment of domesticity, maternal instruction, and sentiment," 119; depiction of women performing